WHITHER UKRAINE?

Whither Ukraine?
Weapons, state building, and international cooperation

SCOTT A. JONES
*Center for International Trade and Security,
The University of Georgia*

LONDON AND NEW YORK

First published 2002 by Ashgate Publishing

Reissued 2018 by Routledge
2 Park Square, Milton Park, Abingdon, Oxon OX14 4RN
711 Third Avenue, New York, NY 10017, USA

Routledge is an imprint of the Taylor & Francis Group, an informa business

Copyright © Scott A. Jones 2002

Scott A. Jones has asserted his right under the Copyright, Designs and Patents Act, 1988, to be identified as the Author of this work.

All rights reserved. No part of this book may be reprinted or reproduced or utilised in any form or by any electronic, mechanical, or other means, now known or hereafter invented, including photocopying and recording, or in any information storage or retrieval system, without permission in writing from the publishers.

Notice:
Product or corporate names may be trademarks or registered trademarks, and are used only for identification and explanation without intent to infringe.

Publisher's Note
The publisher has gone to great lengths to ensure the quality of this reprint but points out that some imperfections in the original copies may be apparent.

Disclaimer
The publisher has made every effort to trace copyright holders and welcomes correspondence from those they have been unable to contact.

A Library of Congress record exists under LC control number: 2002103119

ISBN 13: 978-1-138-71722-0 (hbk)
ISBN 13: 978-1-138-71721-3 (pbk)
ISBN 13: 978-1-315-19646-6 (ebk)

Contents

Foreword   *vi*
Acknowledgements   *viii*
List of Acronyms   *x*
Map of Ukraine   *xii*

1. Introduction   1

2. Why Do States Develop Systems of Export Control?   18

3. Describing and Measuring the Ukrainian Export Control System: The Explication of Method   44

4. Tools and Methods for Measuring Nonproliferation Export Controls: An Application in Ukraine   60

5. Explaining Ukrainian Export Control Development   98

6. Incentives, Coop(t)eration, and Evolving Self-Interest in the Development of the Ukrainian Export Control System: The Bushehr Case   166

7. Conclusion: The Evolution of Ukrainian Export Control System: State Building and International Cooperation   191

Bibliography   *203*
Index   *219*

Foreword

The stabilization and gradual revival of Ukraine's economy are closely related to the solution of problems of foreign trade. In this sense, maximum utilization of the export potential of Ukraine acquires a particular importance. The reduction of Ukraine's Armed Forces and a sharp decrease in their demand for armaments have objectively necessitated dedicated efforts to promote Ukrainian arms and military equipment on foreign markets. The reliance on military and defense-related items is enlarged owing to the overly militarized nature of the Ukrainian economy. As such, arms exports have turned into a factor of critical economic relevance for easing the economic burden of the transition from a centrally planned economy to one based on free market principles and practices.

As of 2001, Ukraine ranked number ten among the ten leading exporters of military hardware.[1] For the period from 1997 through 2000, Ukraine ranked eighth in such deliveries, with a total of $1.5 billion. Ukraine's continued dependence on arms exports can be an indication that the economies of Belarus and Ukraine may be stagnating. For example, the amount of military hardware that Ukraine delivered to foreign customers in 2000 shows that its economy has not evolved properly from Soviet times.

Ukraine inherited the second largest and, some have argued, the most advanced sector of the former Soviet missile industry. Military production in the Ukrainian Soviet Socialist Republic (SSR) constituted an estimated one-third of the total Soviet military production and 38 percent of Ukraine's total industrial production. Government sources suggest that 1,840 research centers and enterprises and 2.7 million people – 5 percent of Ukraine's total population – are engaged in military production, with 700 of these enterprises, employing 1.3 million people, producing exclusively for the military. Ukraine also possesses significant nuclear, chemical, biological, and missile/space capabilities.

All of the former Soviet Republics did not, however, equally inherit the means controlling and monitoring these locations or the movement of sensitive materials and technologies. Moreover, all of these former Republics have difficulty controlling their borders. Consequently, sensitive items may find their way from or through these states to other regions of the world. Developing effective export control systems for all the NIS, therefore, has become an important objective in the effort to reduce the risk of proliferation of weapons of mass destruction. Because Ukraine possesses the industrial facilities for producing components for weapons of mass destruction (WMD) and related military goods, developing and implementing effective controls there are crucial to world security.

This book examines the development of and rationale behind the Ukrainian export control system. Using a theoretically informed case study methodology, the study explains how and why Ukraine – a new state constrained by inexperience, limited political and economic resources, and relations with Russia – has continued to emphasize the importance of not only maintaining but augmenting its export control system, especially in light of waning international support after nuclear divestiture.

Furthermore, this book assesses the utility of four international relations approaches in explaining nonproliferation export control development. By examining the driving forces behind the development of nonproliferation export control policies, practices, and procedures in Ukraine, we come to better appreciate what is prompting Kyiv to address the potential leakage of weapons and weapons-related items from its territory. In particular, we can ascertain the importance of varying factors, such as security threats, democracy, identity, material inducements, and domestic politics, for explaining the development of nonproliferation policies.

Names, institutions, and circumstances have of course changed since the original writing of this book. However, the theoretical findings and policy recommendations are still valid even if Ukraine – since it divested itself of nuclear weapons and began cooperating with the West on export control development – occupies a less prominent place on the international security agenda of most Western countries. In essence, this study endeavors to approximate an answer to a question that lies at the very heart of the study of international relations: "Why do states cooperate?"

Note

[1] Richard Grimmet, *Conventional Arms Transfers to Developing Nations, 1993 to 2000*, U.S. Congressional Research Service (Washington, DC: 2001).

Acknowledgements

> After such knowledge, what forgiveness?
> T. S. Eliot, *Geronition*

The single heading author line is misleading. This piece, and the obscured time and effort, represents a group effort in the truest sense of the phrase. I am indebted to so many people that upon further reflection my endeavor to thank them all would seem to require a document similar in length, but, mercifully, dissimilar in content. That being said, I would like to note particular individuals.

At the outset, I will try to express to my family the deep humility and gratitude with which I am beset when contemplating how best to thank them for their assorted support and, God only knows, infinite patience while I pursued my bookish infatuations. The plain truth of the matter is that without their encouragement, this effort could not have occurred. Their love and persistence means more than can or should be expressed through so poor a medium.

Dr. Gary Bertsch deserves as much credit for the present product as my family. Gary has been a positive, wholly supportive influence in my life since as an undergraduate I attended his classes on all things communist. Gary has been central in my experience as a world-traveling scholar and published author. We are fortunate in life if we meet a mentor. I count myself, therefore, amongst the fortunate.

Special thanks are due also to my colleagues at the Center for International Trade and Security, especially Dr. Mike Beck. Mike patiently endured many a dark night of the soul while I mused aloud about the impossibility or pointlessness of completing this book. Mike's scholarly eye and abiding friendship was more crucial than his modesty will allow him to realize. I would also like to thank Dr. Jonathan Benjamin-Alvarado for his strategic sense of humor and critical voice, Dr. Igor Khripunov for his patient advice, and Dr. Victor Zaborsky for his lay and professional portrayals of Ukraine and assistance in developing Ukrainian contacts.

My advisors – Drs. Gary Bertsch, John Duffield, Loch Johnson, Igor Khripunov, Han Park, and Victor Zaborsky – provided this study with concerned and insightful guidance. Also, I would like to acknowledge the support and friendship of Dr. Sergey Yatskevitch of the Kyiv Institute for

Nuclear Research. I met Sergey while working as a Los Alamos employee in the summer of 1995. Even then we discussed my ideas for a book along the present lines. His guidance in this endeavor kept the whole process honest and precise.

Surpassing my ability to articulate is my appreciation for the unqualified love and support of my little family, Bryan, Tucker, and Terrell.

Hearty thanks also for the guidance and support of my editors at Ashgate: Amanda, Kirstin, and Sarah.

I must also acknowledge my colleagues at Los Alamos National Laboratory, Argonne National Laboratory (thanks especially to Dr. Basil Picologlou), and the US Department of Energy for providing me with unparalleled access to Ukrainian decision makers and government officials – especially Dr. Gene Taylor. I would like to recognize also the National Research Council's generous financial support for book research and travel. Special thanks are due to my contacts and friends at the State Service for Export of the Cabinet of Ministers of Ukraine, the Ukrainian Scientific and Technical Center, and Dr. Sergey Galaka and Dr. Volodymyr Chumak of Kyiv State University.

List of Acronyms

AG	Australia Group
AIOC	Azerbaijan International Oil Consortium
BSEC	Black Sea Economic Cooperation Organization
BWC	Biological Weapons Convention
CFE	Conventional Forces in Europe Treaty
CIS	Commonwealth of Independent States
COCOM	Coordinating Committee for Multilateral Export Controls
CSCE	Conference on Security and Cooperation in Europe
CTR	Cooperative Threat Reduction (Nunn-Lugar) Program
CWC	Chemical Weapons Convention
DOC	US Department of Commerce
DOD	US Department of Defense
DOE	US Department of Energy
DOS	US Department of State
DSWA	US Defense Special Weapons Agency
EBRD	European Bank for Reconstruction and Development
ECO	Economic Cooperation Organization
ETC	Expert and Technical Committee
EU	European Union
FREEDOM	Freedom for Russia and the Emerging Eurasian Democracies and Open Markets
FSA	Freedom Support Act
FSU	Former Soviet Union
GCEC	Government Commission on Export Controls
GCECP	Governmental Commission on Export Control Policy
GUUAM	Georgia, Ukraine, Uzbekistan, Azerbaijan, and Moldova
HEU	Highly Enriched Uranium
IAEA	International Atomic Energy Agency
ICBM	Inter-Continental Ballistic Missile

List of Acronyms

IMF	International Monetary Fund
IR	International Relations
ITAR	International Traffic in Arms Regulations
JCTI	Joint Commission on Trade and Investment
KEDO	Korean Energy Development Organization
MFA	Ministry of Foreign Affairs
MFER	Ministry of Foreign Economic Relations
MIC	Military-Industrial Complex
MINATOM	Russian Ministry of Atomic Energy
MOD	Ministry of Defense
MOU	Memorandum of Understanding
MPC&A	Materials Protection, Control and Accounting
MTCR	Missile Technology Control Regime
NADR	Nonproliferation, Antiterrorism, Demining and Related
NATO	North Atlantic Treaty Organization
NDF	Nonproliferation and Disarmament Fund
NELRS	Nuclear Export License Review System
NGO	Non-Governmental Organization
NIS	New Independent States
NNWS	Non-Nuclear Weapons State
NPT	Nuclear Nonproliferation Treaty
NSG	Nuclear Suppliers Group
NWFZ	Nuclear Weapons Free Zone
OIC	Organization for the Islamic Conference
OSCE	Organization for Security and Cooperation in Europe
PfP	Partnership for Peace (NATO)
SEED	Support for East European Democracy
SNM	Special Nuclear Materials
SOCAR	State Oil Company of Azerbaijan
SSEC	State Service on Export Control
SSR	Soviet Socialist Republic
STCU	Scientific and Technology Center of Ukraine
UN	United Nations
USD	United States Dollar
USG	United States Government
USSR	Union of Soviet Socialist Republics
WA	Wassenaar Arrangement
WMD	Weapons of Mass Destruction
WTO	World Trade Organization

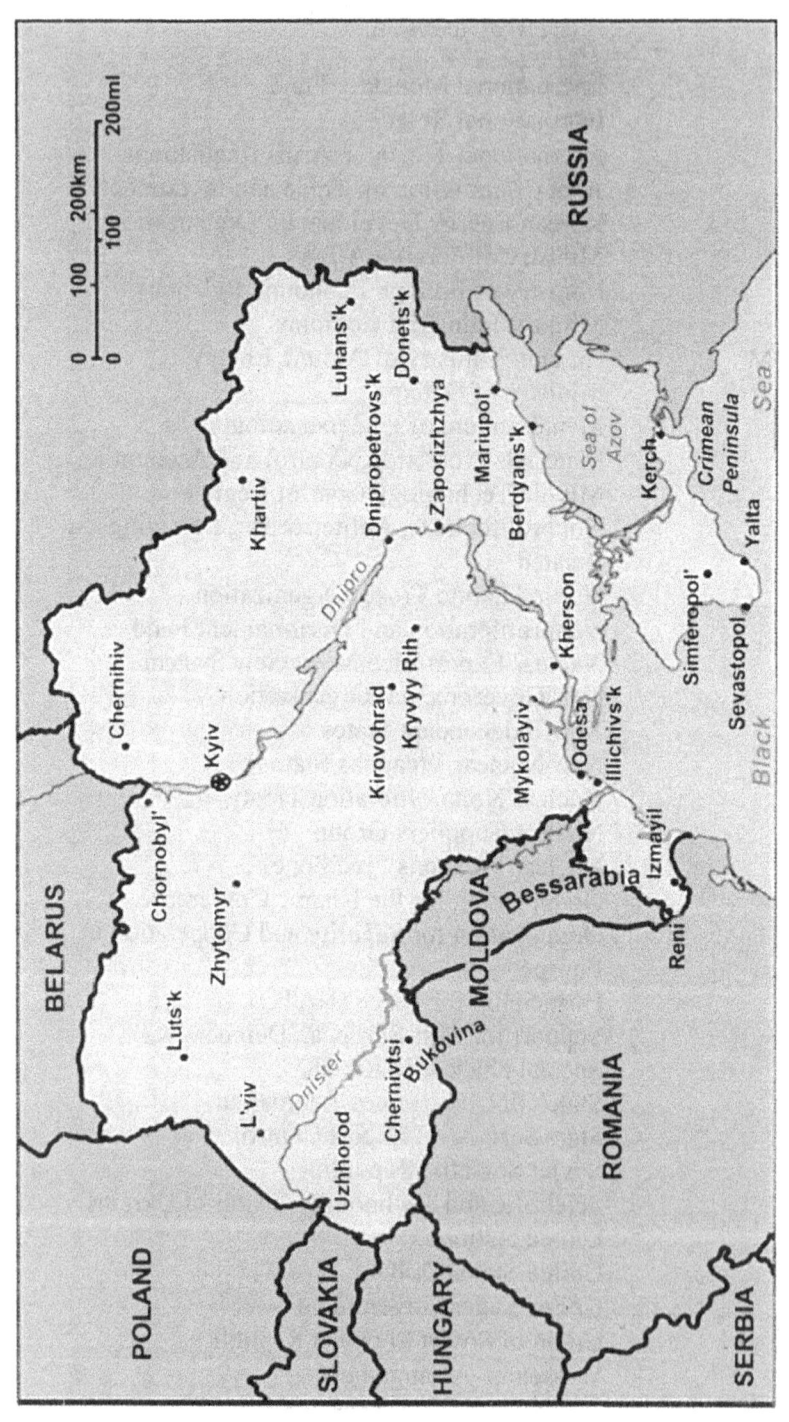

Map of Ukraine

Source: *Perry-Castañeda Map Collection*, University of Texas at Austin, 1998.

Chapter 1

Introduction

1.1 Problem: The Proliferation of Weapons of Mass Destruction and Related Technologies

> The proliferation of weapons of mass destruction and their delivery systems threatens the security of every nation. [W]e reaffirm our commitment to ensure the effective implementation of export controls, in keeping with our undertakings within the nonproliferation regimes. We will deny any kind of assistance to programmes for weapons of mass destruction and their means of delivery. To this end, we will where appropriate undertake and encourage the strengthening of laws, regulations and enforcement mechanism. We will likewise enhance amongst ourselves and with other countries our cooperation on export control, including for instance on the exchange of information. We will ask our experts to focus on strengthening *export control* implementation. And we will broaden awareness among our industrial and business communities of export control requirements.[1]

> The end of the Cold War – and the dissolution of the Soviet Union – has meant that the world has moved from an era of high risk and high stability to one of low risk but also low stability.[2]

Since the demise of the Soviet Union and subsequent end of the Cold War, government and scholarly communities have increasingly paid attention to the potential proliferation threat emanating from the former Soviet region.[3] Almost overnight, the massive military-industrial assets of the Soviet Union came under the jurisdiction of fifteen fledgling states instead of one established government. Who would inherit and control the stockpile of weapons of mass destruction (WMD) and the associated materials, equipment, technology, and expertise posed problems for the security relations of both the newly independent states (NIS) and the globe. Of special concern was how to construct export controls for military and dual-use items (goods, services and technologies with both military and commercial applications) that would reduce the risk of proliferation.

While only Russia, Belarus, Ukraine and Kazakhstan inherited weapons of mass destruction from the Soviet Union, all but three of the fifteen states of the former Soviet Union can produce sensitive materials, technologies, equipment, or have requisite expertise. Moreover, all these states may serve as transit points for legal commerce and illegal smuggling of these items, and several border potentially undesirable end-user states.

Ukraine inherited the second largest and, some have argued, the most advanced portion of the former Soviet defense industry.[4] Military production in the Ukrainian Soviet Socialist Republic (SSR) constituted an estimated one-third of the total Soviet military production and 38 percent of Ukraine's total industrial production.[5] Government sources suggest that 1,840 research centers and enterprises and 2.7 million people – 5 percent of Ukraine's total population – are engaged in military production, with 700 of these enterprises, employing 1.3 million people, producing exclusively for the military. Ukraine also possesses significant nuclear, chemical, biological, and missile/space capabilities.[6]

All of the NIS did not, however, equally inherit the means by which to control and monitor these locations or the movement of sensitive materials and technologies.[7] Moreover, all of the NIS have difficulty controlling their borders. Consequently, sensitive items may find their way from or through these states to other regions of the world.[8] Developing effective export control systems for all the NIS, therefore, has become an important objective in the effort to reduce the risk of proliferation of weapons of mass destruction.[9] As Ukraine possesses the industrial facilities for producing components for weapons of mass destruction (WMD) and related military goods, developing and implementing means of control are crucial to world security.

1.2 Export Controls: The Intertwining of Security and the Economic

The animating object of this study is nonproliferation export controls. For the purposes of study, nonproliferation export controls are defined as a policy tool employed by states to regulate the transfer of WMD, their means of delivery and related technologies. As the name suggests, the term refers to the elaborate set of institutions and provisions that a state establishes to exercise effective control over its weapons-related resources – whether human, physical, or technical. The intrinsic aim of export controls is to erect a selectively permeable membrane that regulates the inflow and outflow of goods, technologies, and related informational resources in a manner consistent with the national laws and international obligations of state.[10] Export controls therefore concern simultaneously national *and* international trade *and* security.

With the end of the Cold War, concerns about the proliferation of WMD and their means of delivery have increased considerably. Concerns have been caused principally by the recent experiences with Iraq and North Korea, and, following the disintegration of the Soviet Union, by the smuggling of fissile material and the potential spread of nuclear weapons technology and expertise.[11] The protracted negotiations over a successor regime to the Coordinating Committee on Multilateral Export Control (COCOM), which have so far only led to the non-committal, unavailing Wassenaar Arrangement, also highlight the difficulty for a state in finding a balance between security and commercial concerns.

1.3 Ukraine: The Onus of Independence

Since gaining independence in 1991, Ukraine, a country of 50 million sitting astride a critical geopolitical juncture,[12] has undergone tremendous political, economic, and social change. Like many of the Eastern European, former Soviet satellite states, Ukraine has struggled to retain its viability as a sovereign state. Moreover, the state-building process in Ukraine began in a history from which a coherent Ukrainian nation-state was absent. As such, the continuing political and accompanying economic crises have made stable governance and economic development into goals unachieved and have completely dominated the political scene in Kyiv.

Since independence, Ukraine undertook four transitions:

1) Moving from a command administrative system to a social-market economy (a market economy with a social welfare safety net);
2) Shifting from a totalitarian political system to a pluralist democracy;
3) Making the transition from a subject of empire to an independent state;
4) Evolution from a country possessing an uneven national identity to one with a civic, unified nation and political culture.

It was generally accepted and acknowledged that comprehensive reforms in several areas of economic life would be required to achieve a successful transition, and that the reform process would extend over several years, and that it would involve profoundly fundamental economic and political – to say nothing of the social – changes.[13] Unfortunately, while several Central and East European countries have made great progress with their political and economic reforms, Ukraine has been one of the slowest to improve.[14] For example, Ukraine, a country of 51 million, has garnered only $2.8 billion (1998) in foreign investment since 1991.[15] A telling comparison is Hungary, a country of 10 million, which has received over $18.5 billion in foreign investment since independence.[16]

One would expect that given the acute political and economic turmoil besetting Ukraine, the development of an export control system would be relegated to the lower rungs of political priorities. However, as my previous research indicates, Ukraine has evinced a clear and consistent pattern of export control development over time.[17] Export control development and international nonproliferation cooperation have increased despite the on-going political and economic difficulties. Many in both the West[18] and Ukraine viewed Ukraine's considerable military-industrial and dual-use goods and technology capacity as the means whereby to stabilize and augment the Ukrainian economy. The conversion of defense enterprises, however, has been – by any measure – a complete failure.[19] Nevertheless, despite considerable domestic political and economic pressure, Ukraine persists in restraining from illicit military trade and in developing its export control system and nonproliferation policies.[20]

Inset 1

The Yuzmash Missile Factory

The Yuzhnoe research production organization and the Yuzmash manufacturing plant, also known as the Southern Machine Building Association, is the largest integrated rocket design and production facility in the world and once produced some of the Soviet Union's most powerful strategic missile systems.[21] Its technological advancement and long history have made it a point of national pride – President Leonid Kuchma was head of the facility for several years – and the residents of Dnipropetrovs'k depend heavily on the plant for their livelihood.[22] Though 50,000 people were once employed on the production side of the plant, and that figure has since dropped to about 30,000 to 34,000,[23] the plant's closure would clearly be an economic disaster. The plant has been producing non-military goods such as space boosters, trolleybuses, washing machines, but financial strain has led to reports that the plant is seeking arms and technology transfer arrangements with China and Iraq as well as technology development with and conversion options – specifically the development of a missile with a range of up to 500 kilometers and use of military missiles as space launchers – that are not supported by proponents of the Missile Technology and Control Regime (MTCR).[24] Thus, Ukraine finds itself with the ability to address an enormous economic burden by taking advantage of its technological capabilities and generating export revenue but consequently

> spurning the nonproliferation agendas of western powers that may attach adherence to agreements such as the MTCR as preconditions for assistance and access to key markets.

1.4 Accounting for Restraint

> We are a civilized government, and it is inappropriate for us to become involved directly in the military business, but, at the same time, we are trying to get around the economic problems without selling complex military technology overseas.
> Viktor Antonov, former director of the Ministry of Machine Building, Military-Industrial Complex, and Conversion[25]

> To help our economy, we are ready to supply missiles [sic] to any republic of the CIS or any other country.
> Leonid Kuchma, director general, Yuzmash Missile and Space Agency, now President of Ukraine[26]

> Today we possess enormous scientific, technical and staff potential and are able to produce competitive products for both domestic and foreign customers. And the armaments market has always existed and will exist for many more years, and it would be unwise not to take advantage of this fact.
> Victor Petrov, former Minister of Machine Building, the Military-Industrial Complex and Defense Conversion[27]

Why would Ukraine attempt to control any export for which it could gain much needed hard currency? Similarly, why would Ukraine feel obligated to add the administrative burden of an export control system when the government continues to face severe financial constraints and other pressing domestic challenges? (See Inset 1.)

These questions are puzzling for various reasons. First, nearly all the NIS are dependent on exports for economic growth, and this is especially the case for Ukraine.[28] Intuitively, one could argue that a high level of export dependence would lead to a low priority being placed on export controls in general and on subsequent progress on export control development in particular. Ukraine, however, is continuing to develop its export control system and to carry out its nonproliferation obligations.[29] Second, Ukraine has experienced significant negative economic growth rates yet is still making significant progress in developing a system of export control (see Table 1.1). For example, President Kuchma recently commented that "the economic and financial situation is complicated in the country and is showing a trend towards worsening. This situation threatens to undermine the viability of the Ukrainian state."[30] This is counter-intuitive because one would expect countries undergoing economic difficulties to balk at any legal, institutional, or behavioral commitments that would hinder, rather than promote, economic activity (exports). This is especially true in high value-added sectors of the economy typical of proliferation-related WMD and dual-use technology.[31]

Other liabilities associated with developing an export control system include economic and domestic political costs. Social dislocation and unemployment may result from imposing any restrictions on exports. Coupled with the failure of defense conversion programs, the resulting unemployment, especially in a highly militarized economy, can bring considerable political pressure to bear on an already unstable government and further social instability.[32] Furthermore, being a "new" state, the relatively significant policy attention devoted to developing the export control system that exists is intriguing.

Table 1.1 Various Economic Indicators: Ukraine 1997-2000[33]

	1997	1998	1999	2000
GDP per head (USD)	985	829	607	638
GDP (% real change pa)	-3.02	-1.93	-0.42	5.97
Government consumption (% of GDP)	23.92	21.56	19	17.8
Budget balance (% of GDP)	-6.64	-1.97	-1.18	2.2
Consumer prices (% change pa; avg.)	15.9	10.6	22.7	28.2
Public debt (% of GDP)	27.09	37.24	48.78	45.5
Labor costs per hour (USD)	0.51	0.42	0.3	0.31
Recorded unemployment (%)	2.74	4.3	5.38	5.3
Current-account balance/GDP	-2.66	-3.09	5.39	4.6
Foreign-exchange reserves (m$)	2,341	761	1,046	1,353

For many years, Western scholars have debated why states develop, implement, and cooperate on systems of export control.[34] Some have suggested that states cooperate on export controls through participation in multilateral fora because the United States compels them to do so, while others have argued that security considerations or domestic political calculations motivate states to cooperate on these policies.[35] More recently, others have argued that a state's liberal identification affects export control cooperation.[36] Still others suggest that some mixture of these and other factors are most appropriate for understanding why states control sensitive exports.[37] Understanding how and why Ukraine developed and continues to augment an export control system (as well as continued international nonproliferation cooperation), therefore, should provide not only a basis for policy prescriptions to improve the Ukrainian system, but also broader theoretical insights about international cooperation and NIS security and economic relationships.

With respect to examining the causal mechanisms behind the behavioral outcome, this study sets forth competing explanations from which behavioral expectations are delineated and then compared against the empirical record. Specifically, four theoretical approaches – Realism/Neorealism, Domestic Political Processes, Rational Institutionalism, and Liberal Identity – provide accounts as to why states would develop export control systems. Each of the perspectives differs in that they would lead us to expect observably different behavior. The subsequent review of the four approaches is limited to how states would behave regarding export controls. The goal is to determine which of the rival approaches helps us better understand the Ukrainian effort.[38] The theoretical approaches guide both data collection and empirical testing. In this respect, case study methods prove quite apropos.

In summary, this study has two primary objectives: to explore how and to what extent Ukraine has developed its export control system; and to explain what drives export control behavior in Ukraine.

1.5 Expectations

The above noted theories and derivative hypotheses suggest that states develop export control systems for a variety of motives. Applied to Ukraine, moreover, we expect to find that some approaches better explain:

1) the initial establishment of the Ukrainian export control system; and
2) the maintenance and continued development thereof.

Specifically, we would expect the founding of the system to best explained by Rational Institutionalism, as evidenced by significant side-payments, the influence and recognition of nonproliferation norms, and a positive cost-benefit analysis undertaken by policy makers, and the inordinate political and economic influence of the United States. The Liberal Identity approach also explain, albeit partially, why Ukraine developed and is developing a system, especially when considering the inchoate and impressionable nature of the Ukrainian political identity.[39] Given the lack of imminent security threats to Ukraine, Neorealism offers little explanatory weight. Further, the absence of export controls as a pressing domestic political issue and the relatively isolated scope of export control policy making and active policy makers, means the domestic politics approach is of little heuristic value.

With regards to the maintenance and continued development of the Ukrainian export control system – despite continued economic stagnation – Rational-Institutionalist and liberal identity explanations should offer more cogent explanations than do behavioral expectations derived from Neorealism or Domestic Politics. Especially persuasive are propositions from the Constructivist (or "sociological") aspect of liberal identity. Constructivism explores the ways in which shared norms and identities shape actors' understandings of their interests.[40] As Ukraine is a "new" state, one cannot assume its interests *a priori*. The Western states, primarily the United States, first raised and continue to stress the importance of the nonproliferation issue to Kyiv. Furthermore, Constructivism allows us to assume that, through such continuous and structured interaction on export control issues, Ukraine came to see the further development of its export control system as part of what it is to be a member of what Anatoly Golubchenko, First Vice Prime Minister of Ukraine, Head of the Governmental Commission on Export Control Policy, referred to as the "community of civilized nations," rather than due to independent national preferences – which were themselves in the process of development and articulation – arising from security concerns or domestic political interests.[41]

In summary, the preliminary expectations are as follows:

1) The impetus and capabilities to construct a nonproliferation export control system in Ukraine arose from Western (primarily US) influence and accompanying financial and technical incentives, and "soft" political-economic pressure[42] and not from security concerns or internally-born domestic political imperatives; and
2) The continued development of the export control system and increased international nonproliferation cooperation are the result of an increasing identification with the Western states (and the norms associated therewith) and continued material and promissory inducements.

1.6 Research Procedure

To analyze and examine the expectations highlighted in the previous section, this study employs the case study method (an elaboration of which is to be found in chapter 2). The case study method is most appropriate for this project as it is preferred when researchers: (1) ask "how" and "why" questions; (2) do not and cannot control the subjects and/or events being studied; and (3) focus on contemporary events in their natural context.[43] Moreover, case studies are useful when investigators attempt to illuminate particular decisions, processes, institutions and events, why and how each of these operated and/or are made, and what resulted.[44] This study presents a case study of Ukraine which compares the behavioral expectations (outlined above) against the empirical record of Ukraine's export control development. The behavioral expectations served as a common guide for data collection and analysis.

The objective of this study is to determine which approach, if any, best explains the development of nonproliferation export control measures in Ukraine. An explication of the methodology, review of relevant literature and derivative hypotheses are to be found in the subsequent chapters.

Specifically concerning the measurement of export control development (dependent variable), this study will analyze and evaluate Ukrainian export control measures using a general quantitative tool based on Western nonproliferation export control "common standards" that have emerged over the past several decades.[45] The independent variables of an export control system – and therefore suggestive of development *vis-à-vis* a standardized measure – are found in Table 1.2. Because individual states develop and implement national systems of export control, it is possible that states may inconsistently create and apply export control measures. Such inconsistencies or gaps in export control systems decrease the effectiveness of export control as an international nonproliferation tool. Multilateral action is, therefore, necessary.

Table 1.2   Elements of an Export Control System

•	Licensing System	•	Control Lists
•	Regime Adherence	•	Catch-All Clause
•	Training	•	Bureaucratic Process
•	Customs Authority	•	Import/Export Verification
•	Penalties	•	Information Gathering/Sharing

1.7 Significance

> The dark ages may return, the Stone Age may return on the gleaming wings of science, and what might now shower immeasurable material blessings upon mankind, may even bring about its total destruction.
> Sir Winston Churchill, "The Sinews of Peace," 5 March 1946, Fulton, Missouri

Although much voiced, the proliferation of WMD material and technology is truly a profoundly global and critical threat to world security. In this respect, nonproliferation export controls have played, and continue to play, an important role in the realm of international security. Because the new states of the former Soviet Union inherited vast stockpiles of weaponry, as well as sensitive materials and technologies, but did not equally inherit the means for controlling such an inheritance, it is important to evaluate, examine and explain nonproliferation export control behavior in the region generally, and in Ukraine specifically. This study seeks to do just that. Through this analysis, the overall objective of the study is to provide practical and theoretical insights regarding Ukrainian export control behavior. An enhanced understanding of export control development should in turn enhance the ability to further control and prevent the proliferation of the world's most deadly weapons.

1.8 Outline of the Book

> We ourselves often spoil our reputation because of lack of experience in these matters [export controls] and sometimes because of our foolishness. Crooks from the far and near abroad are flocking into our country to offer their brokerage in the export of controlled goods.
> Volodomyr Radchenko, Chief of Ukrainian Security Service [46]

The book continues with six chapters. Chapter two reviews various theoretical perspectives in international relations (hereafter: IR) accounting for state behavior in terms of export control policy. Behavioral expectations – which serve as research guides in this study – are derived from the theoretical approaches, thereby allowing a formal comparison of the theoretical expectations with the empirical record. Chapter three outlines the research methodology. Chapter four explains the evaluative method for measuring export control systems and applies the methodology to the Ukrainian case. Chapter five seeks to test the behavioral expectations with the historical record of behavior. Moreover, chapter five attempts to explain why Ukraine developed and continues to augment a nonproliferation export control system, using the various perspectives as heuristic guides. Chapter six expands on the conclusions reached in the preceding chapter; specifically, elaborating on the relationship between expectations derived from the Rational Institutional and Liberal Identity approaches. Chapter seven, the concluding chapter, canvasses the theoretical and policy implications of the study. Chapter seven also assesses the general applicability of the findings to other venues and issues of international relations.

Notes

[1] Excerpt from "Final Communiqué from G-8 Birmingham Summit," 17 May 1998.

[2] "Terrorism Meets Proliferation: A Post-Cold War Convergence of Threats," speech by Senator (ret.) Sam Nunn at the Inaugural *Sam Nunn Policy Forum*, "Terrorism, Weapons of Mass Destruction, and US Security" (organized by the Center for International Trade and Security), University of Georgia, 29 April 1997.

[3] See, for example, Graham Allison, et al., *Avoiding Nuclear Anarchy: Containing the Threat of Loose Russian Nuclear Weapons and Fissile Material* (Cambridge: The MIT Press, 1996); William Potter, "Before the Deluge: Assessing the Threat of Nuclear Leakage from the Post-Soviet States," *Arms Control Today* 25, 8 (October 1996), pp. 9-16; Zachary Davis and Jason Ellis, "Nuclear Proliferation: Problems in the States of the Former Soviet Union," *CRS Report for Congress* IB91129 (June 28, 1995); United States General Accounting Office, "Weapons of Mass Destruction: Reducing the Threat From the Former Soviet Union: An Update," GAO/NSIAD-95-165 (June 1995); United States General Accounting Office, "Nuclear Nonproliferation: US Assistance to Improve Nuclear Material Controls in the Former Soviet Union," GAO/NSIAD/RCED-96-89 (March 1996); US Congress, Office of Technology Assessment, *Proliferation and the Former Soviet Union*, OTA-ISS-605 (Washington, DC: US Government Printing Office, September 1994); and *Combat Proliferation of Weapons of Mass Destruction: [Deutsch] Commission Report of the Commission to Assess the Organization of the Federal Government to Combat the Proliferation of Weapons of Mass Destruction* (Washington, DC: US Publishing Office, 1999).

[4] See, William Potter, *Nuclear Profiles of the Soviet Successor States*. Monograph No. 1. Monterey Institute of International Studies. May 1993, pp. 83-90.

[5] Robert Keatley, "Ukraine Arms Makers Seek Civilian Pursuits," The Wall Street Journal, 20 April 1992; Christopher Hummel, "Ukrainian Arms Makers Are Left on Their Own," *Radio Free Europe/Radio Liberty (RFE/RL) Research Report*, 14 August 1992, pp. 33-37.

[6] See, Gary K. Bertsch and William C. Potter, eds., *Dangerous Weapons, Desperate States: Russia, Belarus, Kazakstan, and Ukraine* (New York: Routledge, 1999); *Proliferation and Export Controls: An Analysis of Sensitive*

Technologies and Countries of Concern, Deltac & Saferworld Report (Surrey, 1995); and *Proliferation Concerns: Assessing US Efforts to Help Contain Nuclear and Other Dangerous Materials and Technologies in the Former Soviet Union*, Office of International Affairs, National Research Council (Washington, DC: National Academy Press, 1997) – Dr. Bertsch was a contributor to this report.

[7] See Potter, *Nuclear Profiles of the Soviet Successor States* (Monterey, CA: Monterey Institute of International Studies, 1993).

[8] Many cases have already been documented. In Ukraine, for example, 100 kg of mercury was confiscated along with falsified documents from Armenia, Tajikistan, Moldova and Russia. See "Attempt to Smuggle Radioactive Material Thwarted," *Radio Ukraine World Service*, 22 December 1993, JPRS-TND-93-003, 1/31/94, p. 28. Reportedly, an Azeri, who made his way to Turkey via Armenia, was detained in Istanbul as he attempted to sell 750 grams of enriched uranium. See "Azeri Detained in Turkey with Uranium For Sale," *Reuters* 10/20/94. For cases of smuggling throughout the former Soviet region, see Craig Whitney, "Germans Seize More Weapons Material," *The New York Times* 17 August 1994; Julia Rubin, "Nuclear Nightmare: A Soviet Legacy," *Sunday Age* 27 November 1994, p. 16; and the Statement of William Potter Before the Permanent Subcommittee on Investigations, Committee on Government Affairs, United States Senate, March 13, 1996.

[9] On the importance of export control as a long-term challenge requiring continuous development and modification to address the changing domestic and international environment, see Gary Bertsch and Igor Khripunov, "Restraining the Spread of the Soviet Arsenal: Export Controls as a Long-Term Nonproliferation Tool," *Status Report*, Center for International Trade and Security, University of Georgia, March 1996; and the Statement of Gary Bertsch Before the Permanent Subcommittee on Investigations, Committee on Government Affairs, United States Senate, March 13, 1996.

[10] See, Gary K. Bertsch, Richard T. Cupitt, and Steven Elliott-Gower, eds., *International Cooperation on Nonproliferation Export Controls: Prospects for the 1990s and Beyond* (Ann Arbor: University of Michigan Press, 1994), pp. 3-25.

[11] See, for example, Mark Phythian, *Arming Iraq: How the US and Britain Secretly Built Saddam's War Machine* (Northeastern University Press: 1996); Mitchell Reiss and Robert Litwak, *Nuclear Proliferation after the Cold War* (Washington, Johns Hopkins University Press, 1994); and Scott A. Jones "Post-Warsaw Pact Arsenal Unbound: Managing Weapons Flows to Conflict Zones," Center for International Trade and Security Occasional Paper, August 1999 (Athens: The University of Georgia).

[12] A study outlining the geostrategic importance of Ukraine to regional security is Sherman W. Garnett, *Keystone in the Arch: Ukraine in the Emerging Security Environment of Central and Eastern Europe* (Washington, DC: Carnegie Endowment for International Peace, 1997). See especially pp. 41-82.

[13] On the continuing structural problems facing a newly independent Ukraine, see Jozef Darski, "Quo Vadis Ukraine?" *Uncaptive Minds*, 5/1 (Spring 1992), pp. 59-

74; Paula Dobriansky, "Ukraine: A Question of Survival," *The National Interest*, 36 (Summer 1994), pp. 65-72; Stephen Larrabee, "Ukraine: Europe's Next Crisis?" *Arms Control Today*, July/August 1994, pp. 14-19; and John Jaworsky, *Ukraine: Stability and Instability, McNair Paper 42* (Washington DC, August 1995). Dobriansky, for example, describes Ukraine as a "crisis state," a state in which its fundamental existence is perpetual "semi-collapse."

[14] Paul Hare, "Ukraine: the Legacies of Central Planning and the Transition to a Market Economy," in Taras Kuzio, *Contemporary Ukraine: Dynamics of Post-Soviet Transformation* (New York: M.E. Sharpe, 1998), pp. 181-199.

[15] David Dyker, "FDI in Ukraine: First Results, Tendencies and Prospects," in David Dyker, ed., *Foreign Direct Investment and Technology Transfer in the Former Soviet Union* (London: Edward Elgar Publishers, 1999).

[16] Mohammed Ishaq, "Foreign Direct Investment in Ukraine Since Transition," *Communist & Post-Communist Studies* 32, no. 1 (March 1999), pp. 91-109; *Foreign Direct Investment in Ukraine*, OECD Working Papers, vol. 5, no. 83 (Paris: OECD, 1997); and *United Nations Development Report: Ukraine 1998*, United Nations, Kyiv, 1999.

[17] See Scott Jones and Victor Zaborsky, "Ukraine," in *Restraining the Spread of the Soviet Arsenal: A Status Report*, Center for International Trade and Security, University of Georgia, October 1995; "The Evolution of the Ukrainian Export Control System: State Building and International Cooperation," in Gary K. Bertsch and Suzette R. Grillot, eds., *Arms on the Market: Reducing the Risk of Proliferation in the Former Soviet Union* (New York: Routledge, 1998); and Scott Jones, "Ukraine," Global Evaluation of Nonproliferation Export Controls: 1999, Center for International Trade & Security, University of Georgia, 1999.

[18] The "West" is a generic historical, political, and economic term, seldom explicitly defined, used to designate an ostensibly distinct "civilization." This term is, needless to say, problematic at best. Nevertheless, for the sake of this study, the "West" is understood to be a political-economic community of similar states sharing the primary tenets of Western society. David Gress presents an apropos description of these central tenets: "With the end of the Cold War and the collapse of the Soviet empire. the *market economy* and *democracy* appear to have triumphed. Universally praised, these two central values of Western society have become the prerequisite for any nation seeking acceptance by the international community or assistance from international financial institutions." David Gress, "The Modern Western Identity: Its Fit in World Politics," *Current*, no. 398, December 1997, pp. 7-18. Recent studies of the "West" include: Samuel Huntington, *The Clash of Civilizations and the Remaking of World Order* (New York: Simon and Schuster, 1996); Thomas C. Patterson, *Inventing Western Civilization* (New York: Monthly Review Press, 1997); Jacques Attali, "The Crash of Western Civilization: The limits of the Market and Democracy," *Foreign Policy*, no. 107, Summer 1997, pp. 54-64.

[19] Marget B. McClean and Deborah Palmieri, "Marketization through Defense Conversion: A Policy Prescriptive on the Ukrainian Case," in Deborah Palmieri,

ed., *Russia and the NIS in the World Economy: East-West Investment, Financing, and Trade* (Westport, CT: Præger, 1996) pp. 149-60. See also, Stacy Larsen, "An Overview of Defense Conversion in the Ukraine," Bonn International Center for Conversion, *BICC paper 9*, June 1997; and, Center for Peace, Conversion and Foreign Policy of Ukraine, "Conversion in Ukraine: Problems and Prospects," Analytical Paper Series, October 1998, Kyiv.

[20] A senior Ukrainian export control official noted: "The government of Ukraine continues to stress the importance of export control development, in conformity to international nonproliferation norms. Recently, the main export control agency [the Ukrainian State Service for Export Control] was accorded ministerial status." Author's interview: Athens, GA. See also, See, Robert Keatley, "Ukraine Arms Makers Seek Civilian Pursuits."

[21] John Baker, *Nonproliferation Incentives for Russia and Ukraine*, Adelphi Paper 309 (Oxford: International Institute for Strategic Studies, 1997), pp. 14-15.

[22] Much of the Ukrainian political elite hail from Dnipropetrovsk. See, Taras Kuzio, *Ukraine: State and Nation Building* (New York: Routledge, 1998), pp. 60-62. Kuzio, as well as other analysts, refer to the Kuchma administration as the "Dnipropetrovsk clan."

[23] Baker, p. 10. See also, George Quester, ed., *The Nuclear Challenge in Russia and the New States of Eurasia* (London: M.E. Sharpe, 1996).

[24] See, Gary K. Bertsch and Victor Zaborsky, "Bringing Ukraine Into the MTCR: Can US Policy Succeed?" *Arms Control Today* 27, 2 (April 1997), pp. 9-14.

[25] *Ekonomicheskaya Gazeta*, July 1992.

[26] *Pravda Ukrainy*, 23 June 1992.

[27] *FBIS-SOV-95-050*, 15 March 1993.

[28] See, Nicholas Stern, "The Future of the Economic Transition," *EBRD Working Paper*, No. 30, July 1998, and *Economist Intelligence Unit Report*, Ukraine, 1st Quarter 1999.

[29] In 1998, Ukraine ranked a score of 35.41 out of an ideal 41.82, or a 83 per cent compliance rate with western export control standards. Furthermore, when examining overall development over time, a longitudinal study also suggests a progressive pattern. In other words, since 1992, there has been a steady evolutionary path in the development of its export control system. For an explanation of the scoring methodology, see Suzette R. Grillot, "Explaining the Development of Nonproliferation Export Controls: Framework, Theory and Method," in Gary K. Bertsch and Suzette R. Grillot, eds., *Arms on the Market: Reducing the Risk of Proliferation in the Former Soviet Union* (New York: Routledge, 1998). In this volume, see also, Scott A. Jones, "The Evolution of the Ukrainian Export Control System: State Building and International Cooperation," pp. 57-88.

[30] Mikhail Melnik, "Kuchma Says Economic Situation in Ukraine 'Explosive,'" *Itar-Tass, FBIS-SOV-99-169*. Official figures put the overall size of Ukraine's economy in 1999 at US$30.8 billion, only around two-thirds the size of Hungary's economy in US dollar terms despite a population that is five times larger. Even in

purchasing parity terms, Ukraine ranks well below its central European neighbors and Russia. Ukraine's GDP per head in terms of purchasing power parity stood at around US$2,100 in 1999, compared with around US$4,400 in Russia, US$7,300 in Poland, US$8,400 in Hungary and US$10,500 in the Czech Republic. See, *Economist Intelligence Unit: Ukraine 2001, 2nd Quarter, The Economist*, Summer 2001 and International Monetary Fund: Ukraine: Fifth and Sixth Review under the Extended Arrangement - Staff Report; Staff Supplement and News Brief on the Executive Board Discussion, Series: Country Report No. 01/216, November 2001, http://www.imf.org/external/pubs/cat/longres.cfm?sk=15515.0.

[31] For an examination of economic costs attendant with export controls, see Kathleen Bailey, "Nonproliferation Export Controls: Problems and Alternatives," in Kathleen Bailey and Robert Rudney, eds., *Proliferation and Export Controls* (New York: University Press of America, 1993), pp. 49-55. Bailey also argues that there are opportunity costs to developing export control systems, so that such development may come at the expense of other governmental activities. A recognition of the value of sensitive exports is evidenced by a recent statement of the Ukrainian Industrial Policy Minister, Vasyl Hureyev. Hureyev noted that military export makes up the major part of the export potential of Ukrainian industry. He said that military items have the most export potential among industrial branches. According to the minister, Ukraine "has chosen the course of increasing the number of types of armament with closed production cycles." Hureyev named some examples: aviation, shipbuilding, the production of armored vehicles, and warheads. "Ukraine: Industrial Policy Minister Outlines Military Export Plans," *Unian*, 3 July 2001.

[32] See, Stacy Larsen, "An Overview of Defense Conversion in the Ukraine," *Working Paper 9*, June 1997, Bonn International Centre on Conversion, pp. 32-33.

[33] Source: *Economist Intelligence Unit Report*, Ukraine, 2nd Quarter 2000 and *EBRD 2000 Transition Country Report: Ukraine* (London: EBRD, 1998).

[34] See, for example, Gary K. Bertsch, Richard T. Cupitt, and Steven Elliott-Gower, eds., *op. cit.*; Gary K. Bertsch and Steven Elliott-Gower, eds., *Export Controls in Transition: Perspectives, Problems, and Prospects* (Durham: Duke University Press, 1992); Peter Sullivan, *Export Controls: Conventional Arms and Dual-Use Technologies* (Washington, DC: National Defense University, Institute for National Strategic Studies, 1996); William J. Long, *US Export Control Policy: Executive Autonomy vs. Congressional Reform* (New York: Columbia University Press, 1989), Homer E. Moyer and Linda A. Mabry, *Export Controls as Instruments of Foreign Policy: The History, Legal Issues, and Policy Lessons of Three Recent Cases* (Lanham, MD: International Law Institute, 1988). A recent study of export control developments in the FSU is Gary K. Bertsch and Suzette Grillot, *Arms on the Market*; see especially, pp. 1-31, 213-228.

[35] See Gunnar Adler-Karlsson. *Western Economic Warfare* (Stockholm: Alquist and Wiksell, 1968); Michael Mastanduno. *Economic Containment: CoCom and the Politics of East-West Trade* (Ithaca: Cornell University Press, 1992) or Hendrik Roodbeen, *Trading the Jewel of Great Value: The Participation of the*

Netherlands, Belgium, Switzerland, and Austria in the Western Strategic Embargo versus the Socialist Countries (Rijksuniversiteit Leiden, The Netherlands, 1991).

[36] Michael Lipson, "The Reincarnation of COCOM: Explaining Post-Cold War Export Controls," *The Nonproliferation Review* 6, no. 2 (Winter 1999), pp. 33-51 and Richard Cupitt and Suzette Grillot, "COCOM is Dead, Long Live COCOM: Persistence and Change in Multilateral Security Institutions," *British Journal of Political Science*, 27 (July 1997), pp. 361-389. Lipson contends: "States would be expected to join export control regimes and establish COCOM-like national export control systems out of a sense that this is part of what it is to be a proper state, rather than due to independent national preferences arising from security concerns or domestic political interests (45)." See also, Glenn Chafetz, "The End of the Cold War and the Future of Nuclear Proliferation: An Alternative to the Neorealist Perspective," in Zachary Davis and Benjamin Frankel, eds., *The Proliferation Puzzle: Why Nuclear Weapons Spread and What Results* (London: Frank Cass, 1993), pp. 127-158.

[37] See Bertsch et al., eds. *International Cooperation on Nonproliferation Export Controls: Prospects for the 1990s and Beyond* (Ann Arbor: University of Michigan Press, 1994); and Claus Hofhansel, *Commercial Competition and National Security: Comparing US and German Export Control Policies* (Westport, CT: Præger, 1996).

[38] The present study is built upon on-going FSU export control research at the Center for International Trade and Security at the University of Georgia. A recent study is, Bertsch and Grillot, *Arms on the Market*; see especially, Scott Jones, "The Evolution of the Ukrainian Export Control System," pp. 57-89.

[39] On the unsettled nature of Ukrainian political identity, see Taras Kuzio, *Ukraine: State and Nation Building*, Routledge Studies of Societies in Transition, 9 (New York: Routledge, 1998), pp. 107-55. Kuzio maintains that the Ukrainian political identity has been profoundly influenced by Western – and US in particular – involvement and assistance. Furthermore, he notes, "the Ukrainian elite view relations with the West as indispensible to political and economic development," pp. 75-76.

[40] See, for example, Martha Finnemore, *National Interests in International Society* (Ithaca: Cornell University Press, 1996).

[41] For a similar argument, see Martha Finnemore, "Norms, Cultures, and World Politics: Insights from Sociology's Institutionalism," *International Organization*, 50 (Spring 1996). Glenn Chafetz, for example, argues that liberal state identity resulting from institutional interaction helps explain export control cooperation and consonance. See, Glenn Chafetz, "The End of the Cold War and the Future of the Nonproliferation Regime: An Alternative to the Neorealist Perspective," in Davis and Frankel, *The Proliferation Puzzle*, pp. 127-58. A recent study attempting to explain the disparate levels of export control in the FSU notes: "The evidence demonstrates that the countries that have made more progress toward establishing a liberal, democratic government tended to have made more headway in developing

national export control systems." See Bertsch and Grillot, eds., *Arms on the Market*, p. 223.

[42] "Soft power" is an expression coined by Joseph Nye. Nye contends that power, popularly conceived, need not be limited to direct application of material advantage. Nye defines "soft," or "co-optive," power – as opposed to "command" power – is an "indirect way to exercise power. A country may achieve outcomes it prefers in world politics because other countries want to follow it or have agreed to a system *that produces such effects. Co-optive power can rest on the attraction of one's ideas or on the ability to set the political agenda in a way that shapes the preferences the others express.*" See, Joseph Nye, "The Changing Nature of World Power," *Political Science Quarterly*, vol. 105, no. 2 (1990), p. 181; and *Bound to Lead: the Changing Nature of American Power* (New York: Basic Books, 1990). The issue of co-optive power – as it applies to US-Ukrainian relations – will be examined in chapter 6.

[43] Robert Yin, *Case Study Research: Design and Methods* (Newbury Park, CA: Sage Publications, Inc., 1989), p. 4. For more on the case study method, see Harry Eckstein, "Case Study and Theory in Political Science," in Fred I. Greenstein and Nelson W. Polsby, eds., *Handbook of Political Science, Volume 7: Strategies of Inquiry* (Reading, MA: Addison-Wesley Publishing Company, 1975), pp. 79-137; and Alexander L. George, "Case Studies and Theory Development: The Method of Structured, Focused Comparison," in Paul Gordon Lauren, ed., *Diplomacy: New Approaches in History, Theory, and Policy* (New York: The Free Press, 1979), pp. 43-68.

[44] Joe R. Feagin, Anthony M. Orum, and Gideon Sjoberg, eds., *A Case for the Case Study* (Chapel Hill: University of North Carolina Press, 1991).

[45] For a complete and detailed description of this measurement tool for export control development, see Cassady Craft and Suzette Grillot with Liam Anderson, Michael Beck, Chris Behan, Scott Jones, and Keith Wolfe, "Tools and Methods for Measuring and Comparing Nonproliferation Export Control Development," Occasional Paper of the Center for International Trade and Security (Athens: The University of Georgia, 1996); and Grillot and Craft, "How and Why We Evaluate Systems of Export Control," *The Monitor: Nonproliferation, Demilitarization and Arms Control* 2, 4 (Fall 1996).

[46] Leonid Frosvych, "New Ukrainian Arms Trade Company Profiled," *Kyivskiye Vedmosti, FBIS-TAC-98-257*, 14 September 1998.

Chapter 2

Why Do States Develop Systems of Export Control?

The problematic character of modern theories of international relations has been widely discussed, especially in relation to the presumed bankruptcy of established intellectual traditions, the untidy proliferation of research strategies, an unseemly dependence on the interests of specific states and cultures, and the hubris of empirical social science. Very often, the more far-reaching epistemological problems posed by those who seek to understand what is involved in making knowledge claims about social and political processes have been pushed aside in favor of even more restricted concerns about method and research techniques. This approach limits the types of questions we may ask of these processes. However, these questions remain interesting despite the socio-scientific attempt to reduce them problems of utilitarian calculation and empirical testing.[1]

At least four theoretical approaches – Realism/Neorealism, Domestic Political Processes, Liberal Identity, and Rational Institutionalism – offer explanations as to why states would develop export control systems. Each of the perspectives differs in that they would lead us to expect observably different behavior. This chapter review of the four approaches is limited to how states would behave regarding export controls. The derived expectations sets are heuristic devices that frame the explanation effort. In the subsequent chapter, these expectations will be weighed against the empirical record. From this assessment, conclusions will be drawn regarding state behavior; specifically, explaining why Ukraine developed an export control system.

2.1 Realism/Neorealism[2]

Systems theories, whether political or economic, are theories that explain how the organization of a realm acts as a constraining and disposing force on the interacting units within it. Such theories tell us about the forces the units are subject to. From them, we can infer some things about the expected behavior and fate of the units: namely, how they will have to compete with and adjust to one another if they are to survive and flourish. To the extent that dynamics of a system limit the freedom of its units, their behavior and the outcomes of their behavior become predictable.[3]

The Realist/Neorealist approach to international relations suggests that because of the lack of a central governing authority in world politics, whose role it is to execute and enforce rules, laws and norms, states operate and interact in an international system characterized by anarchy.[4] In an anarchical system, therefore, states must rely on their own wits and abilities as they attempt to achieve national security and maintain survival. States are overwhelmingly motivated by their primary objective of guaranteeing their security through the pursuit of power.[5] Acquiring military capability, then, is important for achieving this objective. Moreover, states are compelled to balance the power of other, potentially adversarial, states. To do so, they rely either on internal balancing measures by focusing on their own capabilities, or on external balancing by forming or joining military alliances.[6]

Gilpin (in Keohane 1986:304-5) suggests that three assumptions about political life are common to all Realists:

1) The nature of international affairs is essentially conflictual;
2) The essence of social reality is the group rather than the individual, and particularly the conflict group, whether tribe, city-state, kingdom, empire, or nation-state; and
3) The prime human motivation in all political life is power and security.

Keohane (1986:164-65) identifies the following hard core assumptions of *Classical* (i.e. mid-twentieth century) Realism:

1) States are the most important actors in world politics;
2) States are unitary rational actors, albeit operating under conditions of stress, uncertainty and imperfect information; and
3) States seek power and calculate their interests in terms of power.

In addressing threats to international stability, neorealism – or "structural"[7] realism posits the following central assumptions:

1) International politics is characterized by systemic anarchy;

2) States, as rational unitary entities, are the central actors in international politics;
3) States seek to maximize their security above all else, considering other factors only when security is assured; and
4) States try to increase their power if doing so does not put their security at risk.

Anarchy means that there is no supranational authority that can enforce agreements between states. Consequently, international politics involves self-help above all else. No state can count on any other for help except to the extent that others expect to benefit themselves by helping. The assumption of anarchy is equivalent to saying that international politics is played out as a non-cooperative game. Non-cooperative games are games in which promises are not binding and contracts are enforced by self-interest rather than by some external authority.[8]

The second assumption claims that domestic politics within states are largely irrelevant to international politics. It is because of this assumption that neorealists argue that foreign policy needs to be considered separately from international politics.[9] By assuming that the state is the central actor and that it is unitary and rational, neorealism puts aside internal factors, like those highlighted by bureaucratic or interest group perspectives, when dealing with issues that might jeopardize the state's survival.

The third assumption establishes the primacy of security above all other possible goals. It also establishes that states are not willing to trade away any of their currently assured security for other benefits. Other things of value are only pursued once security is assured. This assumption lends considerable predictability to behavior if international affairs in reality is consistent with these assumptions. Because all states are assumed to have the same goal, there is no need to worry about idiosyncratic factors like the personalities of individual leaders or the domestic political institutions that govern state behavior. Every state is a role player with the role dictated by its security needs and its position in the distribution of power among states.[10]

The final assumption tells us that states are always interested in increasing their influence over other states. No state is content to be weak, but states accept being weaker than they might otherwise be if pursuit of greater power could place their security at risk. This assumption places restrictions on the pursuit of power. The idea is that if a state becomes sufficiently powerful that other states foresee the prospect that their security will be threatened by it in the future, then they join together to deprive the growing state of the power to threaten them. So, an increase in a state's power can actually make the state weaker in the long run if the increase in power alarms rivals and mobilizes them to form an opposition alliance.[11] A coalition or alliance of states is expected to come together to beat back a growing state if that state's power threatens to become large enough that others face a possible loss of sovereignty as a result of the growing power of the first state. This well-known element of the security dilemma which bedeviled earlier realist theories, is solved in the neorealist formulation by the presence of the third and fourth assumption. These two assumptions place a brake on the pursuit of power. Morgenthau argued that, "Since the desire to attain a maximum of power is universal, all nations must always be afraid that their own miscalculations and the power increases of other nations might add up to an inferiority for themselves which *they must at all costs try to avoid.*"[12]

With his third and fourth assumptions, Waltz, for example, sets out an important innovation over earlier realist thought. States are not assumed to seek power or to avoid a decrease in power at all costs. Specifically, the quest for power is assumed not to be worthwhile if it costs the state its current security. Power becomes an instrument for security in neorealism, while it was the goal of states in realism.

Because states operate in a "self-help" environment under anarchy, pursue power as a means for achieving security, and seek to balance against other powers, realists and neorealists suggest that states are necessarily concerned with the relative gains of both friends and foes. The anarchical nature of the international system, after all, breeds distrust. Security-minded states, in other words are inherently wary of the actions of others as states may very well take advantage of each other in the daily struggle to survive. Because all states are striving to maintain their sovereignty, they find it difficult to be certain of other states' intentions. States must always anticipate the dangers of offensive actions and are, therefore, aware of and sensitive to the capabilities of others.[13]

According to the Realist/Neorealist perspective, we would expect states to have a more developed export control system if they are particularly concerned about external threats to their security and perceive export control development as a way to diminish those threats by limiting the diffusion of military related items, technology and know-how.[14] We would also expect to see a greater commitment to export control development in those states that are seeking to balance the power of a particular state or group of states by controlling the flow of weapons, materials, and technology to them. States may, however, focus export control measures toward certain target states whom they wish to balance against, and away from allies who are participating in such balancing efforts. The Realist/Neorealist approach also leads us to expect that states concerned about the relative gain in other states' military capabilities would seek to stem the transfer of military relevant equipment and technology to others. Moreover, export control systems will be more developed in those states that see such behavior as a way to *enhance* their security in relation to others (see Table 2.1).

Table 2.1 Realism/Neorealism: Expected Behavior

- Concern about external threats to security as a result of weapons, equipment and technology proliferation;

- Desire to balance the power of others by controlling the export of military items, possibly steering controls towards particularly threatening states and away from friendly states;

- Interest in preventing gains in other states' military capabilities;

- Attempt to use export controls as a means for enhancing state security.

2.2 Domestic Politics

Scholars have often found that various Domestic Political variables have a profound effect on foreign policy choices. To date, no single theory of Domestic Politics exists to explain state behavior, international cooperation, or (especially) export control policies. There are, however, at least four Domestic Political approaches that may enlighten and inform us as to the decision state leaders make and the policies they employ.[15] Below I review four domestic theories (pluralist, elitist, institutional and bureaucratic theories), and elicit from each various expectations for state action regarding export control behavior in the NIS.[16]

Pluralist approaches to foreign policy suggest that domestic interest groups matter. Findings on the specific impact of interest groups have, however, been mixed. Some scholars argue that domestic pressure groups play a limited role in the construction of state policies, while others find that they significantly affect state behavior.[17] The pluralist approach centers on the competition and struggle between various groups with various interests, each vying for influence over particular policy choices.

In the realm of nuclear policy, for example, Etel Solingen explains state decisions to develop and maintain nuclear weapons according to the relative strength or weakness of two broad interest groups – a "liberalizing coalition" and an "inward-looking coalition." The first group, which prefers less state intervention in economic affairs, and seeks economic opportunities outside state boundaries, is less willing to support a state's nuclear status if it inhibits access to external markets. The second group, which supports the extension of state power into economic (and other) affairs and opposes state openness beyond national borders, is more willing to herald nuclear weapon status if such a stance enhances state independence, and prevents the intrusion of external influences in state affairs.[18] These groups, therefore, struggle to influence state decisions. Ultimately, their pressure places constraints on the choices and strategies of state decision-makers, and subsequently shape state behavior.[19]

Elite approaches to foreign policy focus on national decision-makers themselves as the source of state behavior. According to this perspective, the perceptions, beliefs, and interests of state leaders influence policy choices. The approach emphasizes the goal-oriented behavior of elite decision-makers as they address both internal and external pressures in an effort to shape policy in accordance with their preferences.[20] Their preferences are tied to and define the "national interest," and rest on the belief of overall general welfare.[21] Moreover, recent literature on "two-level games" and foreign policy choices suggests that elite decision-makers manipulate domestic constraints, including pressure groups. Where the pluralist approach emphasizes the independent effect of societal groups, an elite approach emphasizes a leader's ability to construct coalitions among groups to serve their needs, enhance their position, and enable them to select policies that are consistent with their preferences.[22]

The "black box opened" model of international relations suggests that domestic politics matters precisely because the state is not a unitary actor.[23] Elites within it have different policy preferences because they are differentially affected by government policies both immediately and over time. Any change in policies, as might occur because of international cooperation, has domestic distributional and electoral consequences.[24] These domestic consequences constitute, to this line of theory, the essence of the political. First, they mean that some societal actors oppose and others favor cooperation.[25] These groups will pressure the government to cooperate or not; they will promise to increase or threaten to withdraw their electoral or otherwise political support. In turn, political actors will favor or oppose cooperative policies depending on their relationship to these societal actors. There is, moreover, unlikely to be a unified view of the "national interest" as such and of the effect of cooperation upon it.[26] Second, policy choices have electoral ramifications. When choosing amongst policy options, a state's political leaders will not only be buffeted by pressure groups with conflicting interests but will also have to consider the electoral consequences of those choices.[27] Policies that favor, for example, the economy will be favored by political actors because they will enhance their likelihood of retaining office or consolidating power. Hence cooperative policies that improve some aspect of an economy will gain favor; those that harm the economy by increasing unemployment or inflation will be opposed. Political leaders' policy preferences *vis-à-vis* international cooperation will be shaped by these two forces.[28]

An *institutional* approach to state behavior centers on the specific institutional characteristics of states and how they influence policies.[29] According to this "domestic structures" approach, states "differ in the extent to which their states and societies are centralized, and in the range of policy instruments available to state officials. They also differ in the degree of autonomy state officials enjoy relative to societal forces."[30] Based on these differences, states can be placed along a continuum where one extreme is characterized as "weak" and the other as "strong." Weak and strong states are differentiated as to the degree to which the state is centralized. Weak states, for example, are "decentralized and fragmented along bureaucratic or institutional lines."[31] Due to the number of domestic constraints in weak states, policy-makers do not have the range of policy instruments available to them that policy-makers do in strong states. As a result, decision-makers "find it difficult to act purposefully and coherently, to realize their preferences in the face of significant opposition, and to manipulate or restructure their domestic environment."[32]

Finally, theories of *bureaucratic politics* highlight the effect that competition between governmental agencies and bureaucracies have on policy choices.[33] According to this approach, state behavior is the result of a tug-and-pull between government officials that represent various agency interests. Multiple governmental bodies engage in bargaining strategies to see that their institution's interests are addressed in the policy process, thereby enhancing their relative position of power. Such inter-governmental struggles ultimately influence the array of policy options available to decision-makers, as well as the policy selections.[34]

These various theories each highlight Domestic Political variables that have an effect on state foreign policy decisions. From these domestic perspectives, we may expect certain state behavior regarding export control policies in the NIS. We should see states have more developed systems of export control if domestic interest groups exist and seek to influence export control decisions. "Liberalizing coalitions," for example, may pressure the government to select policies that would allow greater access to international markets, while "inward-looking coalitions" would exert pressure to choose a course of action that enhances independence and prevent openness.[35] Moreover, we would expect the governments of Ukraine to be responsive to such domestic pressure and act accordingly. We expect that states will have more developed systems of export control if the perceptions and beliefs of elite decision-makers suggest to them that the control of sensitive exports is consistent with their notion of the "national interest." From an institutional perspective, we expect "weaker," more decentralized and fragmented states may find it more difficult to commit to, develop and coordinate export control activities. On the other hand, we expect that "stronger" states will have more developed export control systems. Finally, we expect that states with more influential export regulation agencies as actors (as opposed to the relative influence of agencies with competing functions, such as trade promotion) will have more developed systems of export control (see Table 2.2).

Table 2.2 Domestic Politics: Expected Behavior

- Interest groups pressure government to develop export control policies and procedures in-line with international standards;
- Elite decision-makers perceive and believe export control policies to be in the "national interest;"
- More centralized states will be better equipped to develop and coordinate export control activities;
- Agencies with export control functions are more powerful and influential than agencies with trade promotion functions.

2.3 Liberal Identity

Recent scholarship on state behavior suggests that states choose cooperative policies, not because of some rational calculation of security threats, costs or benefits, but because they "identify" with others in a community of states.[36] Borrowing from theories of social identity, some international relations scholars argue that states, like people, can and do come to share a common identification.[37] Just like individuals, states develop a group identity and a "sense of community" through interaction, communication and "transaction flows."[38] Group identity enables individual actors to act collectively in solving common dilemmas. Moreover, group identity allows members of the group to behave toward one another in a cooperative manner. Partners in a community, in other words, operate based on "mutual obligation," loyalty and trust.[39]

Forty years ago, Karl Deutsch and his colleagues offered one of the first significant pieces of research on community in the security arena to help understand, explain, and proscribe behavior for the elimination of violent conflict.[40] "Security-communities," differ in the degree of integration and institutionalization from fully integrated (amalgamation) to fully autonomous (pluralistic). Either way, members of a security community have achieved a sense of common identity, and believe that they together can solve common problems in a peaceful manner.[41] Recently, scholars have employed this concept of security community to explain the so-called "democratic peace."[42] They suggest that states do create communities based on a common identification, but more often than not it is *liberal* states that form such communities. Liberal democratic governments feel a common bond with other liberal democratic states based on similar normative and institutional foundations. The belief that domestic conflict should not be resolved with violence, for example, is extended to relations with other democratic states – for leaders in one state are more certain that their democratic partners also value non-violent conflict resolution, and can, therefore, be more certain of their partners' potential actions.[43]

Because individuals, as do states, gain self satisfaction and esteem from group membership, they also tend to discriminate based on their group identity.[44] Psychologically, the concepts of self and other are important to one's mental well-being. Further distinguishing between self and other only enhances that well-being.[45] Group identity, being an extension of individual identity, predisposes one to specifically target members of your group (in-group) with cooperative behavior, or members of another group (out-group) with non-cooperative behavior.[46] Members of a community of liberal states, therefore, may target illiberal states with more restrictive behavior than they would liberal states.

An aspect of group-informed identity is the concept of legitimacy. Apart from coercion and self-interest (narrowly and generally conceived) compliance with a rule may be motivated by a belief in the normative legitimacy of the rule (or in the legitimacy of the body that generated the rule). Legitimacy contributes to compliance by providing an internal reason for an actor to follow a rule. When an actor believes a rule is legitimate, compliance is no longer motivated by the simple fear of retribution, or by calculation, but instead by an internal sense of moral obligation: control is legitimate to the extent that it is approved or regarded as "right."[47] Mark Suchman, an organizational sociologist, defines legitimacy as a "generalized perception or assumption that the actions of an entity are desirable, proper, and appropriate within some socially constructed systems of norms, beliefs, and definitions."[48] When several individuals (or states) share a common definition of what is legitimate, we say they constitute a community.[49]

This theoretical emphasis on identity also includes a sub-approach: constructivism. For the past decade a central locus of contention within international relations has been the neorealist-neoliberal debate. This exchange has been fruitful and cumulative, allowing proponents of the two research programs to sharpen arguments while simultaneously shedding light on key issues of world politics, for example, the conditions under which relative or absolute gains-seeking behavior occurs.[50]

The constructivist critique of neorealism and neoliberalism reaches well beyond the level-of-analysis argument of either Image I (individual) or Image II (domestic politics) theorists.[51] Constructivism is concerned not with levels per se but with underlying conceptions of how the social and political world works. It is not a theory but an *approach* to social inquiry based on two assumptions: (1) the environment in which agents/states take action is social as well as material; and (2) this setting can provide agents/states with understandings of their interests (it "constitutes" them).[52] Put differently, these scholars question the materialism and methodological individualism upon which much contemporary IR scholarship has been built.

The first assumption reflects a view that material structures, beyond certain biological necessities, are given meaning only by the social context through which they are interpreted. Consider nuclear weapons – the ultimate material capability. Constructivists argue that it is not such weapons themselves that matter. After all, the United States worries very little about the large quantity of nuclear weapons held by the British; however, the possibility that North Korea might come into possession of even one or two generates tremendous concern.[53]

The second assumption addresses the basic nature of human agents and states, in particular, their relation to broader structural environments. Constructivists emphasize a *process of interaction between agents and structures*; the ontology is one of mutual constitution, where neither unit of analysis – agents or structures – is reduced to the other and made "ontologically primitive."[54] This opens up what for most theorists is the "black box" of interest and identity formation; state interests emerge from and are endogenous to interaction with structures.[55]

Constructivists thus question the methodological individualism that underpins both neoliberalism and neorealism. This agent-centered view asserts that all social phenomena are explicable in ways that involve only individual agents and their goals and actions; the starting point of the analysis is actors (states) with given properties. Ontologically, the result is to reduce one unit of analysis – structures – to the other – agents.[56] The term *identity* here is intended as a useful label, not a signal of commitment to studies that seek to privilege the theoretical (and therefore explanatory) primacy of this designation – however configured. Quite simply, actor designation is routinely assumed away. However, explicit designation is fundamental to any study of the international system.[57]

Early in the development of regime theory, for example, Stephen Kranser suggested that regimes could change state interests, that an "institutional" approach would problematize the "very nature of the actor: their endowments, utilities, preferences, capacities, resources, and identity."[58] And Robert Keohane, too, has called for a more "sociological" approach to state interests, in which transformations of interests become an important effect to be investigated.[59]

Also implicit in many constructivist accounts is a model of human and state behavior where rule-governed action and logics of appropriateness prevail. Such logics involve reasoning by analogy and metaphor and are not about ends and means. Under them, agents ask "What kind of situation is this?" and "What should I do now?" – with norms helping to supply the answers. In other words, to act, to be doing something, is to be committed to a context in which it makes sense to speak of actions being correctly done or not.[60] Norms therefore constitute states/agents, providing them with understandings of their interests.[61] Scholars of rational choice, by contrast, use a behavioral model based on utility maximization: when confronted with various options, an agent picks the one that best serves its objectives and interests. Much rational choice research ("thick" rationalism) also makes assumptions about the content of these interests, typically that they are material goods such as power or wealth. State (agent) interests are given a priori and exogenously. Norms and social structures at most constrain the choices and behavior of self-interested states, which operate according to a logic of consequences (means-ends calculations).[62]

As used in this work, a norm is used to describe collective expectations for the proper behavior of actors with a given identity. In some situations, norms operate like rules that define the identity of an actor, thus having "constitutive effects" that specify what actions will cause relevant others to recognize a particular identity. In other situations, norms operate as standards that specify the proper enactment of an already defined identity. In such instances, norms have "regulative" effects that specify standards of proper behavior. Norms thus either define (or constitute) identities or prescribe (or regulate) behavior, or they do both.[63] The norm of nonproliferation, for example, affects the behavior of actors in more than a purely instrumental or material way.[64]

It is important to note that constructivists do not reject science or causal explanation; their quarrel with mainstream theories is ontological, not epistemological. The last point is key, for it suggests that constructivism has the potential to bridge the still vast divide separating the majority of IR theorists from the post-modernists. With the latter, constructivists share many substantive concerns (e.g., role of identity and discourse) and a similar ontological stance; with the former, they share a largely common epistemology. Constructivists thus occupy a middle ground between rational choice theorists and postmodern scholars and between traditionally divided mainstream IR theories.[65]

From the perspective of Liberal Identity, then, we can expect that states who interact regularly on export control matters may develop a "sense of community" and a common group identification. As members of the liberal community tend to promulgate the virtues of nonproliferation export controls, we expect that those states in the NIS – especially Ukraine – who interact regularly with the liberal community will have more developed systems of export control. One could reasonably expect that states in the NIS, for example, which are developing the normative and institutional bases of a liberal democratic government may see themselves as part of the liberal security community, and will, therefore, have more developed export control systems. Finally, one could expect that the budding democracies of the NIS who are interested in focusing export controls on illiberal states will have more developed export control practices (see Table 2.3).

Table 2.3 Liberal Identity: Expected Behavior

- Acknowledgment of a "sense of community" in export control matters;

- Importance of regular interaction with the liberal community, and its advocacy of nonproliferation export controls;

- Development of the normative and institutional bases of a liberal, democratic government;

- Interest in targeting the control of sensitive materials toward illiberal states.

2.4 Rational Institutionalism

Contrary to the Realist/Neorealist notion that cooperation among states is limited, the Rational Institutional approach suggests that, even under anarchy, states can and do cooperate in the international system.[66] Rational Institutionalist scholars have argued that together states create and maintain explicit patterns of behavior, from which emerge various rules and norms that constrain future policy choices.[67] These international institutions or regimes facilitate cooperation among nations for many reasons. They enlighten states as to the policy preferences of partners, thereby decreasing uncertainty in international interactions. Institutions reduce the transaction costs inherent in international relations as states may link issues from one area to another. Moreover, regimes (i.e., institutionalized regimes) provide opportunities for the use of side-payments and enhance the credibility of state commitments.[68] This approach posits a rationally-calculating strategic utility-maximizing subject reflexively monitoring its conduct and weighing up alternatives. Rational choice institutionalism is broadly deductive in approach, and, in form at least, intentionalist and voluntarist. Accordingly, rather than account for what a situated subject actually chose, rational choice institutionalism provides a description of what any utility maximizing chooser would do in a given situation. In other words, rational choice analysis oscillates from an apparently agent-centered individualism exhibited in choice to a deep structuralism, deriving action from context.[69]

The Rational Institutional approach to international cooperation highlights how states rationally calculate the costs and benefits of cooperation based on their self-interests. Because state actors may better achieve their individual goals through collaborative action, states come together to solve perceived common problems and maximize joint and, where possible, individual interests. Institutionalized means of interaction are important because they create efficiencies that may contribute to the redefinition of interests and thus modify behavior. For example, this approach interprets the partial pooling of sovereignty in Europe as a series of nested games that link states in on-going interactions that limit the range of their bargaining tactics. Political elites make strategic use of international institutions to escape from both the democratic controls and the political fragmentation of domestic societies.[70]

Promises of future interaction based on reciprocity enhance state willingness to cooperate.[71] According to Robert Axelrod, cooperation cannot prosper unless there is reciprocal cooperative reactions on the part of all involved.[72] Cooperation evolved among states because they move toward "mutually awarding strategies based on reciprocity." According to Keohane:

> The rationalistic theory implies hypotheses that could be submitted to systematic, even quantitative, examination. For instance, this theory predicts that the incidence of specific international institutions should be related to the ratio of benefits anticipated from exchange to the transaction costs of establishing the institutions necessary to facilitate the negotiation, monitoring, and enforcement costs of agreements specifying the terms of exchange. This theory could also help us to develop a theory of compliance or noncompliance with commitments. For international regimes to be effective, their injunctions must be obeyed.[73]

Reciprocity implies that actions are "contingent on rewarding actions from others and cease when these expected reactions are not forthcoming."[74] Furthermore, such interaction "spills-over" into other issue areas creating a wider array of opportunities for cooperation among nations. Ultimately, within the scope of international institutions, states are induced to develop more cooperative policies because their interests are tied to the interests of others; international rules and norms limit their policy choices;[75] the costs of defection and benefits of cooperation are increased; uncertainty is decreased; issues are linked; and material incentives in the form of side-payments are used.[76]

From the Rational Institutional perspective we expect that states' systems of export control will be more developed when they perceive greater benefits and fewer costs (such as the benefit of access to markets and technology in the West versus the cost of developing and maintaining a bureaucracy) associated with export controls. We expect that states with more developed export control systems will emphasize the role the rules and norms of the nonproliferation regime played in constraining their policy choices.[77] We would also expect states to have more developed export control systems when they perceive that transaction costs and uncertainty in their future interactions with others may be reduced by joining, or adhering to, the international nonproliferation regime.[78] Moreover, we expect that states will have more developed systems of export control when they receive favorable material incentives in the form of side-payments – even from one issue to another – to do so (see Table 2.4).

Concerning material inducements, this study considers two types to be especially important. First, aid generally targeted toward nonproliferation policies, and specifically toward the development of nonproliferation export controls, should obviously affect state actions.[79] Second, aid, such as technology incentives,[80] not targeted toward proliferation (such as monies available via the US Department of State's FREEDOM Support Act [FSA]) may be considered an inducement if it is *explicitly* linked to the development of nonproliferation policies, activities, or norms.[81]

Table 2.4 Rational Institutionalism: Expected Behavior

- Explicit calculations of costs and benefits that will be in favor of export control development;

- Acknowledgment of nonproliferation regime's rules and norms as constraints on behavior;

- Interests in reducing transaction costs and uncertainty, and in increasing future interaction and reciprocity;

- Receives material incentives in the form of direct and/or side payments.

Conclusion

> I have endeavoured rather to show exactly what is the meaning of the question and what difficulties must be faced in answering it, than to prove that any particular answers are true.
>
> G.E. Moore, *Principia Ethica*

At the outset, the expectations of the overall study were recorded as:

1) The impetus and capabilities to construct a nonproliferation export control system in Ukraine arose from western (almost exclusively US) influence and attendant financial and technical incentives, and "soft" political-economic pressure[82] and not from security concerns or internally born domestic political imperatives; and
2) The continued development of the export control system and increased international nonproliferation cooperation are the result of an increasing identification with the western states (and the norms associated therewith) and continued material and promissory inducements.

These expectations will then applied to those listed in the above, assessing which of expectations best explain the Ukrainian case. Applying behavioral expectations derived from a wide array approaches is a methodological hedge against measurement and theoretical bias and against overdetermination.[83]

In attempting to account for why Ukraine developed an export control system, the preceding review of relevant international relations literature will serve as heuristic guide in the subsequent examination of the historical evidence. Further, the behavioral expectation derived from said approaches help frame the explanation. The subsequent chapters will investigate the data and draw explanatory conclusions on the basis of hypotheses confirmation or inapplicability. The end result is an explanation systematically enframed and therefore made more discernible than would a purely anecdotal account.

At this juncture, it is important to note that the point of this study is *not* testing theory. In other words, the operative assumptions of the respective IR approaches are not being contested, for "Testing theories is precisely a way of evaluating the assumptions that underlie them."[84] While deeply important and interesting, the "grand debates" of the IR canon are better left to another study.

The next chapter outlines the research methodology.

Notes

[1] R.B.J. Walker, *Inside/Outside: International Relations as Political Theory* (Cambridge: Cambridge University Press, 1993), p. 82. Walker contends that theoretical debates about how studies of international relations relate to the social sciences suggest that commonly made analytical distinctions – for example, between international and domestic politics, security issues and economic issues, facts and values – often hinder rather than help our description and explanation of real world events. These analytical distinctions often pose conceptual barriers that reflect a synchronic, binary view of the world. However, the author would simply like to note that the operative theoretical premise of this study is that the various IR theories are by no means mutually exclusive. The approach is therefore syncretic, a view supporting the nomothetic *and* idiographic aspects of social science. For an explanation of the use of the nomothetic and idiographic aspects, see Immanuel Wallerstein, *Unthinking Social Science: The Limits of Nineteenth Century Paradigms* (Oxford: Blackwell Publishers, 1991), pp. 223-225. See also, Marysia Zalewski, "All these theories yet the bodies keep piling up: Theories, Theorists, Theorising," in Ken Booth, Steve Smith, and Marysia Zalewski, eds., *International Relations Theory: Positivism and Beyond* (Cambridge: Cambridge University Press, 1997), pp. 340-355.

[2] "Realism," "Neorealism," and "Structural Realism," as conceptual terms, often needlessly complicate theory identification. "Realism," which contains the latter variations of a central worldview, is a coherent school of thought insofar as it enjoys an epistemological and ontological core consensus. That said, for the purposes of this study, the term of choice is the Realism/Neorealism affixation. The point is to convey the previously mentioned epistemological and ontological consensus on core assumptions animating all variants of "Realism." On the distinctions and core assumptions between schools of Realism, see Barry Buzan, Charles Jones and Richard Little, *The Logic of Anarchy: Neorealism to Structural Realism* (New York: Columbia University Press, 1993), pp. 1-20.

[3] Kenneth Waltz, "Reductionist and Systemic Theories," in Robert Keohane, ed., *Neorealism and Its Critics* (New York: Columbia University Press, 1986), p. 60.

[4] On the anarchical nature of the international system, see Kenneth Waltz, *Man, the State, and War: A Theoretical Analysis* (New York: Columbia University Press, 1959); Waltz, *Theory of International Politics* (Reading, MA: Addison-Wesley, 1979); Raymond Aron, *Peace and War: A Theory of Peace and War*, translated by Richard Howard and Annette Fox (Garden City, NY: Doubleday, 1966); and Stanley Hoffmann, *The State of War: Essays in Theory and Practice of International Politics* (New York: Praeger, 1965). For a complete explication of realism see Hans Morgenthau, *Politics Among Nations: The Struggle for Power and Peace* (New York: Alfred A. Knopf, 5th ed., 1973); and Edward Carr, *The Twenty Years Crisis, 1919-1939* (New York: Harper Torchbooks, 1964).

[5] In *Theory of International Politics*, Kenneth Waltz, by focusing on security maximization rather than power maximization, appeared to fix the fundamental problem of Morgenthau's realism, namely the existence of the security dilemma.
[6] See Waltz, *Theory of International Politics*, pp. 117-123; and Waltz, "The Emerging Structure of International Politics," *International Security* 18, 2 (Fall 1993), pp. 44-79. Stephen Walt argues that states not only balance the power of other states, but they balance specific threats. See Stephen M. Walt, *The Origins of Alliances* (Ithaca: Cornell University, 1987); and Walt, "Alliance Formation and the Balance of Power," *International Security* 9, 4 (Spring 1985), pp. 3-43.
[7] See Patrick James, "Neorealism as a Research Enterprise: Toward Elaborated Structural Realism," *International Political Science Review* 14, no. 2 (1993): p. 127. See also Stephen G. Brooks, "Dueling Realisms," *International Organization* 51, no. 3 (Summer 1997): pp. 445–477, for a useful effort to differentiate among strands of realist theory.
[8] See, in particular, J.M. Grieco, "Anarchy and the Limits of Cooperation: A Realist Critique of the New Liberal Institutionalism," *International Organization* 42, no. 3 (1988), pp. 485-508.
[9] Robert Gilpin, *War and Change in World Politics* (Cambridge: Cambridge University Press, 1981).
[10] Randolph M. Siverson and Michael P. Sullivan, "The Distribution of Power and the Onset of War," *Journal of Conflict Resolution* 27, pp. 473-94.
[11] On alliances see, for example, Stephen M. Walt, *The Origins of Alliances* (Ithaca: Cornell University Press, 1987); Edward Gulick, *Europe's Classical Balance of Power* (New York: Norton, 1955), pp. 58-62; Glenn Snyder, "Alliance Theory: A Neorealist First Cut," in Robert Rothstein, ed., *The Evolution of Theory in International Relations*, pp. 83-104 (Columbia: University of South Carolina Press, 1992); Kenneth N. Waltz, Theory of International, chs. 6, 8; and Randall Schweller, "Bandwagoning for Profit: Bringing the Revisionist State Back In," *International Security* 19, no. 1 (Summer 1994), pp. 72-107.
[12] Morgenthau, *Politics Among Nations*, p. 215.
[13] John Mearsheimer, "The False Promise of International Institutions," *International Security* 19, 3 (Winter 1994/95), pp. 7-11; and Robert Gilpin, "The Richness of the Tradition of Political Realism," in Robert Keohane, ed., *Neorealism and Its Critics* (New York: Columbia University Press, 1986), pp. 304-5.
[14] The military term for this is "blow back," or, in other words, when a state's military exports are used against them – as was the case in the Gulf War. See, Mark Phythian, *Arming Iraq: How the US and Britain Secretly Built Saddam's War Machine* (Northeastern University Press: 1996).
[15] It is not my intention in this project to determine the value (strength or weakness) of each domestic approach, but rather to establish whether domestic variables matter concerning state export control behavior.
[16] This study examines only these four domestic political approaches. I acknowledge that these are not the only domestic politics approaches available for

analysis, but appear to be the four that are more often employed in the study of foreign policy and international cooperation. See Helen Milner, "International Theories of Cooperation Among Nations: Strengths and Weaknesses," *World Politics* 44, 3 (April 1992), pp. 494-495.

[17] See, respectively, Steven Miller, "Politics Over Promise: Domestic Impediments to Arms Control," in Charles Kegley, Jr. and Eugene Wittkopf, eds., *The Domestic Sources of American Foreign Policy: Insights and Evidence* (New York: St. Martin's Press, 1988), pp. 166-177; and Etel Solingen, "The Political Economy of Nuclear Restraint," *International Security* 19, 2 (Fall 1994), pp. 126-169.

[18] Solingen, "The Political Economy of Nuclear Restraint," pp. 130-133. See also, Peter Lavoy, "Nuclear Myths," *Security Studies* 4 (Spring/Summer 1993).

[19] See Peter Gourevitch, *Politics in Hard Times* (Ithaca: Cornell University Press, 1987); Helen Milner, *Resisting Protectionism* (Princeton: Princeton University Press, 1988); David Truman, *The Governmental Process: Political Interests and Public Opinion* (New York: Knopf, 1951); and Robert Dahl, *Who Governs?* (New Haven: Yale University Press, 1963).

[20] Andrew Moravcsik, "Introduction: Integrating International and Domestic Theories of International Bargaining," in Peter B. Evans, Harold K. Jacobson, and Robert D. Putnam, eds., *Double-Edged Diplomacy: International Bargaining and Domestic Politics* (Berkeley: University of California Press, 1993), pp. 3-42; especially p. 30. The notion behind elite approaches to foreign policy are similar to Kenneth Waltz's concept of the "first image." See Kenneth Waltz, *Man, The State, and War: A Theoretical Analysis* (New York: Columbia University Press, 1959).

[21] Stephen D. Krasner, *Defending the National Interest: Raw Materials Investments and US Foreign Policy* (Princeton: Princeton University Press, 1978); and John Odell, *US International Monetary Policy* (Princeton: Princeton University Press, 1982).

[22] Moravcsik, "Introduction," p. 436. See also, Jeffrey Frieden and Ronald Rogkowski, "The Impact of the International Economy on National Policies," in Helen Milner and Robert Keohane, eds., *Internationalization and Domestic Politics* (Cambridge: Cambridge University Press, 1996), pp. 25-47.

[23] On the theoretical role played by assuming a "black box," see Peter B. Evans, "The Eclipse of the State? Reflections on Stateness in an Era of Globalization," *World Politics* 50.1 (1997) 62-87 and Robert Powell, "Anarchy in International Relations Theory: The Neorealist-Neoliberal Debate," *International Organization* 48 (Spring 1994). See also, Leif Lewin, "Man, Society, and the Failure of Politics," *Critical Review* 12 (Winter–Spring 1998). In particular, Lewin contends: "The better we understand what happens in the black box of politics, the better able we surely will be to make long-term calculations."

[24] See, Helen Milner, *Interests, Institutions, and Information: Domestic Politics and International Relations* (Princeton: Princeton University Press, 1997), p. 16.

[25] Of course, this heavy assumption leaves aside consideration of the overall political environment. Namely, the question of stability, identity and commonly

agreed upon methods by which to collectively address difference in preferences that arise in fluid (i.e., 'transition') political environments. For example, see Russell Bova, "Political Dynamics of the Post-Communist Transition: A Comparative Perspective," F.J. Fleron & E.P. Hoffman, eds., *Post-Communist Studies and Political Science: Methodology and Empirical Theory in Sovietology* (Boulder: Westview Press, 1993), pp. 239-265.

[26] See Milner, *Interests, Institutions, and Information*, pp. 16-17.

[27] Models of 'polyarchy' are especially pronounced in the domestic politics approach. For an illustrative sampling of this model see, Robert Dahl, *Modern Political Analysis* (New York: Prentice Hall, 1984).

[28] See Jack Knight, *Institutions and Social Conflict* (Cambridge: Cambridge University Press, 1992), pp. 2-3; and James Morrow, "Electoral and Congressional Incentives and Arms Control," *Journal of Conflict Resolution*, 35 (1991), pp. 245-265.

[29] See, in particular, G. John Ikenberry, David A. Lake and Michael Mastanduno, eds., *The State in American Foreign Economic Policy* (Ithaca: Cornell University Press, 1990); Peter J. Katzenstein, *Between Power and Plenty: Foreign Economic Policies of Advanced Industrialized States* (Madison: University of Wisconsin Press, 1978); Peter J. Katzenstein, *Small States in World Markets: Industrial Policy in Europe* (Ithaca: Cornell University Press, 1985); and Hofhansel, *Commercial Competition and National Security*.

[30] Ikenberry, et al., *The State in American Foreign Economic Policy*, pp. 10-11.

[31] Ibid., p. 11.

[32] Ibid.

[33] See Graham Allison, *Essence of Decision Making* (Boston: Little, Brown and Company, 1971); and Morton H. Halperin, *Bureaucratic Politics and Foreign Policy* (Washington, DC: The Brookings Institution, 1974).

[34] Allison, *Essence of Decision Making*, pp. 162-177.

[35] Arguably, in the area of export control development, both "liberalizing coalitions" and "inward-looking coalitions" may or may not pressure state actors to develop systems of export control. "Liberalizing coalitions" may perceive export controls as consistent with international nonproliferation standards that may place their state in favor and open access to new markets with new partners; or they may see export controls as an obstacle and constraint on trade and, therefore, will pressure government to forego export control practices. "Inward-looking coalitions" may disregard the importance of export controls as trade with the world is not a priority; or they may support them in an attempt to control economic activity. Regardless, these are empirical questions with which this project is not concerned at this point. I am simply evaluating whether domestic pressure groups did indeed influence state officials to choose one export control strategy over another, and whether the officials did indeed respond.

[36] For an excellent overview of this approach see Emanuel Adler and Michael Barnett, "Governing Anarchy: A Research Agenda for the Study of Security Communities," *Ethics and International Affairs* 10 (1996), pp. 63-98. Relatedly,

this approach is in theoretical agreement with the "society of states" model or IR, popularly known as the "English School." According to international society theorists, by an international society we mean "a group of states (or, more generally, a group of political communities) which not merely form a system, in the sense that the behavior of each is a necessary factor in the calculation of others, but also have established by dialogue and consent common rules and institutions for the conduct of their relations, and recognize their common interest in maintaining these arrangements" (Bull 1997). Hedley Bull, *The Anarchical Society: A Study of Order in World Politics* (New York: Columbia University Press, 1977), especially pp. 254-55. See also, Tim Dunne, *Inventing International Society: History of the English School* (New York: St. Martin's Press, 1998). A useful comparison of the theoretical constructs of the American and British academies within the large umbrella of the realist tradition of international relations scholarship is found in Barry Buzan, "From International System to International Society: Structural Realism and Regime Theory Meet the English School," *International Organization* 47 (3) (1993), pp. 327–52.

[37] On theories of social identity, see Glynis M. Breakwell, ed., *Social Psychology of Identity and the Self Concept* (London: Surrey University Press, 1992).

[38] For one of the earliest and most influential works on community among states, and the importance of transactions in the development of such communities, see Karl Deutsch, Sidney A. Burrell, Robert A. Kann, Maurice Lee, Jr., Martin Lichterman, Raymond E. Lindgren, Francis L. Loewenheim and Richard W. Van Wagenen, *Political Community and the North Atlantic Area: International Organization in the Light of Historical Experience* (Princeton: Princeton University Press, 1957). Also see Bruce Russett, *Power and Community in World Politics* (San Francisco: W.H. Freeman and Company, 1974); and Claudio Cioffi-Revilla, Richard L. Merritt, and Dina A. Zinnes, eds., *Communication and Interaction in Global Politics* (Beverly Hills: Sage Publications, Inc., 1987).

[39] Alexander Wendt, "Anarchy is What States Make of It: The Social Construction of Power Politics," *International Organization* 46 (1992), pp. 395-421; Wendt, "Collective Identity Formation and the International State," *American Political Science Review* 88 (1994), pp. 384-396. See also, Joseph S. Nye, Jr., *Peace in Parts: Integration and Conflict in Regional Organization* (Boston: Little, Brown and Company, 1971), pp. 16-44.

[40] Deutsch, *et al.*, *Political Community and the North Atlantic Area*.

[41] Ibid., pp. 5-6. A recent study on export control cooperation amongst COCOM members in the post-Cold War period in which the liberal identity approach is discussed is found in Richard Cupitt and Suzette Grillot, "COCOM is Dead, Long Live COCOM: Persistence and Change in Multilateral Security Institutions," *British Journal of Political Science* 27 (Fall 1997), pp. 361-389 (377).

[42] Bruce Russett, *Grasping the Democratic Peace: Principles for a Post-Cold War World* (Princeton: Princeton University Press, 1993): Michael Doyle, "Kant, Liberal Legacies, and Foreign Affairs," Parts I and II, *Philosophy and Public Affairs* 12, 3-4 (Summer/Fall 1983); and Doyle, "Liberalism and World Politics,"

American Political Science Review 80, 4 (December 1986), pp. 1151-1170; and Jens Bartelson, "The Trial of Judgement: A Note on Kant and the Paradoxes of Internationalism," *International Studies Quarterly* 39 (1995), pp. 255-279.
[43] Doyle, "Liberalism and World Politics," pp. 1166-1168.
[44] Jonathan Chase, "The Self and Collective Action: Dilemmatic Identities," in Breakwell, ed., *Social Psychology of Identity and the Self Concept*, pp. 101-127, especially p. 107.
[45] For a classic work on social identity theory, see Michael Hogg and Dominic Abrams, *Social Identifications: A Social Psychology of Intergroup Relations and Group Processes* (New York: Routledge, 1988). For its application to international relations, see Alexander Wendt, "Anarchy is What States Make of It," pp. 391-425.
[46] H. Tajfel, "Social Identity and Intergroup Behavior," *Social Science Information* 14 (1974), pp. 101-118; and Tajfel, "Differentiation Between Social Groups: Studies in the Social Psychology of Intergroup relations," *European Monographs in Social Psychology, No. 14* (London: Academic Press, 1978).
[47] Robert Dahl and Charles Lindblom, *Politics Markets, and Welfare*, 2nd edition (New York: Transaction Publishers, 1992), p. 114.
[48] Mark Suchman, "Managing Legitimacy: Strategic and Institutional Approaches," *Academy of Management Review* 20, no. 3 (1995), pp. 571-610 (574). See also, Jürgen Habermas, *Communication and the Evolution of Society* (Boston: Beacon Press, 1979), Chapter 5.
[49] Ian Hurd, "Legitimacy and Authority in International Politics," *International Organization* 53, no. 2, Spring 1999, pp. 379-408 (387-388).
[50] Robert Keohane, *After Hegemony: Cooperation and Discord in the World Political Economy* (Princeton: Princeton University Press, 1984); David Baldwin, ed., *Neorealism and Neoliberalism: The Contemporary Debate* (New York: Columbia University Press, 1993); Robert Powell, "Anarchy in International Relations Theory: The Neorealist-Neoliberal Debate (Review Article)," *International Organization* 48 (Spring 1994); and "Promises, Promises: Can Institutions Deliver?" *International Security* 20 (Summer 1995).
[51] David Singer, "Level of Analysis Problems in International Relations," in Klaus Knor and Sidney Verba, eds., *The International System: Theoretical Essays* (Princeton: Princeton University Press, 1961).
[52] Interestingly, Morgenthau's discussion of power acknowledges that international politics operates within a framework of rules and through the instrumentality of institutions: "The kinds of interests determining political action in a particular period of history depend upon the political and cultural context within which foreign policy is formulated." Hans Morgenthau, *Politics Among Nations: The Struggle for Power and Peace* (New York: Alfred A. Knopf, 5th ed., 1973).
[53] Alexander Wendt, "Constructing International Politics," *International Security* 20 (Summer 1995), 73. See also, Peter L. Berger and Thomas Luckmann, *The Social Construction of Reality: A Treatise in the Sociology of Knowledge* (New York: Anchor Books, 1966).

[54] Anthony Giddens' "structuration theory" explicitly defines the necessarily reciprocal and co-equal relationship between agent and structure in *The Consitution of Society* (Berkeley: University of California Press, 1984). For an IR-based application of Giddens' theory, see Barry Buzan, Charles Jones, and Richard Little, *The Logic of Anarchy: Neorealism to Structural Realism* (New York: Columbia University Press, 1993), pp. 102-113.

[55] On the theoretical role played by assuming a black box, see Peter B. Evans, "The Eclipse of the State? Reflections on Stateness in an Era of Globalization," *World Politics* 50.1 (1997) 62-87 and Robert Powell, "Anarchy in International Relations Theory: The Neorealist-Neoliberal Debate," *International Organization* 48 (Spring 1994).

[56] On neoliberalism's methodological individualism, see Volker Rittberger, Andreas Hasenclever, and Peter Mayer, "Interests, Power, Knowledge: The Study of International Regimes," *Mershon International Studies Review* 40 (October 1996), 183-87. For that of neorealism, see Alexander Wendt, "The Agent-Structure Problem in International Relations Theory," *International Organization* 41 (Summer 1987), 340-44.

[57] On problems in designating actorship, see Frederick Frey, "The Problem of Actor Designation in Political Anlaysis," *Comparative Politics* 17, no. 2 (January 1985), pp. 127-152.

[58] Stephen Krasner, "Sovereignty: An Institutional Perspective," *Comparative Politics* 21 (1988), p. 72; and *International Regimes* (Ithaca: Cornell University Press, 1983), pp. 362-364.

[59] Robert Keohane, "International Liberalism Reconsidered," in John Dunn, ed., *The Economic Limits of Modern Politics* (Cambridge: Cambridge University Press, 1990), p. 183.

[60] Roger Spegele, *Political Realism in International Theory* (Cambridge: Cambridge University Press, 1996), pp. 184-185.

[61] On logics of appropriateness, see James March and Johan Olsen, *Rediscovering Institutions: The Organizational Basis of Politics* (New York: Free Press, 1989).

[62] On the last point, see Barry Weingast, "A Rational Choice Perspective on the Role of Ideas: Shared Belief Systems and State Sovereignty in International Cooperation," *Politics and Society* 23 (December 1995); and Dennis Chong, "Rational Choice Theory's Mysterious Rivals," in Jeffrey Friedman, ed., *The Rational Choice Controversy: Economic Models of Politics Reconsidered* (New Haven: Yale University Press, 1996). Useful introductions to rational choice are Jon Elster, "The Market and the Forum," in Elster, ed., *Foundations of Social Choice Theory* (Cambridge: Cambridge University Press, 1986); James Morrow, *Game Theory for Political Scientists* (Princeton: Princeton University Press, 1994), chap. 2; and Donald Green and Ian Shapiro, *Pathologies of Rational Choice Theory: A Critique of Applications in Political Science* (New Haven: Yale University Press, 1994), chap. 2.

[63] See, Peter J. Katzenstein, "Introduction," in Peter J. Katzenstein, ed., *The Culture of National Security: Norms and Identity in World Politics* (New York: Columbia University Press, 1996), p. 5.

[64] Colin Gray, "The Second Nuclear Age: The Search for Political Context," in Colin Gray, *The Second Nuclear Age* (New York: Lynne Rienner Publishers, 1998); and Richard Price and Nina Tannenwald, "Norms and Deterrence: The Nuclear and Chemical Weapons Taboo," in Peter Katzenstein, *The Culture of National Security: Norm and Identity in World Politics* (New York: Columbia University Press, 1996), pp. 114-143.

[65] See, among others, Alexander Wendt, *Social Theory of International Politics* (New York: Cambridge University Press, forthcoming), chaps. 1-2. There is a good bit of confusion regarding these central tenets of constructivism; see, for example, John Mearsheimer, "The False Promise of International Institutions," *International Security* 19 (Winter 1994-95), 37-47.

[66] Kenneth Oye, ed., *Cooperation Under Anarchy* (Princeton: Princeton University Press, 1986); Oye, "Explaining Cooperation Under Anarchy: Hypotheses and Strategies," *World Politics* 38 (1985), pp. 1-24; Robert Axelrod, "The Emergence of Cooperation Among Egoists," *American Political Science Review* 75 (June 1981), pp. 306-18; Axelrod, *The Evolution of Cooperation* (New York: Basic Books, 1984); and Robert Axelrod and Robert O. Keohane, "Achieving Cooperation Under Anarchy: Strategies and Institutions," *World Politics* 38 (October 1985), pp. 226-54.

[67] International regimes are commonly defined as "set[s] of implicit or explicit principles, norms, rules, and decision-making procedures around which actors' expectations converge in a given area of international relations." See Stephen D. Krasner, ed., *International Regimes* (Ithaca: Cornell University Press, 1983), p. 2.

[68] Robert O. Keohane, "The Demand for International Regimes," *International Organization* 36 (Spring 1982), pp. 325-56; Keohane, *After Hegemony*; Krasner, ed., *International Regimes*; and Lisa L. Martin, "Institutions and Cooperation: Sanctions During the Falklands Island Conflict," *International Security* 16 (Spring 1992), pp. 143-178.

[69] Peter Hall and Rosemary Taylor, "Political Science and the Three New Institutionalisms," *Political Studies* 44, no. 4 (1996), pp. 936-57.

[70] Wayne Sandholtz, "Choosing Union: Monetary Politics and Maastricht," *International Organization* 47, no. 1 (Winter 1993), pp. 1-39.

[71] On the importance of future interaction and the "shadow of the future," see Axelrod, *The Evolution of Cooperation*; and Oye, ed., *Cooperation Under Anarchy*. On the importance of reciprocity see Robert Keohane, "Reciprocity in International Relations," *International Organization* 40 (Winter 1986), pp. 1-27. Keohane highlights two kinds of reciprocity: specific and diffuse. Specific reciprocity centers on expectations of exact returns for that which is given; and diffuse reciprocity focuses on an actor's willingness to give more and receive less from issue to issue. Nonetheless, both specific and diffuse reciprocity highlight the state's rational actions based on future returns.

[72] Robert Axelrod, *The Evolution of Cooperation*, p. 175. On the concept of "diffuse" reciprocity, see Robert Keohane, "Reciprocity in International Relations," *International Organization* 40 (Winter 1986), pp. 1-27.
[73] Keohane, *International Institutions and State Power* (Boulder: Westview Press, 1989), p. 167.
[74] Peter Blau, *Exchange and Power in Social Life* (New York: Wiley and Sons, 1964), p. 6.
[75] R. Weaver and Bert Rockman, eds., *Do Institutions Matter? Government Capabilities in the United States and Abroad* (Washington, DC, Brookings, 1993). See also, Robert Cox and Harold Jacobson, *The Anatomy of Influence* (New Haven: Yale University Press, 1973).
[76] Robert O. Keohane, *International Institutions and State Power* (Boulder, CO: Westview Press, 1989); Robert O. Keohane and Joseph Nye, Jr., *Power and Interdependence: World Politics in Transition* Second Edition (Boston: Little, Brown, 1989); and Keohane and Nye, "Power and Interdependence Revisited," International Organization 41 (1987), pp. 723-53. See also, John Ikenberry and Charles Kupchan, "Socialization and Hegemonic Power," *International Organization* 44 (Winter 1990), pp. 283-315.
[77] The international nonproliferation regime is comprised of various international arms control treaties (e.g., the Nuclear Nonproliferation Treaty [NPT], Biological Weapons Convention [BWC] and Chemical Weapons Convention [CWC]), and supplier organizations that control the proliferation of weapons of mass destruction and their component parts, material, equipment and expertise (e.g., the Nuclear Suppliers Group [NSG], Australia Group [AG], Missile Technology Control Regime [MTCR] and Wassenaar Arrangement).
[78] Activities such as signing and ratifying the NPT and joining such institutions as the International Atomic Energy Agency (IAEA), Wassenaar Arrangement, AG, MTCR, NSG, BWC and CWC.
[79] Aid from the United States for nonproliferation activities, for example, comes from the Cooperative Threat Reduction/Safe and Secure Dismantlement program (CTR), and/or the Nonproliferation Disarmament Fund (NDF).
[80] On the use of technology transfers as incentive tools, see William Long, *Economic Incentives and Bilateral Cooperation* (Ann Arbor: University of Michigan Press, 1997).
[81] Section 498A(a)(6) of the FREEDOM Support Act requires each state to: "implement responsible security policies, including: (A) adhering to arms control obligations derived from agreements signed by the former Soviet Union; (B) reducing military forces and expenditures to a level consistent with legitimate defense requirements; (C) not proliferating nuclear, biological, or chemical weapons, their delivery systems, or related technologies; and (D) restraining conventional weapons transfers."
[82] "Soft power" is an expression coined by Joseph Nye. Nye contends that power, popularly conceived, need not be limited to direct application of material advantage. Nye defines "soft," or "co-optive," power – as opposed to "command"

power – is an "indirect way to exercise power. A country may achieve outcomes it prefers in world politics because other countries want to follow it or have agreed to a system that produces such effects. Co-optive power can rest on the attraction of one's ideas or on the ability to set the political agenda in a way that shapes the preferences the others express." See, Joesph Nye, "The Changing Nature of World Power," *Political Science Quarterly*, vol. 105, no. 2 (1990), p. 181; and *Bound to Lead: the Changing Nature of American Power* (New York: Basic Books, 1990). The issue of co-optive power – as it applies to US-Ukrainian relations – will be examined in chapter 6.

[83] On the problem of overdetermination, see Eugene Mills, "Interactionism and Overdetermination," *American Philosophical Quarterly* 33, no. 1 (January 1996) pp. 105-117.

[84] Jeffrey Legro and Andrew Moravcsik, "Is Anybody Still a Realist?" *Columbia International Affairs Working Paper Series* (www.ciao.org), October 1998, Weatherhead Center for International Affairs, Harvard University.

Chapter 3

Describing and Measuring the Ukrainian Export Control System: The Explication of Method

This project presents a case study that focuses on the Ukrainian decision to create and further augment a system of nonproliferation export controls upon independence from the Soviet Union. The study sets forth competing explanations from which behavioral expectations are delineated and then compared against the empirical record. The goal is to determine which of the rival approaches helps us better understand the Ukrainian effort.

In the social sciences, there are two basic ways to test theories: experimentation and observation.[1] Observational tests come in two varieties: large-n and case study. In the study of international relations, case studies are usually more useful than large-n approaches because of the structure of the international historical record, which serves as a primary source of data, better lends itself to deep study of a few cases or single case than to exploration of many cases.[2] The case study method is employed here.

3.1 Case Study Research

> Those who have handled sciences have been either men of experiment or men of dogmas. The men of experiment are like the ant, they only collect and use; the reasoners resemble spiders, who make cobwebs out of their own substance. But the bee takes a middle course; it gathers its materials from the flowers of the garden and field, but transforms and digests it by a power of its own.
>
> Francis Bacon, *Novum Organum* I xcv

To analyze and examine the expectations highlighted in the previous section, this study employs the case study method. The case study method is most appropriate for this project as it is preferred when researchers: (1) ask "how" and "why" questions; (2) do not and cannot control the subjects and/or events being studied; and (3) focus on contemporary events in their natural context.[3] Moreover, case studies are useful when investigators attempt to illuminate particular decisions, processes, institutions and events, why and how each of these operated and/or are made, and what resulted.[4] Unlike in a controlled laboratory, the researcher studying social/political phenomena in its real-life context is unable to manipulate or otherwise control the subject of study.[5] The export control policy making of Ukrainian elites is an exemplary case for such an investigation.

The purpose of case study research is, in the final analysis, to contribute to "knowledge." Jürgen Habermas classified the processes of scientific enquiry into three categories, each of which produces its own kind of knowledge (see Table 3.1).[6] Knowledge "enhancement" is ideally done through theory construction.[7] There is, however, considerable scholarly debate as to whether or not case studies can and do contribute to theory-building.[8] That being said, many have suggested that case studies contribute to knowledge in the following manner: they can (a) generate hypotheses thereby beginning the scientific process; (b) test inferences in different contexts; (c) establish correlations that lead to questions of causal relationships; (d) eliminate spurious relationships; and (e) test the boundaries of generalizable theory.[9]

Table 3.1 Processes of Scientific Enquiry

Type of Science	Underlying Interests	Aspects of Social Existence
Empirical-Analytical	Prediction and Control	Work (instrumental action)
Historical-Hermeneutic	Understanding	Interaction (language)
Critical Theory	Emancipation	Power

Alexander George argues that case studies can and should be employed when seeking to develop theory. Case studies, George suggests, contribute to theory generation because such studies are usually "focused" in that they are generally concerned with only certain aspects of some historical phenomenon, and "structured" as they use general questions for guidance in the collection and analysis of data.[10] Most importantly, however, is that through case study research, it is possible to evaluate alternative or rival theories or explanations. The strength of one explanation is enhanced when it is found to be the most consistent with the data after alternative explanations have been considered and found to be less consistent.[11] This process allows a researcher to build on cases and, therefore, "knowledge."[12] Furthermore, some scholars suggest that without high-quality case research, the development of good theory is, at the least, problematic and, at the most, unlikely.[13]

This study presents a case study of Ukraine which compares the behavioral expectations (outlined above) against the empirical record of Ukraine's export control development. The objective of this study is to determine which approach, if any, best explains the development of nonproliferation export control measures in Ukraine.

3.2 A Case for the Single-Case Case Study

> The separation of concepts applicable to groups from those applicable to individuals is a powerful tool for eliminating the solipsism characteristic of traditional methodologies. Science becomes intrinsically a group activity, no longer even idealizable as a one-person game.[14]

The debate about the utility of the case study research method is particularly salient when one considers a single-case case study. Although many scholars argue that single cases are useful in many ways – even for creating and testing generalizable theories – others suggest that single-case case studies do not constitute grounds for generalization nor a basis for proving or disproving an existing generalizable proposition.[15] For single case projects to be useful, however, the case must be *critical*, *unique*, or *revelatory*.

First, when a single case represents a critical case, it can be used "to determine whether a theory's propositions are correct, or whether some alternative set of explanations might be more relevant."[16] Graham Allison's well-known study of American and Soviet decision-making during the 1962 Cuban Missile Crisis is an excellent example of a critical case.[17] In that study, Allison relied on a single-case in his evaluation of three well-formulated theories. In so doing, he was able to contribute significantly to disciplinary knowledge and the building of theory regarding foreign policy decision-making processes.

Second, a single case may represent a unique or extreme case when the subject of study focuses on some rare phenomena, such as the use of atomic weapons during war.[18] Unique cases are particularly useful for intensive exploration of an event. Such exploration may generate some hypotheses or propositions that may be relevant for future studies. Unique cases, however, may also allow for the evaluation of established explanations to determine their strength or weakness in a new and challenging area. Unique cases, therefore, may offer "hard" tests for existing theories.[19]

Lastly, a single case may be considered a revelatory case "when an investigator has an opportunity to observe and analyze a phenomenon previously inaccessible to scientific investigation."[20] For example, a study of the Soviet Union's nuclear weapons industry may be considered a revelatory case as researcher access to such a subject was heretofore impossible.[21]

This case focuses on the single case of the development of the Ukrainian export control system. The Ukrainian export control decision process represents a critical case rather than a unique or revelatory case.[22] It is critical in that Ukraine's decision to develop and augment its export control system presents an opportunity to evaluate existing rival theories that offer explanations and expectations regarding state behavior, although the thrust of this study is not theory testing *per se*. The matter to be explained is why Ukraine, despite direct and indirect immediate political and economic costs, created and continues to develop an internationally-compatible nonproliferation export control system. Ukraine is a complex case for existing theories insofar as its transitional, "fluid" nature problematizes data collection and theory testing. Such complexity is unique to post-Soviet and post-Communist systems. For example, noted Sovietologist Erik Hoffman notes:

> More problematical is the attempt to construct conceptual frameworks prior to data collection. This research strategy is most useful in relatively well-defined and data-rich fields. It is generally inappropriate for an analyst new to a rapidly changing subject. And it is counterproductive if it distorts political actors' perceptions of their aims and environment or homogenizes the political behavior of groups and individuals, thereby minimizing or disregarding contexts such particular geographical and issue areas or time periods.[23]

Furthermore, Ukraine, being a new state, is a difficult case insofar as the investigator cannot assume Ukrainian interests *a priori*, as state "interests" are still in the process of maturation.[24]

Given its initial and present context, conventional wisdom may suggest that Ukraine would forego the direct and indirect costs of constructing, maintaining, and operating a nonproliferation export control system. However, that a comprehensive system was created, received high-level policy attention, and continues to develop, Ukraine therefore presents a critical case for the evaluation of existing theoretical approaches to determine which has the most explanatory power in this case. The case of the Ukrainian export control system offers a compelling and useful critical, single-case study.

3.3 Case Study Types: Descriptive, Explanatory, Exploratory

Case study projects have a purpose of either describing, exploring, or explaining some event or phenomenon, each of which can be categorized as to the role theory plays in the research process (see Table 3.2). Ordinarily, the research question one asks dictates what type of approach one employs. Descriptive studies focus on the details of an event, often tracing a sequence or series of events. These studies tend to be atheoretical in nature. They are neither guided by general hypotheses nor motivated to formulate such. The cases are selected because of the researcher's interests in the subject at hand rather than for reasons of formulating or examining generalizable theories.[25]

Table 3.2 Case Study Types

Yin	Descriptive	Exploratory	Explanatory
Eckstein	Configurative-Idiographic & Disciplined-Configurative	Heuristic	Plausability Probe & Crucial Case
Lijphart	Atheoretical Interpretive	Hypothesis-Generating	Theory-Confirming Theory-Infirming Deviating

Regarding actual procedural methods, case studies offer three formats for testing theories: controlled comparison, congruence procedure, and process-tracing. Controlled comparison uses across-cases comparative observation to test theories. Congruence procedures are of two types: one type uses across-cases comparative observation to test theories, the other uses within-case observations. Process-tracing tests theories within-case observations. Congruence procedure and process-tracing are generally viewed as stronger test methods than controlled comparison.[26] In each format the same three steps are followed: (1) statement of theory(-ies); (2) statement of expectation(s) about what should be observed in the case if the theory is valid, and what should be observed if it is false; and (3) explore the case(s) looking for congruence or incongruity between expectation and observation.

Case studies are often undertaken because the researcher expects that the clarification of causal mechanisms in one case will have implications for understanding causal mechanisms in other cases. However, whether a causal account that fits one historical circumstance will fit another is an open question.[27] What matters here is that a causal mechanism has been identified, and the researcher has some framework within which to begin to investigate the external validity of the causal claims.[28] Such a framework permits initial judgements about which cases theoretically, plausibly explain the case. Furthermore, case studies are often more important for their value in clarifying previously obscure theoretical relationships than for providing an additional observation to be added to a sample. In the words of one ethnographer, for example, a good case is not necessarily a "typical" case, but rather a "telling" case, in which "the particular circumstances surrounding a case serve to make previously obscure theoretical relationships sufficiently apparent."[29] McKeown likens this aspect of case study research to Max Weber's well-known "ideal types." Weber viewed such types as deliberately "one-sided" constructs intended to capture essential elements of causation and meaning in a particular setting, without regard to whether they adequately represented all relevant situations.[30]

In process-tracing, the selected format for this case study, the investigator explores the chain of events or the decision making process by which initial case conditions are translated into case outcomes. The general method of process-tracing is to generate and analyze data on the causal mechanisms, or processes, events, actions, expectations, and other intervening variables, that link putative causes to observed effects Within the general method of process-tracing there are two very different approaches. The first, "process verification," involves testing whether the observed processes among variables in a case match those predicted by previously designated theories. The second, "process induction," involves the inductive observation of apparent causal mechanisms and heuristic rendering of these mechanisms as potential hypotheses for future testing.[31] This particular case study is of the former approach. Accordingly, the project attempts to confirm or negate the generalizable expectations that are derived from each theoretical approach. The predictions of each approach are delineated and then compared to the empirical record to determine which approach better explains the Ukrainian export control policy decisions.

The general method of process-tracing is to generate and analyze data on the *causal mechanisms*, or processes, events, actions, expectations, and other intervening variables, that link putative causes to observed effects.[32] Causal mechanisms are defined here as the causal processes and intervening variables through which causal or explanatory variables produce causal effects. While the notion of causal mechanisms is often explicated in terms of physical causal processes, it is applicable as well to social processes, including intentions, expectations, information, small group and bureaucratic decision making dynamics, coalition dynamics, strategic interaction, and so on.[33]

It should be noted that process-tracing is no guarantee that a study can establish internal validity, or that it will uncover only relationships that are truly causal. Both false positives, or processes that appear to fit the evidence even though they are not causal in the case at hand, and false negatives, processes that are causal but do not appear to be so, are still possible through measurement error or under-specified or *mis*-specified theories. External validity, or the ability to generalize results to other cases, also remains a difficult standard. The findings of single case studies can only be contingent generalizations that apply to typologically similar cases, but even then, cases that appear to be typologically similar may differ in an as-yet unspecified causal variable that leads to different outcomes.[34] Disagreements over measurement of qualitative variables can also limit the cumulation of case study results, just as disagreements over how to define and quantify variables can limit the cumulation of statistical findings.

Objections may arise – as maintained, for example by King, Keohane, and Verba (1994) – that in attempting to describe completely the causal mechanisms in a concrete situation (i.e., a/the "case") leads to explanations that are in principle infinitely large.[35] However, this charge is irrelevant since explanations do not aim at being complete, but merely at answering the questions the researcher asks.[36] Human decision making is inherently limited in the number of factors that impinge on the awareness of the decision maker, thus making possible the construction of explanations that are reasonably complete representations of the decision situations facing historical actors, as those actors actors see them. For instance, Alexander George and McKeown argue, "Because the limitations on the perceptual and information-processing capabilities of humans are well known and pronounced, the process-tracing technique has a chance of constructing reasonably complete account of the stimuli to which the actor attends."[37]

Despite these limits and problems, process-tracing is a useful method for generating and analyzing data on causal mechanisms. It can be used in studies of a single case and those involving many cases whose processes can be traced individually. It can greatly reduce the risks of the many potential inferential errors that can arise from the use of Mill's methods of comparison, from congruence testing, and from other methods that rely on studying covariation.[38] Process-tracing is particularly useful at addressing the problem of equifinality by documenting alternative causal paths to the same outcomes, and alternative outcomes for the same causal factor. In this way, it can contribute directly to the development of differentiated typological theories. Finally and most generally, process-tracing is the only observational means of moving beyond covariation alone as a source of causal inference.[39] Whether it is pursued through case studies, correlations, experiments, or quasi-experiments, it is an invaluable method that should be included in every researcher's repertoire.

3.4 Data Sources

Important for case study analysis is the use of multiple sources of evidence. Multiple sources allow a researcher to consider a broad range of issues. Furthermore, utilizing varied data sources is advantageous insofar as "converging lines of inquiry" may develop.[40] To bolster the strength of this case study, therefore, more than one source of information was sought to confirm and corroborate each piece of evidence.

Primary and secondary sources that concern the Ukrainian decision to create and develop an export control system – and that are publicly available[41] – include authored articles, books, reports, government and other official reports and documents, and news sources that provide official statements and analyses of Ukrainian export control issues. Data was also gathered from many open sources including published books and articles; official government documents, reports, and speeches;[42] and other primary news and information sources such as the Foreign Broadcast Information Service Daily Reports, which offers English translations of news reports and official documents for the entire former Soviet region. Data were also collected from Ukrainian, Russian, and other language sources.

More importantly, I have independently conducted a number of personal interviews with officials, researchers, and other experts involved in and/or knowledgeable of Ukrainian export control policy development, as well as with key counterparts in the United States who have been integrally involved in promoting and assisting Ukrainian export control activities.[43] I have also relied on extensive note taking of US-Ukrainian official interactions on export control issues and from US and Ukrainian fieldwork both in my official and academic capacities. Interviews were guided by a research protocol designed to systemize data collection. The behavioral expectations served as a common guide for data collection and analysis.

3.5 Strategies for Data Analysis

Specifically concerning the measurement of export control development (dependent variable), this study will analyze and evaluate Ukrainian export control measures using a general quantitative tool based on Western, nonproliferation export control "common standards" that have emerged over the past several decades.[44] The independent variables of an export control system – and therefore suggestive of development *vis-à-vis* a standardized measure – are found in Table 1.2. Because individual states develop and implement national systems of export control for various reasons,[45] it is possible to explore motivational aspects of a respective state's decision in light of the attendant circumstances in which decisions were made. The proceeding chapter, chapter 4, will measure and describe the Ukrainian export control system.

With respect to examining the causal mechanisms behind the behavioral outcome, this study sets forth competing explanations from which behavioral expectations are delineated and then compared against the empirical record. Specifically, four theoretical approaches – Realism/Neorealism, Domestic Political Processes, Rational Institutionalism, and Liberal Identity – provide accounts as to why states would develop export control systems. Each of the perspectives differs in that they would lead us to expect observably different behavior. The antecedent review (chapter 2) of the four approaches is limited to how states would behave regarding export controls. The goal is to determine which of the rival approaches helps us better understand the Ukrainian effort.

The theoretical approaches guide both data collection and empirical testing. In this respect, case study methods prove quite apropos. Case study methods are theory-driven rather than blindly empirical. As Andrew Bennett and Alexander George notes, "Without prior theories, or at least proto-theories, it is impossible to select which of the thousands of facts about cases should be analyzed for purposes of comparison or within-case analysis."[46] Case comparisons, congruence testing, and process-tracing are all set up by prior theories, and their results should be weighted or discounted by our existing level of confidence in these theories.

3.6 Enhancing the Quality of Case Study Research: A Brief Note

"Case studies, as theoretical stand-alones, are useless."
Bruce Bueno de Mesquita[47]

So-called "large-N" studies luxuriate in the virtue of institutional preference, a default status enjoyed by the decidedly quantitative methodological approaches of "rigorous" social *science*. While the point of this project is not to defend the methodological validity of the case study, a few words on the quality of case study research are warranted.

The quality of any given case study can be evaluated by four general tests: construct validity, internal validity, external validity, and reliability.[48] Construct validity concerns establishing correct operational measures for the concepts being studies. Yin suggests three tactics by which to improve construct validity: the use of multiple sources of evidence; the establishment of a chain of evidence; and the review of the draft study report by key informants.[49] This study adopts these three tactics in order to enhance construct validity.

Internal validity concerns causal or explanatory studies, where one is trying to determine whether event X led to event Y.[50] To improve internal validity, the dual tactics of "pattern-matching" and "process-tracing" (as discussed in the above) procedures are applied. According to Yin, the analytic strategy of pattern-matching enhances internal validity as it sets out possible explanations for some occurrence(s) and then matches the observed with the predicted outcomes. Process-tracing retroactively traces the causal process by which the case outcome was produced, thereby leading to a primary cause(s).[51]

Reliability means that the operations of study can be repeated – repeatability being one the hallmark qualities of the scientific method – culminating in the same or approximate result(s). In order to produce similar results, a researcher must document research procedure clearly enough to replicate the same study. Apart from tautologically underwhelming, this observation highlights a necessary condition for the elaboration of a methodologically sound case study.

3.7 Summary

This study presents a case study of Ukraine which compares the behavioral expectations (examined in chapter 4) against the empirical record of Ukraine's export control development. The objective of this study is to determine which approach, if any, best explains the development of nonproliferation export control measures in Ukraine. Process-tracing, the selected format for this case study, the investigator explores the chain of events or the decision making process by which initial case conditions are translated into case outcomes. The general method of process-tracing is to generate and analyze data on the causal mechanisms, or processes, events, actions, expectations, and other intervening variables, that link putative causes to observed effects.

Process tracing, which involves the inductive observation of apparent causal mechanisms and heuristic rendering of these mechanisms as potential hypotheses for future testing, is the chosen approach. Process tracing also lends itself to the study of the intentional behavior of individuals and organizations because this often involves the use of qualitative variables that are difficult though not necessarily impossible to quantify in a fruitful way.[52] Moreover, because the decision making at any level beyond the individual is a social process, it necessarily leaves behind at least some kinds of evidence – documents, participant recollections, public communications – even though this evidence may be far from complete or unbiased.[53] Accordingly, this project attempts to confirm or negate the generalizable expectations that are derived from each theoretical approach. The predictions of each approach are delineated and then compared to the empirical record to determine which approach better explains the Ukrainian export control policy decisions.

In terms of dissertation "types," this work is best represented by the "historical explanatory" type.[54] A historical explanatory dissertation uses theory (academically recognized theory, folk theory, or "common sense") to explain the causes, patterns, or consequences of historical cases. The following chapter will explain the methods used to assess system development and a general description thereof.

Notes

[1] Arguably, the seminal exposition of research ontology in the social sciences is Imre Lakatos, "Falsification and the Methodology of Scientific Research Programs" in Lakatos and Musgrave, eds., *Criticism and the Growth of Knowledge* (Cambridge: Cambridge University Press, 1970). Although Karl Popper – chiefly in *The Logic of Scientific Discovery* (*Der Logik der Forschung*) (New York: Basic Books, 1959) – is credited with establishing the "falsification criteria" of scientific research as the standard measure.

[2] See, *Methodology and Epistemology for Social Science: Selected Papers* (Chicago: University of Chicago Press, 1988), pp. 377-388.

³ Robert Yin, *Case Study Research: Design and Methods* (Newbury Park, CA: Sage Publications, Inc., 1989), p. 4. For more on the case study method, see Harry Eckstein, "Case Study and Theory in Political Science," in Fred I. Greenstein and Nelson W. Polsby, eds., *Handbook of Political Science, Volume 7: Strategies of Inquiry* (Reading, MA: Addison-Wesley Publishing Company, 1975), pp. 79-137; and Alexander L. George, "Case Studies and Theory Development: The Method of Structured, Focused Comparison," in Paul Gordon Lauren, ed., *Diplomacy: New Approaches in History, Theory, and Policy* (New York: The Free Press, 1979), pp. 43-68.
⁴ Joe R. Feagin, Anthony M. Orum, and Gideon Sjoberg, eds., *A Case for the Case Study* (Chapel Hill: University of North Carolina Press, 1991).
⁵ For a critical examination of the attempt to "scientize" political enquiry, see Peter Winch, *The Idea of a Social Science and its Relation to Philosophy*, second edition (London: Redwood Press, 1990), see especially p. 83. See also, Immanuel Wallerstein, *Unthinking Social Science: The Limits of Nineteenth Century Paradigms* (Cambridge: Basil Blackwell, Ltd., 1991), see pp. 242-243 wherein Wallerstein examines the innate tension between the nomothetic and idiographic strains in contemporary social science research, a tension, he contends, resulting from a decidedly behavioralist or "natural science" operative methodology. See also, James Rosenau, "Probing Puzzles Persistently: A Desirable But Improbable Future for IR Theory," in S. Smith, K. Booth, M. Zalewski, *International Theory: Positivism and Beyond* (Cambridge: Cambridge University Press, 1996), pp. 309-320. In particular, Rosenau notes: "Positivism in IR, as in all the social sciences, has essentially been a methodological commitment, tied to a rigid empiricist epistemology: together these results in a in a very restricted range of permissible ontological claims," p. 314.
⁶ Jürgen Habermas, *Knowledge and Human Interests* (London: Heinemann, 1972), pp. 301-317. See also Richard Rorty, *Objectivity, Relativism, and Truth* (Cambridge: Cambridge University Press, 1991), pp. 168-169.
⁷ While the existence of an array of divergent approaches and strategies for social enquiry pose the problem of choice for the social researcher, "it is possible to adopt a pragmatic position and to try to match a strategy to the nature of a particular research project and the kind of research questions that have been selected for consideration." See, Norman Blaike, *Approaches to Social Enquiry* (Cambridge: Polity Press, 1993), pp. 201-202.
⁸ For example, see Gary King, Robert Keohane, & Sidney Verba, "The Importance of Research Design in Political Science," *American Political Science Review*, 89, June 1995, p. 479.
⁹ See, Bruce Russett, "International Behavior Research: Case Studies and Cumulation," in Michael Haas and Henry Kariel, eds., *Approaches to the Study of Political Science* (Scranton: Chandler Publishing, 1970), pp. 428-429.
¹⁰ George, "Case Studies and Theory Development: The Method of Structured, Focused Comparison," in Paul Gordon Lauren, *op. cit.*, pp. 43-68.

[11] See, Stephen Van Evera, *Guide to Methodology for Political Science* (Cambridge, MA: MIT Press, 1991), pp. 29-35.

[12] *Ibid.*, pp. 57-58.

[13] See, William Boulton, "Case Study as a Research Methodology," *Case Research Journal*, 1985, p. 10; and Yin, *op. cit.*, p. 44.

[14] Thomas S. Kuhn, "Foreword," to Paul Hoyningen-Heune, *Reconstructing Scientific Revolutions: Thomas Kuhn's Philosophy of Science* (Chicago: University of Chicago Press, 1993), p. xiii.

[15] Concerning the former argument, see Steven R. Brown, "Intensive Analysis in Political Research," *Political Methodology* 1, Winter 1974, p. 3; on the latter, see Arend Lijphart, "Comparative Politics and Comparative Method," *American Political Science Review* 65, September 1971, p. 691.

[16] Yin, *Case Study Research*, pp. 47-48.

[17] Graham T. Allison, *Essence of Decision: Explaining the Cuban Missile Crisis* (Boston: Little, Brown, & Co., 1971).

[18] See, Douglas Holdstock & Frank Barnaby, eds., *Hiroshima and Nagasaki: Retrospect and Prospect* (Portland: F. Cass, 1995).

[19] Yin, *Case Study Research*, p. 47.

[20] *Ibid.*, p.48.

[21] See, for example, David Holloway, *Stalin and the Bomb: The Soviet Union and Atomic Energy* (New Haven: Yale University Press, 1994) and Gary K. Bertsch, Richard T. Cupitt, and Steven Elliott-Gower, eds., *International Cooperation on Nonproliferation Export Controls: Prospects for the 1990s and Beyond* (Ann Arbor: University of Michigan Press, 1994).

[22] Earlier studies have studied similar cases. See, Bertsch and Grillot, *Arms on the Market*, especially pp. 231-228.

[23] For an examination of these methodological problems and proposed solutions, see Russell Bova, "Political Dyanamics of the Post-Communist Transition: A Comparative Perspective," F.J. Fleron and E.P. Hoffman, eds., *Post-Communist Studies and Political Science: Methodology and Empirical Theory in Sovietology* (Boulder: Westview Press, 1993), pp. 239-265.

[24] The explication of state interests assumes the existence of an established battery of such interests coinciding with a state. In transition political and economic situations, such assumptions are problematized. On the inchoate nature of Ukrainian political identity and interests, see Jeffrey T. Checkel, "International Norms and Domestic Agents: Probing the Dynamics of Socialization," Columbia International Affairs Online, 15 May 1998, www.ciao.org/conf/ssr01.html, pp. 12-18. Also, see chapter 6 for a further elaboration of state interests development.

[25] For a discussion of descriptive, atheoretical case studies, see Yin, *Case Study Research*, p. 15; Lijphart, "Comparative Politics and Comparative Method," pp. 691-692; and Harry Eckstein, "Case Study and Theory in Political Science," in Fred Green Greenstein & Nelson Polsby, eds., *Handbook of Political Science, Volume 7: Strategies of Inquiry* (Reading: Addison-Wesley, 1975), pp. 79-137.

[26] See, Stephen Van Evera, *Guide to Methodology for Political Science* (Cambridge, MA: MIT Press, 1991), pp. 28-29.

[27] Timothy McKeown, "Case Studies and the Statistical Worldview," *International Organization* 53, no. 1, Winter 1999, pp. 161-190.

[28] For a review of the validity issue, see Anita Hubley and Bruno Zumbo, "A Dialectic on Validity: Where Have Been and Where Are We Going," The Journal of General Psychology, 4 (1997), pp. 208-215.

[29] J. Mitchell, "Case Studies," in R.F. Ellen, ed., *Ethnographic Research: A Guide to General Conduct* (Orlando: Academic Press, 1984), pp. 237-241.

[30] McKeown (1999), p. 174. See also, Thomas Burger, *Max Weber's Theory of Concept Formation: History, Laws, and Ideal Types* (Durham: Duke University Press, 1976), p. 127-128.

[31] Andrew Bennett and Alexander L. George, "Process Tracing in Case Study Research," Paper presented at the MacArthur Foundation Workshop on Case Study Methods, Belfer Center for Science and International Affairs (BCSIA), Harvard University, October 17-19, 1997. In particular, the authors note: "Process tracing is the only observational means of moving beyond covariation alone as a source of causal inference. Whether it is pursued through case studies, correlations, experiments, or quasi-experiments, it is an invaluable method that should be included in every researcher's repertoire."

[32] On establishing causality, see Margaret Marini and Burton Singer. "Causality in the Social Sciences" in Clifford Clogg, ed., *Sociological Methodology* (New York: American Sociological Association, 1998), pp. 347-409; and John Jackson, "Political Methodology: An Overview," in Robert Goodin and Hans-Dieter Klingemann, eds., *A New Handbook of Political Science* (Oxford: Oxford University Press, 1997).

[33] See, Daniel Little, *Microfoundations, Method, and Causation* (New Brunswick: Transaction, 1998), pp. 22-30.

[34] For further elaboration of these problems, see Andrew Bennett and Alexander L. George, "Process Tracing in Case Study Research," MacArthur Foundation Workshop on Case Study Methods October 17-19, 1997; and Alexander George, "The Role of the Congruence Method for Case Study Research," Paper presented at the annual convention of the International Studies Association, Toronto (1997).

[35] Gary King, Robert Keohane, and Sidney Verba, *Designing Social Inquiry: Scientific Inference in Qualitative Research* (Princeton: Princeton University Press, 1994) p. 86.

[36] Isaac Levi, *Decisions and Revisions: Philosophical Essays on Knowledge and Value* (Cambridge: University Press, 1984), p. 51.

[37] Alexander George and Timothy McKeown, "Case Studies and Theories of Organizational Decision Making," in R. Coulam and R. Smith, eds., *Advances in Information Processing in Organizations* (Greenwich: JAI Press, 1985), pp. 21-58. See also, Timothy McKeown, "Case Studies and the Statistical Worldview," *op. cit.*, pp. 178-180.

[38] For an explanation of Mill's method of difference, see Andrew Bennett and Alexander L. George, "Process Tracing in Case Study Research."
[39] See, Alexander George and Timothy McKeown, *op. cit.*, p. 56.
[40] Yin, *op. cit.*, p. 97.
[41] As export control issues frequently concern sensitive technologies and attendant official sensitivities, access to complete information is problematic. However, this relative informational lack does not pose an insurmountable methodological obstacle insofar as access to complete information in any setting is well-nigh impossible. For commentary on "incomplete information" and social science, see B.A. Turner, "Some Practical Aspects of Qualitative Data Analysis: One of Organizing the Cognitive Process Associated with the Generation of Grounded Theory," *Quality and Quantity* 15 (1981), pp. 225-247.
[42] For a discussion concerning the strengths and weaknesses of using decisions makers statements and speeches in policy analysis, see Ole Holsti, "Foreign Policy Makers Viewed Psychologically: Cognitive Process Approaches," in James Rosenau, ed., *In Search of Global Patterns* (New York: Free Press, 1976), pp. 120-144; Philip Tetlock, "Psychological Research on Foreign Policy: A Methodological Overview," *Review of Personality and Social Psychology* 4 (1983), pp. 239-262; and Yaccov Vertzberg, *The World in Their Minds: Information Processing, Cognition, and Perception in Foreign Policy Decision Making* (Stanford: Stanford University Press, 1990). Multiple sources of data are crucial to enhancing the quality of a case study. Vertzberg admonishes, "Attempts to explain cognitive operations by a single theory are parsimonious but also reductionist. They fail to grasp the multidimensionality of the personality or the variable contingencies and circumstances in which information processing takes place, thus missing the integrative character of human behavior. It is no coincidence that each single theory finds it difficult to explain inconsistencies between theory and actual behavior," p. 111.
[43] Interviews were conducted primarily with Ukrainian representatives from the Ministries of Foreign Economic Relations, Foreign Affairs and Defense. In the United States, interviewees were situated primarily in the US Departments of Commerce, Customs, Defense, Energy and State. All interviewees were promised anonymity in that their names and titles would not be attributed to their comments in our written report. Through my work with and for Los Alamos National Laboratory and the US Department of Energy, I was closely involved in several high, mid, and working level export control exchanges between the US and Ukraine from 1995-1999. Consequently, I have developed a considerable network of US and Ukrainian government officials and analysts. Furthermore, I also supplemented my research with a Summer 1999 research trip to Kyiv, made possible by a travel grant from the National Research Council.
[44] For a complete and detailed description of this measurement tool for export control development, see Cassady Craft and Suzette Grillot with Liam Anderson, Michael Beck, Chris Behan, Scott Jones, and Keith Wolfe, "Tools and Methods for Measuring and Comparing Nonproliferation Export Control Development,"

Occasional Paper of the Center for International Trade and Security (Athens: The University of Georgia, 1996); and Grillot and Craft, "How and Why We Evaluate Systems of Export Control," *The Monitor: Nonproliferation, Demilitarization and Arms Control* 2, 4 (Fall 1996).

[45] *Ibid.*

[46] Andrew Bennett and Alexander L. George, "Process Tracing in Case Study Research," MacArthur Foundation Workshop on Case Study Methods October 17-19, 1997.

[47] Lecture to the Political Science at the University of Georgia, Athens, May 1998.

[48] Yin, *op. cit.*, p. 20.

[49] *Ibid.*, pp. 42-43.

[50] *Ibid.*, p. 43.

[51] Stephen Van Evera, *op. cit.*, pp. 37-38.

[52] Andrew Sayer, *Method in Social Science* (New York: Routledge, 1992) pp. 25-29. Even for qualitative methods like case studies, the difficulties of collecting and interpreting data on cognitions and intentions are well known, and they are indeed daunting. These difficulties are no doubt one reason that some researchers prefer to treat cognitive variables as a "black box," or dealing with them by making certain restrictive assumptions about individual behavior on the basis of game theories, rational choice models, or other simplifying approaches.

[53] Alexander George and Timothy McKeown, "Case Studies and Theories of Organizational Decision Making," in *Advances in Information Processing in Organizations*, vol. 2. JAI Press (1985), p. 37.

[54] Stephen Van Evera, *Guide to Methodology for Political Science*, p. 50.

Chapter 4

Tools and Methods for Measuring Nonproliferation Export Controls: An Application in Ukraine

4.1 Introduction

After the Soviet Union collapsed and the Cold War ended, the threat of a clearly defined, indisputably capable political and military adversary was much reduced. Nonetheless, the industrialized democracies do confront national and international security threats. Among the most important of these threats is the proliferation of weapons of mass destruction and the technology, equipment, material and know-how helpful in their construction. To address this threat, the West has placed renewed emphasis on nonproliferation policies and tools.[1] Included among these policies and tools are three major strategies for preventing the proliferation of mass destructive weapons and their component parts: (1) physical protection; (2) accounting and control; and (3) export control. Perhaps the most challenging strategy, however, is the development of nonproliferation export controls.[2]

While most western nations have much experience with export control system development and management, many other nations are currently trying to create such systems. To assist their efforts, the West – led primarily by the United States – has been relatively forthcoming in providing resources, inducements and security assistance for the development of nonproliferation export controls.[3] Very little has been undertaken thus far, however, to establish appropriate tools and methods that will allow both the recipients and grantors of aid and assistance to evaluate progress in export control development. This chapter provides a methodology by which to measure and trace the evolution of the Ukrainian export control system. In so doing, we will find that steady enlargement has in fact occurred since independence. By charting quantitative development over time, we then logically ask *why* such development took place, a topic to be discussed in subsequent chapters.

4.2 Why Are Such Evaluations Necessary?[4]

Export controls are ultimately the responsibility of individual states. The effectiveness of such controls, however, depends on multilateral action. For export controls to be a useful tool for combating proliferation, controls must be interpreted and implemented (especially by those within a control regime) with some degree of uniformity.[5] Any state that serves as either a supply or transit point can weaken the effect of international and national export control efforts if it does not commit itself to such controls. In terms of security, multilateral export control efforts are only as strong as the weakest link. It is important, therefore, that states evaluate their systems of export control, as well as those of others. By doing so, they can learn more about and address the gaps in such systems in order to boost the effectiveness of export controls across the board.[6]

In addition to security priorities, there are important economic reasons for evaluating export control systems. Because export controls operate on the basis of "national discretion" and, therefore, the potential for considerable variation in export control policies exists, it is possible for certain states to implement their national systems in such a way as to establish a comparative advantage for their domestic economy. Moreover, one state's manipulation of multilateral controls to serve its purposes will provide other states with an incentive to neglect controls as well. States should be interested in complementary systems of export control because of the potential economic consequences gaps in such systems may create.[7]

The importance of multilateral action in the control of sensitive exports, due to its influence on the effectiveness of export control policies, provides a compelling reason why evaluation of national export control behavior is warranted. Because export control development (as a sign of adherence to nonproliferation norms) is being linked more often to aid and assistance in the post-Cold War environment, however, both grantors and recipients of such aid should be interested in evaluation tools. Grantors of aid, either specifically for export control development or for non-export control purposes, should want to see progress in the recipient country. Grantors will be in a better position, therefore, to evaluate the efficacy of the aid they have provided. Recipients will no doubt be interested in showing evidence of compliance, especially if they are or will be seeking additional aid and assistance.[8]

To present the tools and methods for evaluating the development of nonproliferation export controls, this chapter is organized as follows.[9] First, a short review of the development of Western multilateral nonproliferation export controls, focusing on the emphasis that the West places on the need for export controls and on the "common standards" deemed beneficial – if not absolutely necessary – for multilateral nonproliferation efforts to work. Second, an explanation of tools for the measurement of state export control development. Third, a brief, but important, section on the techniques of comparison useful when the tools are used. An example of such comparisons is offered by presenting preliminary collective research on the Southern Tier states of the former Soviet Union. Fourth, a discussion of the various strengths and weaknesses of the approach. The last section provides an examination of the Ukrainian export control system and its institutional and policy development. An analysis of why such development occurred will be pursued in later chapters.

4.3 The Development of Common Standards in Nonproliferation Export Control

In 1949, the United States and several of its West European allies began coordinating efforts – through the Coordinating Committee for Multilateral Export Controls (COCOM) – for the control of sensitive trade with the Soviet Union, its allies, and (later) China.[10] COCOM developed throughout the Cold War and persisted beyond, both serving as an arena for negotiating the niceties of East-West trade and technology transfer, and also becoming the core component of a larger nonproliferation regime. With the addition of the Nuclear Nonproliferation Treaty in 1968, the Nuclear Suppliers Group (nuclear fuel and reactor transfers) in 1976, the Biological and Toxin Weapons Convention in 1972, the Australia Group (chemical and biological weapons and technology transfers) in 1985, the Chemical Weapons Convention in 1993, and the Missile Technology Control Regime (means of delivery) in 1987, states forged (both formally and informally) a relatively comprehensive nonproliferation regime.[11] This regime seeks to prevent the spread of weapons of mass destruction and the technologies, material and equipment that may prove of aid to states of concern desiring to acquire mass destructive capability.

COCOM, perhaps the most mature and extensive export control arrangement, served as the cornerstone for the regulation of sensitive trade during the Cold War.[12] COCOM members disbanded the organization in March 1994, but replaced it with the Wassenaar Arrangement on Export Controls for Conventional Arms and Dual-Use Goods and Technologies in December 1995.[13] COCOM's importance as a multilateral export control regime was paramount. It established the rules, norms and procedures that allowed Western states to regulate their economic competition in deference to the security threats posed by perceived enemies. Participation in COCOM encouraged states to develop control lists and other mechanisms that evolved into the "common standards" of national export control systems. These common standards provided a means by which members could encourage the development of comprehensive, consistent and (hopefully) effective national export controls systems, which would in turn decrease the mutual suspicion that historically occurred between states involved in such informal regimes with no formal and legally binding enforcement mechanisms at the transnational level.[14]

The concept of "common standards" continued in the post-Cold War nonproliferation environment despite the dissolution of the COCOM arrangement and the inclusion of the Russian Federation and Ukraine in the Wassenaar Arrangement.[15] Indeed, throughout the discussions of COCOM's reorganization in the early 1990s, several members expressed concern regarding the complete removal or liberalization of COCOM multilateral controls. Many of these countries, France, Japan, and Canada for example, depended on the authority provided by international agreements and obligations to control sensitive exports. These countries relied on COCOM control lists and procedures as the basis for their national controls.[16] Moreover, the current international security climate continues to call for means by which additional states can take measures against the dangers of proliferation. The cooperative techniques that helped in part to guarantee the national security of Western states during the Cold War, as well as ensure smooth trade practices between these states, will be duplicated in the future, differing only in the inclusion of non-Western states to make such measures better able to address international security threats and the normalization of trade relations.

The standards for export control practices set forth throughout COCOM's tenure and beyond serve as a point of departure for the development of tools and methods that will allow for the evaluation of export control systems. As the above discussion illustrates, COCOM's common standards serve as a reasonable model of internationally accepted export control policies, practices and procedures. This does not suggest, however, that the COCOM model is a perfect example of export control procedures, nor that it is without flaws. Nonetheless, the multilaterally accepted export control practices that COCOM established have been and continue to be well accepted and can, therefore, serve as a basis for evaluation and comparison.

4.4 Tools for Measuring Nonproliferation Export Control Development

This section surveys the tools for measuring the development of nonproliferation export control systems developed at the Center for International Trade and Security at the University of Georgia.[17] From a set of questions used in the past by Western government officials (i.e., COCOM members) to describe levels of national export control development based on the idea of common standards, ten elements of an export control system were elicited.[18] These elements are distinct, but mutually reinforcing aspects of effective nonproliferation export controls (see Table 4.1).

Table 4.1 Elements of an Export Control System

• Licensing System	• Control Lists
• Regime Adherence	• Catch-All Clause
• Training	• Bureaucratic Process
• Customs Authority	• Import/Export Verification
• Penalties	• Information Gathering/Sharing

Each element is further broken down into three subparts reflecting the existence of export control (a) policy and/or legal ground; (b) institutions and procedures; and (c) behavior (implementation). The first subpart concerns the existence of nonproliferation export control policy. Is there a legal basis – laws and/or decrees – for nonproliferation export controls? The second subpart reflects the intuition that laws are potentially only effective if there are institutions and procedures for putting them into effect. In other words, is there a bureaucracy and/or officials that are responsible for the development and implementation of export controls? Finally, a third subpart addresses the need for compliant behavior or implementation of export controls, asking, are the export control laws and mechanisms actually in use?

Using a questionnaire of said elements, government officials and non-governmental researchers have a powerful tool with which they can measure the level of export control development in a given country. The 72-item questionnaire provides a sensitive measure of export control development through the use of a simple rating scheme using a three level response (no development [0]; some development [.5]; and full development [1]) for evaluation. Because some elements may be of greater significance for the operation of an export control system, weights were created to indicate their relative importance. To obtain the appropriate weightings, government officials, non-governmental experts, and industry representatives were surveyed, asking them to rank the ten elements in order of importance. For example, Licensing System had the most important ranking in the survey which gave it a weight of 7.47; whereas the Catch-All Provision received (as the least important) a weight of 1.2. Once the questionnaire is answered fully, the researcher then simply averages the tallies for the elements, and multiplies the averages by the weights provided.

By summing the weighted element scores, the researcher obtains a figure that represents the state's overall level of export control development. The researcher/official may then compare the state's export control development with an ideal or perfect score; other states in aggregated form (system to system); other states in disaggregated form (element to element); over-time and by subpart. Each of these methods will be considered in more detail below.

4.4.1 Methods for Comparing Export Control Development

Although this particular study is not concerned with comparison per se, it is – all things being equal – an important component in understanding that the measure of a country's development over time is meaningful insofar as it reflects positive or negative change against the tested country itself based on a measurement that is designed on the basis of comparison.

4.4.2 Comparison with an Ideal Type

An ideal type is conceptualized as some approximation of a "perfect score;" i.e. meeting Western multilateral standards in every category on the questionnaire (having a total weighted score of 41.82). This is potentially an extremely high standard to meet; one that only few states with long export control experiences can presently hope to match. However, comparisons along such lines are useful insofar as states will be required to approach such nonproliferation export control development in order to reap the full rewards of inclusion in Western political, military and economic institutions.

4.4.3 Comparison with Other States in Aggregated Form (System to System)

A second potentially useful comparison using the "elements of an export control system" tool is by using the total weighted scores of two or more states in a cross-sectional manner. Simply put, if one state scores higher than another, we may say that it has a more fully developed export control system. As an example of this type of comparison, I have included preliminary scores established for ex-Soviet states in the Transcaucasus (Armenia, Azerbaijan, and Georgia)[19] as part of a larger project that measures, compares and explains the development of export control systems in these states (see Table 4.2).[20]

Table 4.2 Development of NIS Nonproliferation Export Controls (Weighted Scores)

Country	Export Control System Status in 1998 (41.82 possible)
Belarus	34.00
Kazakstan	28.29
Russia	34.70
Ukraine	32.53
Armenia	**19.69**
Azerbaijan	**8.02**
Georgia	**10.07**
Kyrgyzstan	15.30
Tajikistan	4.36
Turkmenistan	4.36
Uzbekistan	7.14

These scores indicate that, while export control systems in the Trancaucasus are largely underdeveloped, there is considerable variation in what development is in evidence. While we make no claims at this point as to the causal factors that determine the level of export control development in the NIS (that is the purpose of the comprehensive, ongoing project by the authors), we believe that our measurement tools allow for a more rigorous examination of this development.

4.4.4 Comparison with Other States in Disaggregated Form (Element to Element)

The "elements of an export control system" tool can be used to compare disaggregations of states' export control elements (see Table 4.3). A researcher or official may compare the level of export control development in the area of Information Gathering/Sharing, Licensing System, and Customs Authority (or any element or combination of elements) for any state or any number of states. This process allows for the specific evaluation of components *within* an export control system rather than a general evaluation of the system as a whole.

Table 4.3 Comparison of Element Scores in Four States, 1996 (Weighted Score/Percentage of Ideal Score)

	Information Gathering/Sharing	Licensing System	Customs Authority
Armenia	.56 (13%)	3.74 (50%)	4.36 (66%)
Azerbaijan	.63 (15%)	2.47 (33%)	2.18 (33%)
Georgia	.63 (15%)	2.47 (33%)	2.18 (33%)

4.4.5 Comparison Over Time

A comparison may be made over time using either the total score for a state's export control system overall, or the individual element scores.[21] By obtaining total weighted scores for a state at two (or more) points in time, we can evaluate the progress (or lack thereof) of that state's nonproliferation export control development. It has been noted in preliminary research that those NIS states that have experienced more rapid export control system development tend to be those that received Western aid specifically for this purpose.[22] Those that lagged behind (the Southern Tier states and Moldova) have been those which posed less indigenous proliferation threat and subsequently only belatedly received Western nonproliferation export control aid. However, given the fact that the Transcaucasus states began with virtually no national nonproliferation export control systems,[23] this type of analysis is omitted here because the rates of change in export control development tend to mislead.[24]

It may be concluded that since the states of the Transcaucasus region had a higher total weighted score at a later point in time, then they have made progress (however rudimentary) in developing a nonproliferation export control system. In addition to comparing the *state* of development of a country's export control system, we can compare the *percent change* in export control system development.[25] In doing so, we provide a tool by which evaluators may assess the amount of effort that has been invested in nonproliferation export control development. With further research one can investigate which particular causal agents influenced change in export control development. For example, one could consider the amount and timing of CTR aid to each country, and examine its effect on the amount of growth in export control development.

4.4.6 Comparison by Subpart (Policy, Institutions, Behavior)

Finally, evaluators can use this method to compare the level of a state's export control development by subparts; i.e. policy, institutions and behavior (see Table 4.4). Such analysis, at least in this example of three NIS states, shows the relative underdevelopment of state compliance with common standards in terms of nonproliferation export control implementation when compared to policy and institutions.

Table 4.4 Export Control Development in the Transcaucasus by Subparts

	Policy	**Institutions**	**Behavior**
Armenia	60%	23%	8%
Azerbaijan	31%	2%	0%
Georgia	35%	4%	4%

4.5 Strengths and Weaknesses of Approach

The measurement tools presented here allow states to address concerns inherent in undertaking cooperative endeavors in a multilateral context where there is no guarantee that some members may neither "cheat" nor "free-ride."[26] In order for a multilateral nonproliferation export regime to be effective, the West – through long experience during the Cold War – deems common standards to be useful, if not necessary.[27] This measurement system helps to promote common standards by providing a tool by which regime members can evaluate the export control development of other members and prospective members, thereby bridging the gap between export control implementation based on national discretion. Just as important, this evaluation system provides a means for states to demonstrate their status as a member in "good standing" with the nonproliferation regime. Thus, if other states can "see" that they have a well-developed export control system, the uncertainty surrounding their future export behavior may be reduced.

The measurement described above is not, however, a measure of *effectiveness* for national export control systems independently. As stated earlier, the tools provided here contribute to an understanding of effectiveness only through comparison and with the awareness of gaps between national systems of export control. It is acknowledged that while national export control systems have been deemed very important by the West, they alone are neither necessary nor sufficient conditions concerning nonproliferation effectiveness. In other words, a state with a perfect total weighted score would not necessarily be more effective at controlling the export of weapons and sensitive technology, material, and equipment than would a state with no system at all (scoring a 0) – especially given that the latter state may have nothing of concern to export. At the same time, certain states may have developed only a few elements of a nonproliferation export control system, but still be equally effective as those that have developed all of them. This may particularly be the case for those states that rely on a centrally planned and controlled military/industrial/political apparatus.

The methodology, apart from providing policy makers a useful means by which to address nonproliferation deficiencies and chart development, it serves also to prompt further empirical and theoretical research, of which this present study is evidence. In other words, in determining the relative development of a national system, we may then examine development over time, the variables driving state behavior, and so forth.

4.6 The Need for Tools and Methods for Evaluating the Development of Nonproliferation Export Controls

Because of the important role that nonproliferation export controls may play in the realm of international security, analysts of export control system development need refined tools with which they can make rigorous evaluations. Such evaluations are needed in order to address the concerns that states have when entering multilateral arrangements such as the nonproliferation regime. They are also valuable insofar as they allow states to reduce the uncertainty surrounding their future export control behavior through the ability to demonstrate in a rigorous manner the extent of their nonproliferation export control development. Such measurement ability is necessary as non-Western states seek admission to the nonproliferation regime that has been created and maintained by the West. Evaluations are also essential as long as non-export control aid is linked to the adherence to nonproliferation norms. While the measurement tools presented here do not address issues such as the effect of any particular export control system on nonproliferation *effectiveness* (although, this would be a rich avenue for further research), they do provide researchers with the ability to make more rigorous evaluations about key elements that are *important* to export control development.

As yet, the development of export control systems in the Transcaucasus states of the NIS has proceeded at an unhurried rate. Recent indications are, however, that an awareness is growing within US policy-making circles of the extent of the proliferation threat presented by these states and of the overall importance of stability in the region to world energy and commercial trade.[28] Many of these states do possess sensitive items that need to be controlled, and moreover, the absence of export controls in these states could significantly undermine nonproliferation initiatives throughout the NIS. Given this, one can anticipate greater efforts on the part of the US government to encourage the development of functioning systems of export controls in these states. As export controls develop across the Transcaucasus, measuring the extent and rate of their development (and the way in which development takes place), all become issues of great importance. Therefore, one may expect that the methodologies and tools outlined in this section (and elsewhere)[29] will, over time, assume ever greater relevance when applied to the Transcaucasus states.

The "common standards" developed during the COCOM era are likely to prevail in the post-Cold War nonproliferation environment just as is the Western commitment to the nonproliferation regime. While the West provides resources, incentives, and security assistance to states that adhere or seek to adhere to the nonproliferation standards created in the West, non-Western states will find it difficult to emulate export control standards with which they are unfamiliar. The West should also provide the tools and methods with which non-Western states may evaluate their nonproliferation export control system and its development so that all concerned will have positive measures of their progress and expected progress. By doing so, the West will not just strengthen the international nonproliferation regime through the broadening of the norms of cooperation, but may also advance its efforts to prevent the spread of weapons of mass destruction and related technology, material and equipment through the more widespread development of internationally accepted export control systems.

4.7 The Domestic Structure of Export Control

The number of necessary or sufficient requirements implemented by governments in pursuit of export control is not as important as their configuration and suitability to the domestic political structure that translates them into effective public policy and adheres to a country's international obligations.[30] Weaknesses in one area, licensing authority for example, may be compensated for in other areas, such as cooperation with industry or an effective criminal justice system. One government's configuration of institutions and statutory regulations is not likely to match of another government, although history has given some governments similar traditions in law and public administration.[31] How and why states structure their export control systems is best understood through the use of abstract models.

A recent study on export control "models" suggests the existence of three approaches to export control architecture: consensus, arbitration, and collaboration.[32]

Consensus Model
A regulatory system requiring review of sensitive exports by numerous official agencies is one that must rely on consensus for controls. Since it is not in the nature of governmental agencies to work together to achieve consensus, the importance of national legislation mandating the statutory responsibilities of component agencies and ministries is important to decision making. Strong laws empower agencies to participate in the export control process. Examples include the United States and Canada.

Arbitration Model
An export control system that places licensing responsibility in the hands of a single review authority or agency can be described as regulation through arbitration. In this model, the responsible government or agency is given the task of judging the merits of the case and taking responsibility for its actions. It may solicit technical or expert analysis and ask for the opinion of other officials or agencies, but the positions of other agencies and ministries is primarily – if not exclusively – advisory. Should differences exist between agencies or ministries, the non-licensing agency

must make an issue of the policy or case at the highest level of authority. An arbitration model might tend to emerge from the existence of a government ruled by a multiparty government coalition, wherein various ministries are held by different parties. This need not generate differences in policies, but does foster a desire for the independence of administrative authority; put simply, bureaucratic fiefs. Examples include Germany, Russia, and Ukraine.[33]

Collaboration Model
If a government relies on a close relationship with exporting industries to review and discuss pending sales and contracts, then collaboration is a prominent component of export control. In this model, the value of the government's "good will" is sufficiently important to the exporting company to motivate it to self-police its sales activities.[34] The value of "good will" is an obvious by-product of a centrally planned economy, when divergence from governmental policy based in a planning agency is risky from an economic and political point of view. The "good will" of the government is also important in economies where government is active in industrial policy, which can be defined as the public promotion of advanced exporting sectors. This is further amplified when there is much public ownership of enterprise. Examples include Sweden and South Korea.[35]

4.8 Assessing Ukrainian Export Control Development: The Elements

This study of the Ukrainian nonproliferation export control system employs an assessment methodology derived from COCOM's "common standards."[36] The common standards were then modified, resulting in a measurement tool that allows for multiple perspective analyses. The tool is comprised of weighted elements, elements regarded as distinct but mutually reinforcing aspects of an effective export control system. By examining each of the elements, one is able to chart progress, stasis, or decline in the development of an export control system, as described in the above.

Overall, lacking an institutional history upon which to draw reference, Ukraine encountered and continues to face many challenges to its export control development effort. Nevertheless, substantial progress has been made.[37] For example, based on a quantitative analysis of export control development, Ukraine's export control system was 39% compliant with Western export control standards in 1992, rising to 78% compliant in

Table 4.5 System Score Per Annum: Ukraine

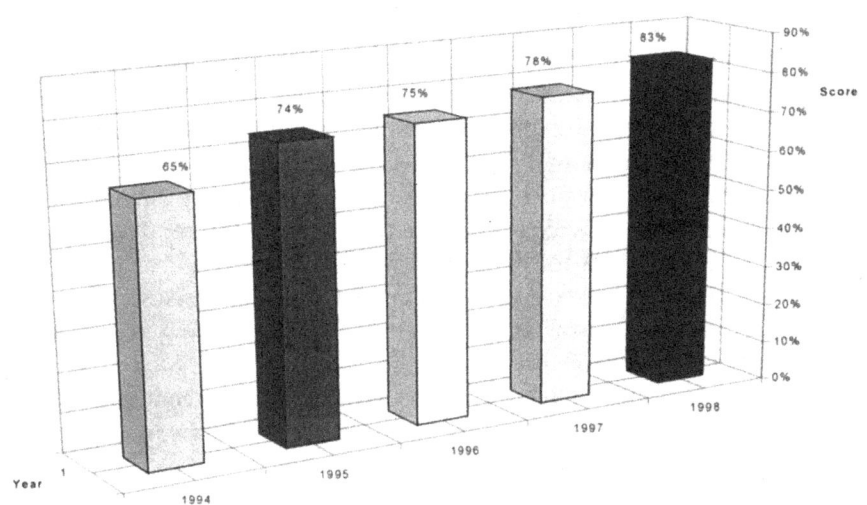

1997.[38] Compared with other newly independent states (NIS), Ukraine ranked below only Russia and Belarus. Furthermore, when examining overall development over time, a longitudinal study reveals a progressive pattern (see Table 4.5).[39] In other words, since 1992, Ukraine has evinced a steady evolutionary path in the development of its export control system. This development is all the more remarkable when considering the political, economic, and social difficulties inherent in the transition from a communist political-economic system to a modern state.

Despite Ukraine's progress, problems and proliferation risks remain to be overcome. Several reports have alleged illicit transfers of sensitive goods and technologies to such destinations as China, Iraq and Libya.[40] The export control agencies are understaffed, underequipped, and undertrained. Furthermore, owing to parliamentary wrangling over the 1998 budget, funds were not disbursed until July of that year, thereby impeding export control activities. Organized crime and government corruption remain formidable obstacles to export control development. For example, in late 1993, top officials in the Ministry of Foreign Economic Relations were arrested for bribe taking and for issuing licenses to export "strategic raw materials."[41] The exporting community in Ukraine is not well-versed in its export control obligations. For example, internal compliance mechanisms are not a common feature of Ukrainian enterprises.[42] Additionally, porous, understaffed borders add to the dilemma. Lax enforcement and limited overseas representation diminish export control developments.

Ukraine is well endowed with sensitive technologies, materials, and equipment. In the absence of a large domestic consumer market and owing to its CIS-interdependent structure, the Ukrainian economy is export-oriented.[43] Consequently, economic privation brings considerable pressure to bear on the export imperative, which in the Ukrainian case involves many internationally controlled items. These economic pressures translate into direct political pressures. For example, the Soviet Union's defense enterprises provided a broad range of social services, such as housing and health care, for their employees and families.[44] Furthermore, Ukraine is home to some 1,870 defense-related enterprises, comprising some 70% of the industrial sector, therefore employing a substantial portion of the working population. In many cases, such enterprises comprise entire towns or regions. Thus, enterprise managers and regional politicians are under considerable pressure to maintain jobs by seeking out clients on the international market.[45]

4.8.1 International Nonproliferation Regime Adherence

Since 1992, Ukraine has joined or adheres to all nonproliferation supplier regimes (see Table 4.6). There are four important institutional arrangements that comprise the supply-side dimension of the nonproliferation regime - the Nuclear Suppliers Group (NSG),[46] the Missile Technology Control Regime (MTCR),[47] the Australia Group (AG),[48] and the Wassenaar Arrangement (WA).[49] The principal concern of the Nuclear Suppliers Group is exercising control over exports of materials and technologies relevant to the production of nuclear weapons; the MTCR regulates the export of missiles and technologies useful in the development of missiles capable of carrying nuclear, biological, or chemical payloads over specified distances; the Australia Group controls exports of chemical precursors and biological agents and related equipment that can be used in producing chemical and biological weapons; finally, the WA addresses potentially destabilizing exports of conventional weapons and "dual-use" technologies.

In terms of institutional structure, all four regimes exhibit similarities, both among themselves, and with COCOM. Specifically, none of the four regimes is grounded in a treaty. They are all informal agreements to control items on the basis of "national discretion," meaning that member states ultimately hold jurisdiction over licensing of exports. Also similar to COCOM, none of the regimes possesses the institutional mechanisms for detecting violations and sanctioning violators. This is left to the discretion of national governments. Compliance with the rules and norms of the regimes is therefore, voluntary.

In an effort to meet its nonproliferation obligations, nuclear, chemical, biological, and conventional weapons and dual-use control lists are now harmonized with those of the multilateral regimes.[50] As of April 1996, Ukraine became a member of the Nuclear Suppliers Group (NSG).

Table 4.6 Nonproliferation Regime Participation

	AG	MTCR	NPT	NSG	WA
Ukraine	+	+	+	+	+

The Missile Technology Control Regime (MTCR) had proven to be the most elusive nonproliferation regime objective. On 13 May 1994, Ukraine signed a Memorandum of Understanding with the US in which it pledged to respect MTCR guidelines. However, membership negotiations have stalled over Ukrainian reservations regarding elements in the arrangement that would adversely affect Ukraine's ability to continue producing Category I missile systems. Washington and Kyiv were attempting in 1997 to move past the impasse to an agreement acceptable to both sides.[51] It was not until 1998 that Ukraine entered the regime. Its accession was facilitated by the United States.[52]

4.8.2 Institutional Developments

The bureaucratic framework of the Ukrainian export control system was not inherited from the Soviet Union. Lacking a vestigial control system and the accompanying personnel trained and conversant in such matters, the present structure has emerged in what can be described as an "adaptive" manner.[53] The present structure is the result of a continuing process by which Ukraine seeks to balance its international obligations, resource capabilities, and political, security, and economic idiosyncrasies and interests. For example, former Head of the State Service on Export Control (SSEC), Victor Vaschilin noted: "Our [SSEC] main objective is to support our national interests and security of Ukraine and to uphold the international norms in the sphere of nonproliferation and export control by preventing the sale or proliferation of weapons of mass destruction and their delivery systems and also monitoring the export of conventional weaponry and military equipment. to regions where they would contribute to the destabilization of the situation."[54]

The first efforts at developing an export control system took place even before independence. On 16 April 1991, the first session of the Ukrainian parliament adopted the "Act on Foreign Economic Activity." Article 20 of the Act specified that the export and import of weapons, special components for their manufacture, explosive agents, nuclear materials, technologies, equipment and installations – along with other kinds of goods and services that could be used for arms production – required authorization by the Ukrainian state. Adoption of the Act took place at the time when the Soviet Union was still formally in existence. Although the primary objective of the Act was to present Ukraine as a formally independent state and prevent uncontrolled withdrawals of commodities from Ukraine to Russia, it included provisions upon which subsequent developments and enhancements of the export control system would be based.[55]

In early 1992, export control responsibilities rested with the Ministry of Foreign Affairs, the Ministry of Foreign Economic Relations, and the Ministry of Defense. Prior to the creation of specific export control agencies, much of the licensing and coordination between buyer and seller was still conducted in Moscow.[56] Subsequently, Ukrainian export control authorities were consolidated into the Governmental Commission on Export Controls (GCEC) and the Expert and Technical Committee (ETC) of the Cabinet of Ministers. Furthermore, there are sections responsible for export control in a number of ministries and agencies.

The Governmental Commission on Export Controls, now the Governmental Commission on Export Control Policy (GCECP), is a broad managerial organ responsible for coordinating state policy in the area of export control, licensing, determining quotas for export and import of commodities subject to export control, and arranging control over legislation implementation. The Commission consists of representatives, usually at the head or deputy head level, from the State Export Control Service and various state ministries.[57]

The Expert and Technical Committee of the Cabinet of Ministers, now the State Export Control Service (SSEC) is the main state executive organ on export control. The Committee conducts its activities in compliance with the decisions of the GCECP, and functions as a permanent body. SSEC examines applications and issues licenses for export, import and the transit of goods subject to export control, submits proposals for renewing the list of commodities subject to export control, provides reports on the implementation of export control legislation, and organizes and maintains cooperation with appropriate organs on export control in foreign countries. SSEC is also responsible for export control enforcement. Enforcement is hampered by finite resources, qualified personnel, and the limited number of overseas missions capable of conducting end-user verification checks. Recently, SSEC expanded its battery of technical experts by establishing a formal working relationship with the Kyiv Institute for Nuclear Research of the Ukrainian Academy of Sciences for the purpose of license, policy, and control lists review.[58]

Cooperation continues between the Ukrainian and US export control communities. Cooperative exchanges, technical and policy seminars, workshops and working agreements (such as the US Department of Energy *Lab-to-Lab* agreements) have increased since early 1996. Activities, involving the US Departments of Commerce, Defense, Energy, and State, as well as Customs include licensing automation plans, border post automation equipment and training, industry outreach programs, and technical exchanges. Finland, Germany, Japan, and Norway have also provided export control assistance to Ukraine.[59]

A clearly identifiable export control culture and community is emerging in Ukraine. SSEC is in the process of developing regional export control offices that will serve local exporters. A center for export control information and assistance, the Ukrainian Scientific and Technical Center, was created in March 1997.[60] Initiated by Ukrainian exporters and the SSEC, the Center will assist Ukrainian enterprises by providing export control information and assistance on developing internal compliance mechanisms.

Although the SSEC was formally granted most of licensing authority, and the Commission was to make licensing decisions only in special cases, in practice, the Commission gradually assumed the major part of licensing responsibilities which created tension between the two bodies. Consequently, the need to restructure the mechanism –and mediate the inherent conflict – became obvious.

As such, President Kuchma issued a decree that signaled the beginning of another reorganization of the arms export control system in the country.[61] The decree, signed on 4 February 1999, renamed the Governmental Commission on Export Control Policy to the Commission on Export Control Policy and Military and Technical Cooperation With Foreign Countries was. The Commission consists of representatives from the following ministries and agencies, at the level of First deputy heads or deputy heads: Foreign Affairs; Foreign Economic Relations and Trade; Defense; Industrial Policy; Internal Affairs; Security Service; the Center for Strategic Planning and Analysis under the Council on National Security and Defense; SSEC; State Customs Service; and the State Committee on Border Protection.

The new Commission has become directly responsible to the President's Council on National Security and Defense. The major responsibility of the Commission has become decision-making on "critical" exports to any country and any military-related exports to "critical" countries. "Critical" exports include exports of "ready-to-go" products, technologies, equipment and materials which may significantly contribute to the importer's ability to develop weapons of mass destruction. Such items are specifically listed in the control lists of the Nuclear Suppliers Group (NSG), Missile Technology Control Regime (MTCR) and Wassenaar Arrangements. "Critical" countries include those against which the UN Security Council and/or the Organization on Security and Cooperation in Europe (OSCE) have imposed sanctions or limitations; those which pose or may pose a threat to Ukraine's national security; and those which "support terrorism."[62]

The newly created Commission is not to interfere in licensing functions beyond the "critical" cases, and the SSEC is the main standing licensing body. As per decree, the number of SSEC employees will increase from current 64 to 80. In October 1998, Lieutenant General Victor Vaschilin, SSEC Chairman, was replaced by Army General Valeriy Gubenko. Gubenko developed close relations with President Kuchma while serving as a General Military Inspector under the President before his subsequent appointment.[63] Gubenko is of higher rank than Vaschilin and is viewed by government officials as bringing a more authoritative element to bear on the export control system.[64]

One of the major perceived weaknesses of the old system was that, since independence, arms exports and imports had been carried out without an "adequate" legal background (i.e., absence of parliamentary legislated export control law) which would clearly define major players and their responsibilities, creating confusion, duplication, and inefficiency.[65] To address this oversight, the President signed Decree No. 422/99 "On Measures to Perfect Military and Technical Cooperation Between Ukraine and Foreign Countries" on 21 April 1999. The Presidential decree on military and technical cooperation (an old Soviet term for international arms transfers)[66] determines that the goals of the arms trade between Ukraine and foreign countries are "to protect national interests and security of the country, provide Armed Forces and other military formations with modern arms, hardware and other military-related goods, develop export potential of the military-industrial complex, increase science and technology potential of the defense industry of Ukraine." The key decision-makers stated in the decree are the Council on National Security and Defense of Ukraine, Commission on Export Control Policy and Military and Technical Cooperation With Foreign Countries, and the Cabinet of Ministers of Ukraine. Although the Cabinet of Ministers is listed among the key players, the actual decision making will be concentrated in the President's Council on National Security and Defense. The numerous responsibilities of the Cabinet of Ministers, specifically stated in the decree, have very little to do with policy making, and downgraded virtually to technical implementation of the decisions made by the Council and the Commission.

4.8.3 Customs Authority

Although the Ukrainian Customs Authority has been substantially augmented since independence – personnel have increased from 2,000 to 17,000 in four years – smuggling and corruption remain formidable problems.[67] Enforcement authority remains weak owing to the uncertain legal environment. Training efforts and equipment upgrades are limited by the acute financial strains facing the government. Border postings are understaffed, ill-equipped and, in most cases, isolated from the central authorities in Kyiv. Borders are not tightly monitored with Russia and Belarus.[68] Furthermore, detection and interdiction efforts are primarily aimed at duty collection. Consequently, Customs officials are more apt to focus on volume rather than types of imports and exports.[69]

The Presidential Decree of November 29, 1996 outlined the ways by which the intensive reforms of the customs system in Ukraine are undertaken. As of today, the customs authority consists of a three-level structure. This three-tiered structure includes the central office of the State Customs Service, regional customs points, and local customs points. Furthermore, the structure of the customs authorities includes a number of specialized organizations and educational institutions, which assist the State Customs Service in terms of developing customs strategy and drafting legal norms in order to improve Ukraine's customs system.

According to the Directive of the Cabinet of Ministers of Ukraine No. 737-R, the central office of the State Customs Service houses a department charged with export control duties. The State Customs Service, through the department of export control, regulates customs control over goods subject to export control.

The department of export control of the State Customs Service:

1) develops legal export control acts;
2) ensures that business entities' export activities are in line with current customs laws;

3) terminates licenses, if exporters violate current customs laws, subsequently informing the Governmental Commission on Export Control Policy for actions against the violator; and
4) coordinates the further organization and implementation of customs control.

US assistance – in the form of training equipment – has been consistent since 1995 and has clearly affected the further development of the export controlling capacity of the Customs Authority.[70]

4.8.4 Verification

According to the *Procedures for State Export Controls in Ukraine* (No. 117/98) of 13 February 1998, in order to obtain an export license, an exporter must first submit an import certificate with its export license application. An authorized government agency in the recipient country must have issued this certificate to the Ukrainian exporter agreeing not to (1) re-export the item(s) without obtaining written consent from Ukraine; (2) use the item(s) to develop weapons of mass destruction; and (3) use the item(s) in any way that contributes to a nuclear-fuel cycle that does not operate under IAEA safeguards. Furthermore, as per Decree of the President of Ukraine No. 117/98 of 13 February 1998: Procedures for State Export Controls in Ukraine, export controls have become ostensibly more comprehensive. Specifically, the Decree states that not only arms transfers, but also initializing negotiations with a foreign customer require special permission from the authorized government agencies. Nevertheless, the lack of resources and inexperience hinder the ability of the government to undertake verification measures. The SSEC is currently in the process of creating a database of export violators, domestic and foreign, that would facilitate such exercises. Furthermore, information gathering at the regime level assists in this development.

Formally, the government has a broad range of investigative powers (inspection of documents, shipments, accounts, seizure of goods, physical inspection of cargoes at border points, etc.) but in practice, the execution of these powers is far from perfect. Sometimes, the SSEC is incapable of verifying submitted documents due to a limited number of qualified officers. Also, if at the pre-license check stage the SSEC reveals intentionally misleading information submitted by the Ukrainian exporter or importer, there is no law to prosecute the violator. Undertaking pre-license checks, the SSEC requests the Foreign Ministry to check end-use and end-user certificates of foreign companies. However, a limited number of Ukrainian embassies abroad (about sixty), inadequate financing, and lack of trained personnel decrease the quality of such checks. Overall, Ukraine has been limited by its lack of information and has had to rely on outside sources. Interpol, for example, has apparently helped Ukrainian authorities check licenses for goods destined for Yugoslavia, and the US Defense Department has been asked to provide information on suspect countries and importers.

4.8.5 Penalties

In compliance with Section 228.6 of the Penal Code of Ukraine, the violation of established procedures for export of commodities, raw materials, equipment and technologies that can be used for creation of missile, nuclear, chemical and other types of armament, special military equipment or services related to creation of arms, military and special equipment and illegal export of above mentioned items and related spare parts and ammunition is punishable by imprisonment up to eight years with confiscation of property. This amendment to the Penal Code was made in 1993, and since that time there has been no precedent of prosecuting violators of export control procedures. Such a precedent is unlikely to occur until a Law on Export Control is adopted. However, there have been cases where Customs officials uncovered smuggling, and the smugglers were subsequently prosecuted. Also, the Ukrainian Security Service revealed cases of spying and attempts to illegally obtain sensitive technology by foreign nationals. In late January 1996, three Chinese nationals were apprehended in Dnipropetrovsk as they attempted to obtain a design schematics for engines on intercontinental ballistic missiles. The Chinese were expelled from Ukraine on the basis of Article 32 of the Law "On the Legal Status of Foreigners" for "actions contrary to the interest of national security" of Ukraine.[71]

The continued development of an "objective" (i.e., a system managed by a state body devoid of portfolio and, therefore, of parochial interest) export control structure is proceeding as quickly as the difficult political and economic environment allow. Since its institutional inception, a clearly progressive line of development through centralization and further empowerment of the export control organs is clearly discernible.

4.8.6 Legal and Regulatory Developments

The legal basis for the Ukrainian export control system continues to be executive branch decrees (issued by both the President and Cabinet of

Ministers). A legal basis for export control in Ukraine was initiated by the "Act on Foreign Economic Activity" adopted by the Verkhovna Rada (Parliament) in 1991. Article 20 of the Act specifies that the export and import of weapons, special components for their manufacture, explosive agents, nuclear material, technologies, equipment and installations, as well as other kinds of goods, technologies, and services that could be used for the production of weapons require authorization by the Ukrainian state. The Cabinet of Ministers of Ukraine, in coordination with appropriate standing committees of the Rada, oversees the nomination of foreign economic policy executives and the regulation of related export and import activities.[72]

As of late Summer 1999, an effort was underway to implement a comprehensive export control law. With the assistance of the Department of Commerce (DOC) Bureau of Export Administration and the Lawyers Alliance for World Security, the SSEC has drafted the "Temporary Provision on Export Controls in Ukraine." Already circulated to the appropriate Ministries for review and comment, the national provision was undergoing a second examination in 1997 before it was to be re-circulated to the Ministries and to the Parliamentary committees (Committee on Foreign Economic Relations and Standing Committee on Defense and Security) for a second perusal. This draft provision will be a prototype of national export control legislation. Until such legislation is drafted and adopted by the Rada, it will have the power of law and was signed by President Kuchma in late 1997.

The draft national export control provision is intended to solidify the legal structure of the export control system by fixing the administration division of labor, consolidating the various control lists, detailing the legal procedures surrounding import and export licensing, specifying criminal and civil violations, and establishing an international agreements protocol. Furthermore, the law is to contain a "catch-all"[73] provision which has heretofore been lacking. An enacted comprehensive export control law would be the most significant advance in the development of the export control system to date.

4.8.7 Licensing

Licensing is the principal responsibility of State Service on Export Controls (SSEC) of the Cabinet of Ministers. SSEC is the working organ of the Governmental Commission on Export Control Policy (GCECP), an interagency body comprised of other ministries and state committees involved in the export control process. Eventually, licensing is to become the sole responsibility of the SSEC. However, as of April 1998, SSEC shares licensing responsibilities with GCECP due to the absence, on a working level, of a clear-cut division of powers between the two bodies. Currently, exports of nuclear goods and technologies and conventional arms are licensed by GCECP, whereas imports and transits of all goods and exports of dual-use items are licensed by SSEC.

In Ukraine, a license is required for: exports; imports; re-export; transits; export of scientific and engineering products related to commodities subject to export control; related agency operations on exports/imports; creation of joint ventures for design, development and production of commodities that can be used for developing arms and military equipment; export and import by passengers; export and import as contribution to the growth of trade and industry enterprises in case of international cooperation. In November 1996, the three primary Ukrainian arms-export firms – *Progress*, *Ukrinmash*, and *Ukroboronservice* – were merged into a single association, *Ukrspetsexport*, in order to increase state control over weapons exports. Furthermore, in Ukraine, not only transactions in sensitive items and technologies require licenses, but certain kinds of industrial activity as well. Thirty-six kinds of industrial activity (mainly related to nuclear, chemical, missile, and conventional arms trade) require licenses.

The issuance of a license can be refused or revoked if: 1) licensing violates or jeopardizes the international commitments of Ukraine; 2) the activity of Ukraine or the foreign side violates international regulations; 3) the sales of goods and technologies jeopardize economic interests or national security of Ukraine; 4) the applicant presents false information in the submitted application and additionally requested documents. Table 4.7 enumerates recent licensing activities.

Table 4.7 Licensing Activities 1995-97[74]

Activities	1995	1996	January-June 1997
License applications reviewed	3507	3824	1363
Total licenses issued	3296	3341	1133
Which makes %	93.9	87.4	83.1
On the amount ($ millions)	1721.7	2171.8	3300.2
Export licenses	2134	2105	920
(including general licenses)	269	340	NA
on the amount ($ millions)	1503,4	1701.5	588.2
Import licenses	688	940	109
(including general licenses)	41	81	NA
on the amount ($ millions)	218.3	470.3	2712
Transit licenses	407	296	105

Previously, the SSEC used to review more than 3,500 license applications annually (more than 14 applications a day). When the national legal basis in the area of export control was brought into accordance with international standards, a large number of goods were dropped from the lists of goods subject to control. Consequently, the number of license applications has decreased by a factor of 2 (for example, 7 applications in October 1997), which ostensibly elevates the quality of the review process. The decreased ratio of issued licenses to the number of submitted applications (from 93.9% in 1995 to 83.1% in 1997) suggests that the license review process has become more exacting. At the same time, the cash value of transfers of controlled goods is increasing. In 1995, 269 general licenses were issued, and 421 in 1996, thereby reflecting the trend of an increasing portion of general licenses in the total number of issued licenses.

The following are the examples of applications declined by the SSEC:

1) application by "Azot" Chemical Plant in Dniprodzerzhinsk to establish a joint venture with a Panamanian company for producing and selling heavy water;
2) application to export high-grade munitions to Croatia;

3) application from "Yuzhmash," missile and space vehicle manufacturer, to export missile technologies to China.[75]

In 1997, 46 individual enterprises applied for the permission to be an independent exporter, but, according to SSEC officials, only two per cent of them qualified for independent trade status.

Enterprises apply for license directly to the SSEC, which, while reviewing the application, may confer with the appropriate ministries. In submitting a license application for export, import and transit of indigenous commodities and technologies controlled by international regimes, the applicant must attach the following documents: international import certificate; end-user certificate; copy of the contract; specifications, if required. When an enterprise applies for a license for the first time, it also must submit to the SSEC a copy of its statute and list of goods it produces for an official registration. Both ministries and the SSEC weigh the technical, political, economic and military factors in making the license decision. According to the Ukrainian Cabinet of Ministers' decrees, regulating exports, import, and transit of commodities which can be used to develop nuclear, chemical/biological, and missile weapons, the following factors are taken into account in making the license decision: nonproliferation standards; capabilities and objectives of the nuclear, chemical/biological, and missile/space programs in the recipient states; criticality of the goods to be exported in terms of ability to develop weapons of mass destruction and their delivery means; assessment of the end-use of transferred goods; applicability of relevant multilateral arrangements.[76] These decrees stipulate that the licensing decision is to be made within 30 days after the submission of complete application. However, due to the submission of incomplete applications and the extensive bureaucratic procedures, the average length of review is 2-3 months, and sometimes up to one year. To provide initial screening and to facilitate the application review, the establishment of nine regional SSEC offices is planned. The final decisions on issuing licenses, however, are to be made by the main SSEC office in Kyiv.

If a decision made by the SSEC is rejected by the GCECP, an exporting firm has the right to appeal by supplying additional information. A state minister can also appeal to the Prime Minister, although this procedure has apparently not been established by decree.

4.8.8 Control Lists

With advisory assistance from the members of the international nonproliferation regime, Ukrainian officials have developed seven lists of controlled commodities that include the following items:

1) nuclear weapons, materials, and equipment; and nuclear-related dual-use technologies;
2) chemical weapons and equipment necessary for their production;
3) biological weapons and equipment necessary for their production;
4) delivery systems for nuclear, chemical and biological weapons;
5) conventional weapons;
6) raw materials, equipment, technologies and expertise related to the development of weapons and military hardware; and
7) dual-use commodities.

To date, the lists are in complete compliance with the international supplier regimes.

4.8.9 Training

The training of export control officials continues to be a liability to export control developments thus far. Owing to considerable economic constraints and the inconsistent place of export controls on the political agenda, export control training is conducted primarily on the job. However, the US, the European Union, Japan, and the IAEA have conducted and/or sponsored training seminars in license processing, identification of controlled items, and investigative and enforcement techniques. Recently, the SSEC sponsored three regional – Zaporizhya, Kyiv, and Dnipropetrovsk – export control conferences in an effort to train enterprise managers, with the larger goal being the development of internal compliance program modules that would be conducted by the SSEC's as yet realized "regional offices." Nevertheless, export control training at all agencies and industries remains seriously inadequate.[77]

4.8.10 Information Gathering/Sharing

After the formal break-up of the Soviet Union in December 1991, the President and the Cabinet of Ministers of Ukraine initiated the development of Ukrainian export controls. Decree No. 153 of the Ukrainian Cabinet of Ministers of March 23, 1992, established the State

Expert and Technical Commission. A principal task of the Commission was to draft export control laws, but it was very slow in performing this duty and had accomplished very little to that end. Presidential Decree No. 3 of January 3, 1993 superseded Decree No. 153 and established two new export control bodies: the Governmental Commission on Export Controls and the Expert and Technical Committee. In order to implement the Presidential decree, the Cabinet of Ministers on March 4, 1993 issued Decree No. 6 "On Establishing State Controls Over Exports/Imports of Arms, Military Material and Materials Needed for Their Production."

The primary difference between the two Presidential Decrees of 1992 and 1993 is that according to Decree No. 3 of 1993, the Governmental Commission on Export Control is a body representing eighteen ministries and agencies on an equal basis, while the Expert and Technical Commission was clearly dominated by Ministry of Machine Building, Military-Industrial Complex and Conversion. This shift to collective decision-making on export control issues indicated the increased importance of export controls on the Ukrainian government's agenda, as well as meeting standards of international export control regimes. Consequently, a greater number of agencies are involved in the sharing and gathering of information germane to export control issues. However, information sharing between the government and industry remains a formidable problem. US Department of Commerce programs and workshops have sought to address this issue. Furthermore, in March 1997, a collective of Ukrainian exporters created the Ukrainian Scientific and Technical Center on the Export and Import of Special Technologies, Hardware, and Materials. The Center serves as a clearinghouse for information on export control policy, undertaking regional conferences for industry on export control obligations and the development of internal compliance mechanisms. SSEC works closely with the Center in the attempt to further educate Ukrainian exporters.

4.9 Why Development?

Clearly, as the above analysis suggests, Ukraine has made substantial progress in the development on an internationally-compatible nonproliferation export control system. Undoubtedly, the present system is, in comparison to systems in the West, underdeveloped. Nevertheless, this system is being built literally from scratch. As such, the distances to be traversed are considerable. That being said, the pattern of progressive development provokes further questions.

Given the limited success, if not large-scale failure, of defense conversion efforts,[78] an active military-industrial complex lobby[79] (especially in the fields of dual-use and missile-related technologies and equipment), an unstable, still unfolding political environment, and overall economic hardship, why would Ukraine devote its limited resources to developing a system that would ostensibly limit its ability to address pressing economic and political issues?[80] This quantitative analysis outlining actual development prompts a theoretical explanation of *why* development.

In examining what has quantitatively changed over time, we then consider the qualitative aspect driving state behavior, behavior contrary to common expectations: namely, why would a fledgling state – burdened with political, economic, and social complexities – allocate material and intellectual efforts in this manner. In order to explain export control development in Ukraine since its 1991 independence, the following chapter will examine the four theoretical approaches – Realism, Domestic Politics, Liberal Identity, and Rational Institutionalism – and derive behavioral expectations therefrom seeking to account for why states develop export control systems. In chapter 5, each approach, with its accompanying behavioral expectations, will then be applied to the Ukrainian historical case with the express aim of exploring the variables driving nonproliferation export control development. The final chapter summarizes the theoretical findings.

Notes

[1] See "White House Fact Sheet on Non-Proliferation and Export Control Policy," *Arms Control Today* 23, 9 (November 1993), pp. 27-28; and US Congress, Office of Technology Assessment, *Export Controls and Nonproliferation*, OTA-ISS-596 (Washington, DC: US Government Printing Office, May 1994).
[2] See Gary Bertsch and Igor Khripunov, "Restraining the Spread of the Soviet Arsenal: Export Controls as a Long-Term Nonproliferation Tool," *Status Report*, Center for International Trade and Security (Athens, GA: University of Georgia, 1996) about the importance of and challenges for export control development.
[3] US resources for the development of nonproliferation export controls are provided to the nuclear successor states of the NIS (Russia, Ukraine, Belarus and Kazakstan) through the Cooperative Threat Reduction/Safe and Secure Dismantlement (CTR) programs of the Nunn-Lugar legislation. For the non-nuclear successor states of the NIS, funding is available through the US State Department's Nonproliferation Disarmament Fund (NDF). Additional financial support has been provided to both nuclear and non-nuclear NIS from US executive agency budgets (e.g., the Departments of Energy, Commerce, State and Customs). Non-American aid has been provided to the NIS by the Japanese ($100 million for

disarmament) and by members of the European Union ($85 million for Material Protection, Control and Accounting). Inducements are provided by limiting access to other sources of US economic aid (e.g. availability of FREEDOM Support Act funding) based on cooperation in nonproliferation efforts. Finally, security assistance is provided by participation in multilateral alliances and quasi-alliances, such as NATO's Partnership for Peace program.

[4] For further information on the tools and methods for measuring nonproliferation export controls, see Suzette Grillot and Cassady Craft, "How and Why We Evaluate Systems of Export Control," *The Monitor: Nonproliferation, Demilitarization and Arms Control* 2 (Fall 1996) and Bertsch and Grillot, eds., *Arms on the Market*, pp. 1-30.

[5] Oran Young, in "The Politics of International Regime Formation: Managing Natural Resources and the Environment," *International Organization* 43, 3 (1989), argues that successful institutional bargaining in international regimes is based on, in part, clear-cut compliance mechanisms that are easy to police. The evaluation tools presented here facilitate institutional bargaining within the nonproliferation regime by providing a means (i.e., "common standards") of assessing export control development in a transparent manner. Such transparency is necessary, according to some scholars, to solve collective action problems in a multilateral environment. See Karl Deutsch, "Power and Communication in International Society," in Anthony de Reuck and Julie Knight, eds., *Conflict in Society* (Boston: Little, Brown, 1966); and Arthur Stein, "Governments, Economic Interdependence, and International Cooperation," in Philip E. Tetlock, *et al.*, eds., *Behavior, Society, and International Conflict* (New York: Oxford University Press, 1993).

[6] See, for example, Michael Mastanduno, *Economic Containment: CoCom and the Politics of East-West Trade* (Ithaca: Cornell University Press, 1992); and Gary Bertsch *et al.*, eds., *International Cooperation on Nonproliferation Export Controls: Prospects for the 1990s and Beyond* (Ann Arbor: University of Michigan Press, 1994) concerning the importance of multilateral coordination of export control policies.

[7] Concerning the economic consequences that may result from unilateral export control policies, see Mastanduno, *Economic Containment*, p. 14, 20; and Stuart MacDonald, *Technology and the Tyranny of Export Controls: Whisper Who Dares* (New York: St. Martins Press, 1990).

[8] For an alternative argument that the creation and usage of evaluation tools such as those developed here to improve the "transparency" of multilateral institutions can be counterproductive or unattractive because of the political sensitivity surrounding the criticism of a partner, see Arthur Stein, *Why Nations Cooperate: A Circumstance and Choice in International Relations* (Ithaca, NY: Cornell University Press, 1990); Duncan Snidal, "Coordination Versus Prisoners' Dilemma: Implications for International Cooperation and Regimes," *American Political Science Review* 79 (1985), pp. 923-42; Kenneth A. Oye, ed. *Cooperation Under Anarchy* (Princeton, NJ: Princeton University Press, 1986); and especially

Joseph M. Grieco, "Anarchy and the Limits of Cooperation: A Realist Critique of the Newest Institutionalism," in Charles Kegley, Jr., ed., *Controversies in International Relations Theory: Realism and the Neoliberal Challenge* (New York: St. Martin's Press, 1995).

[9] For a full explication of the development of our measurement of export control development and its application in the NIS, see Cassady Craft and Suzette Grillot with Liam Anderson, Michael Beck, Chris Behan, Scott Jones and Keith Wolfe, "Tools and Methods for Measuring and Comparing Nonproliferation Export Controls," An Occasional Paper of the Center for International Trade and Security (Athens: University of Georgia, 1996).

[10] Specifically, in 1949 COCOM members included Belgium, Canada, Denmark, France, Italy, Luxembourg, the Netherlands, Norway, the United Kingdom, the United States, and West Germany. Portugal joined in 1951, Japan in 1952, Greece and Turkey in 1953, and Australia in 1989.

[11] For a brief discussion of each of these regimes, see Leonard S. Spector and Virginia Foran, "Preventing Weapons Proliferation: Should the Regimes be Combined?" A Report of the Thirty-Third Strategy for Peace, *US Foreign Policy Conference*, 22-24 October 1992.

[12] Gary Bertsch and Richard Cupitt, "Nonproliferation in the 1990s: Enhancing International Cooperation on Export Controls," *The Washington Quarterly* 16, 4 (Autumn 1993), p. 62. See also Mastanduno, *Economic Containment*, William A. Root, "Trade Controls That Work," *Foreign Policy* 56 (Fall 1984), 61-80; Robert Price, "COCOM after 35 Years: Reaffirmation or Reorganization," in Charles M. Perry and Robert L. Pfalzgraff, eds., *Selling the Rope to Hang Capitalism?* (Maclean, VA: Pergamen-Brassey's International Defense Publishers, 1987), pp. 195-201; Henry R. Nau and Kevin Quigley, eds, *The Allies and East-West Economic Relations: Past Conflicts and Present Choices* (New York: Carnegie Council on Ethics and International Affairs, 1989); and Kevin Quigley and William J. Long, "Export Controls: Moving Beyond Containment," *World Policy Journal* 7 (Winter 1989-90), pp. 165-88.

[13] See Richard Cupitt and Suzette Grillot, "COCOM is Dead, Long Live COCOM: Persistence and Change in Multilateral Security Institutions," *British Journal of Political Science* 27 (July 1997), pp. 361-389. The purpose of COCOM's dissolution and replacement was to include its former targets in the new post-Cold War environment and reorient the regime's focus away from a strategic embargo from West to East. The rationale for a new regime was to move toward a nonproliferation embargo focused on countries of concern such as Iran, Iraq, North Korea, and Libya (although they are not published officially). Members of the Wassenaar Arrangement presently include all COCOM countries plus Austria, the Czech Republic, Finland, Hungary, Iceland, New Zealand, Poland, Russia, the Slovak Republic, Sweden and Switzerland.

[14] The "common standards" approach was also used to evaluate "third countries" who were seeking to cooperate with COCOM controls. On COCOM's "third country initiative" program, see Panel on the Future and Design and

Implementation of US National Security Export Controls, Committee on Sciences, Engineering and Public Policy, *Finding Common Ground: US Export Controls in a Changed Global Environment* (Washington, DC: National Academy Press, 1991), p. 123; and Bertsch, Cupitt and Elliott-Gower, *International Cooperation on Nonproliferation Export Controls*, pp. 34-39; 50.

[15] Michael Lipson, "The Reincarnation of COCOM: Explaining Post-Cold War Export Controls," *The Nonproliferation Review* 6, no. 2 (Winter 1999), pp. 33-51; and Cupitt and Grillot, "COCOM is Dead, Long Live COCOM: Persistence and Change in Multilateral Security Institutions," pp. 375-377.

[16] See "COCOM Rejects US Computer Proposal," *Export Control News* 6, 10 (29 October 1992), pp. 2-3; and "COCOM Deadlocks on List Review," *Export Control News* 6, 12 (12 December 1992), p. 2.

[17] Previous measures of export control development have described the legal bases and some other aspects of export control systems, but have not attempted to rigorously assess the extent of institutional development and implementation. For example, see William Root *et al.*, "A Study of Foreign Export Control Systems," in National Academy of Sciences, *Balancing the National Interests: US National Security, Export Controls and Global Economic Competition* (Washington, DC: National Academy Press, 1987); Finding Common Ground, 1991; *Worldwide Guide to Export Controls* (London: Deltec, Ltd., 1995-6); *Beyond COCOM* (Washington, DC: American Bar Association, 1994); and Richard T. Cupitt and Yuzo Murayama, "Nonproliferation and Export Controls: Malaysia, Singapore, and Taiwan," paper presented at the annual meeting of the International Studies Association, San Diego, April 1996.

[18] See Cupitt and Murayama, "Nonproliferation Export Controls," pp. 7-8 for a description of the COCOM and other export control evaluation questionnaires.

[19] The example is taken from the author's on-going work on export control developments in the Transcaucus states. For more on said research, see Scott A. Jones and Cassady B. Craft, "An Evaluation of Export Controls in the States of the Trancaucasus," in *Global Evaluation of Nonproliferation Export Controls: 1999 Report* (Athens: Center for International Trade and Security at The University of Georgia, 1999) and Scott A. Jones, "Introduction," in Michael D. Beck, Gary K. Bertsch, Cassady B. Craft and Scott A. Jones, eds., *Crossroads and Conflict: Security and Foreign Policy in the Caucasus and Central Asia* (New York: Routledge, 1999).

[20] For more information about this ongoing research project on the development of NIS export controls, see Liam Anderson, Michael Beck, Chris Behan, Cassady Craft, Suzette Grillot, Scott Jones and Keith Wolfe, "In Word and In Deed: Nonproliferation Export Controls in the Former Soviet Union," paper presented at the annual meeting of the International Studies Association, Southern Regional, Roanoke, Virginia, October 1996, or contact the University of Georgia's Center for International Trade and Security. See also, Michael Beck, ed., *Global Evaluation System: Annual Report on Export Controls: 1998 and 1999* (Athens, Center for International Trade and Security).

[21] An additional tool for measuring nonproliferation export control development over time is found in "Tools and Methods for Measuring and Comparing Nonproliferation Export Controls," by C. Craft and S. Grillot, et al., occasional paper of the Center for International Trade and Security (Athens: University of Georgia, October 1996). This questionnaire is designed to facilitate the measurement of the development of nonproliferation export controls in a simplified manner. This is especially useful when data gathering prohibits the use of the comprehensive questionnaire year after year. Again, this tool revolves around the ten elements of an export control system, yet the evaluative questions are simplified and we have suggested a modified system to "score" a country under consideration. This tool has the same limitations as the more extensive survey described above, but has the advantage of brevity.

[22] Bertsch and Grillot, *Arms on the Market*, pp. 213-229.

[23] The one area in which these states "inherited" part of the Soviet nonproliferation export control system was in area of border control/customs. However, given that Russian troops were still acting as border guards, this can hardly qualify as part of a *national* nonproliferation export control system.

[24] For example, Georgia issued decrees in 1992 that gave rudimentary authority to license, develop control lists and customs authority. It would score a weighted 2.78 at this time. By 1996, Georgia still had only a rudimentary system, but scored a 10.07, an increase of about 360%! Given the very low level of export control development, this figure is all but meaningless.

[25] Growth rates are most useful when trying to assess export control development in a single country. Clearly, when one seeks to *compare* the growth in export controls *between* countries, the beginning scores must be taken into consideration as a country that begins with a lower score will have more room to grow than will a country that begins with a higher score.

[26] On the problems of "cheating" and "free-ridership," see Mancur Olson, *The Logic of Collective Action* (Cambridge: Harvard University Press, 1965).

[27] See, Richard T. Cupitt, *Reluctant Champions: US Presidential Policy and Strategic Export Controls, Truman, Eisenhower, Bush and Clinton* (New York: Routledge Press, 2000). See especially, "Introduction."

[28] Scott Jones, "Introduction," *Crossroads and Conflict: Foreign Policy and Security in the Southern Tier* (New York: Routledge, 2000), pp. 1-27.

[29] See Craft and Grillot, "Tools and Methods" and Grillot and Craft, "How and Why."

[30] As a member of the international nonproliferation regimes, Ukraine is obligated to develop, maintain, and harmonize, where appropriate, a national system of export controls.

[31] See, William K. Domke, "Proliferation, Threat, and Learning: The International and Domestic Structures of Export Control," in M. van Leeuwen, *The Future of the Nuclear Nonproliferation Regime* (Amsterdam: Kluwer Academic Publishers, 1995), p. 219.

³² *Ibid.*, pp. 220-225. See also, Claus Hofhansel, "From the Containment of Communism to Saddam: The Evolution of Export Controls," *Arms Control* 14 (December 1993), pp. 371-404.

³³ It should be noted that these models are merely "ideal types." Various aspects of all of the models can be found in a state's system of export control. Further, the use of these models should not suggest that state export control systems are in any way static. The models are simply heuristic, categorizing devices designed to allow for the classification of system architectures. See also, Sergei Kortunov, "National Export Control System in Russia," *Comparative Strategy*, 13 (May 1994), pp. 1-12.

³⁴ *Ibid.*, p. 223.

³⁵ For example, on the South Korean export control system, see Han S. Park, "South Korea's Export Control Policy," in Bertsch, Cupitt, and Elliott-Gower, eds., *International Cooperation on Nonproliferation Export Controls*, pp. 247-261.

³⁶ For an explanation of the scoring methodology and standard measure, see "Tools and Methods for Measuring and Comparing Nonproliferation Export Controls," by C. Craft and S. Grillot, et al., occasional paper of the Center for International Trade and Security (Athens: University of Georgia, October 1996).

³⁷ A description and history of the Ukrainian export control system is found in Jones and Zaborsky, "Ukraine", pp. 17-30; and Jones, "The Evolution of the Ukrainian Export Control System," in Bertsch and Grillot, eds., *Arms on the Market*, pp. 58-63.

³⁸ See, "Tools and Methods for Measuring and Comparing Nonproliferation Export Controls," pp. 1-17.

³⁹ *Ibid.*, pp. 13-15.

⁴⁰ For example, see, Evan Maderios, "US Warns Russia, Ukraine on Missile-Related Sales to China," *Arms Control Today*, 5/96-6/96, p. 24; Bill Gertz, "Ukraine and Libya Forge Strategic Alliance," *Washington Times*, 10 June 1996; Valentin Badrak "Ukraine Charges of Illegal Arms Trade Alleged," *Zerkalo Nedeli*, 27 August 1998; and "Ukraine Customs Detain Two for Nuke Smuggling," *Reuters*, 4 December 1998.

⁴¹ Taras Kuzio, *Ukrainian Security Policy* (Westport: Praeger, 1995), p. 46.

⁴² Jones and Zaborsky, p. 27. See also, John Baker, *Nonproliferation Incentives for Russia and Ukraine*, Adelphi Paper 309 (Oxford: International Institute for Strategic Studies, 1997), pp. 14-15.

⁴³ "Ukraine," *Economist Intelligence Unit: Country Report*, 3rd quarter, 1999. The Ukrainian economy served, as did the other former republics, as a producer of semi-finished goods. Consequently, Ukrainian industry is, by and large, compromised by its lack of full-cycle production facilities, which makes the process of economic transition especially severe. An excellent study exploring the link between the Soviet-era economic system and the present economic challenges in Ukraine is found in: Raphael Shen, *Ukraine's Economic Reform: Obstacles, Errors, Lessons* (Westport: Praeger Press, 1996), see especially pp. 15-140.

⁴⁴ John Baker, *Nonproliferation Incentives for Russia and Ukraine*, Adelphi Paper 309 (Oxford: International Institute for Strategic Studies, 1997), pp. 14-15.

⁴⁵ National Research Council, *op. cit.*, pp. 85-100.

⁴⁶ On the Nuclear Suppliers' Group see, Carlton Thorne, ed., *A Guide to Nuclear Export Controls* (Burke, VA: Proliferation Data Services, 1997 edition); Gary T. Gardner, *Nuclear Nonproliferation: A Primer* (Boulder, CO: Lynne Rienner Publishers, 1994), p. 58.

⁴⁷ On the Missile Technology Control Regime, see Richard H. Speier, "The Missile Technology Control Regime," in Trevor Findley ed., *Chemical Weapons and Missile Proliferation: With Implications for the Asia/Pacific Region* (Boulder: Lynne Rienner, 1991), pp. 15-21; *Tracking Nuclear Proliferation*, Rodney W. Jones and Mark G. McDonough eds. (Washington, DC: Carnegie Endowment for International Peace, 1998), pp. 311-314; Roland Timerbaev and Meggen M. Watt, eds., *Inventory of International Nonproliferation Organizations and Regimes*, 1995 edition (Monterey, CA: Monterey Institute of International Studies, 1995), p. 18.

⁴⁸ On the Australia Group, see *Inventory of International Nonproliferation Organizations and Regimes*, 1995 edition.

⁴⁹ On all regimes, see Gary K. Bertsch, Richard T. Cupitt, and Steven Elliot Gower, "Multilateral Export Control Organizations," in. Bertsch, Cupitt, and Elliot-Gower, eds. *International Cooperation on Nonproliferation Export Controls: Prospects for the 1990s and Beyond* (Ann Arbor: University of Michigan Press, 1994), pp. 33-58.

⁵⁰ Author's interviews with Expert and Technical Committee officials, Washington, DC, October 1996.

⁵¹ Ustina Markus, "US Daily Queries Ukraine's Entry into Missile Pact," *OMRI Daily Digest*, 24 September 1996; and Gary Bertsch and Victor Zaborsky, "Bringing Ukraine into the MTCR: Can US Policy Succeed?" *Arms Control Today*, vol. 27, no. 2, April 1997, pp. 9-14.

⁵² See chapter 5 for a in-depth examination of how and why Ukraine was able to enter the regime on its own terms. Also, see Howard Diamond, "US, Ukraine sign nuclear accord, agree on MTCR accession," *Arms Control Today*, vol. 28 no. 2 March 1998, p. 23.

⁵³ The term *adaptive* is self-consciously fashioned on the "evolution" concept. Moreover, I wish to imply that institutional learning drives the present system shape. Current social science research on complex adaptive systems suggests that collectivities, such as governments, learn as they evolve. Thus, as a new state, Ukraine's state-building effort benefits from the considerable body of the political-economic histories and developmental approaches of other countries. See, Marcelo Alonso, *Organization and Change in Complex Social Systems* (New York: Paragon House, 1990); Warren Bennis, *Beyond Bureaucracy: Essays on the Development and Evolution of Human Organization* (London: Jossey-Bass Publisher, 1993); and Douglas Kiel and Euel Elliott, eds., *Chaos Theory in the Social Sciences: Foundations and Applications* (Ann Arbor: University of

Michigan Press, 1996). Addressing this theme in the IR literature are, for example, Emanuel Adler, "Cognitive Evolution," in Adler and Beverly Crawford, eds., *Progress in Post-War International Relations* (New York: Columbia University Press, 1991); Joseph Nye, "Nuclear Learning and US-Soviet Security Regimes," *International Organization* 41, Winter 1987, pp. 371-402; and Robert Axelrod, *The Evolution of Cooperation* (New York: Basic Books, 1984).

[54] Aleksandr Kluban, quoting Vaschilin,"Ukrainian Official Explain Arms Export Control Procedures," *FBIS-SOV-97-1109, Kyiv Nezavisimost*, 24 September 1997.

[55] Victor Zaborsky, "Export Control Developments in Ukraine," in Gary K. Bertsch and William C. Potter, eds., *Dangerous Weapons, Desperate States: Russia, Belarus, Kazakstan, and Ukraine* (New York: Routledge, 1999); and Scott A. Jones and Glenn Chafetz, *Trip Report: Export Controls in Ukraine, Latvia, and Lithuania, August 1995*, Center for International Trade and Security.

[56] Author's Interview with Ukrainian government official, University of Georgia, April 1997.

[57] Ministries with export control departments are: the Ministry of Foreign Affairs, the Ministry of Machine Building, the Military-Industrial Complex and Conversion, the Ministry of Foreign Economic Relations and Trade, Security Service, State Customs Committee, State Security Service, Ministry of Internal Affairs, State Border Committee, Ministry of Environmental Protection and Nuclear Safety, Committee on State Secrets and Technical Protection of Information, and the Ministry of Economics, Center on Strategic Planning and Analysis (part of the National Security and Defense Committee of the Cabinet of Ministers), and the National Space Commission of Ukraine.

[58] In its export control assistance to Ukraine, the United States government has repeatedly stressed the importance of technical review in export control licensing, policy making and control list fabrication. Los Alamos and Argonne National Laboratories, under the auspices of the US Department of Energy (DOE) provide direct technical and financial assistance to this end.

[59] Also, through the IAEA, limited financial and material assistance is provided by Australia, Finland, France, Hungary, Sweden, and the United Kingdom. See, *IAEA Working Report: Progress Review on Technical Support to Newly Independent States in Non-proliferation Field*, PR 96/24 (Vienna, 1996).

[60] The Center for International Trade and Security at the University of Georgia assisted in the establishment of the Kyiv Center.

[61] The decree is not intended for publication in the open press, and its full name and number are unavailable to the author. All information about the decree included in the article was obtained by the author during his interviews with SSEC officials in July 1999. See also, Mikhail Melnik, "Kuchma Tightens Control Over Arms Exports," *FBIS-SOV-1999-0428, Itar-Tass*, 28 April 1999.

[62] One export control official noted: "Although the interpretation of this term differ from country to country, and Ukraine's list of "terrorists" may not coincide with those of other countries." Author interview, Washington, DC, July 1999.

[63] Victor Zaborsky, "Ukraine Restructures Arms Export Controls," *Jane's Intelligence Review*, 1 November 1999.
[64] Author interview with SSEC and MFA officials, Kyiv, August 1999.
[65] Author interview with US Department of Commerce, Bureau of Export Administration official, Washington, DC, July 1999 and Victor Zaborsky, "Ukraine Restrctures its Arms Export Controls," *Arms Control Today*, forthcoming.
[66] See, Petr Litavrin, "Military-Technical Cooperation: New Image of An Old Business," *The Monitor: Nonproliferation, Demilitarization & Arms Control*, vol. 4, nos. 2-3, Spring-Summer 1998.
[67] National Research Council, *op. cit.*, p. 94.
[68] Interview with US Customs official, Washington, DC, January 1997.
[69] National Research Council, *op. cit.*, p. 95.
[70] "US Customs Continues Training Work in Ukraine," US Customs Service Press Release, 7 December 1998.
[71] Author's interview with Ukrainian Custom officials, Kyiv, November 1997. For open sources, see: *FBIS-SOV*-96-021. January 31, 1996, p. 54; *OMRI Daily Digest*. No. 22, 31 January 1996; and *OMRI Daily Digest*. No. 32, 14 February 1996.
[72] Sergey Svistil, "Ukraine," *Worldwide Guide to Export Controls*, 1994/1995 Edition (London: Deltac), p. 2.
[73] Specifically, with regards to catch-all, the Decree states "the international transfer of military and dual-use goods is prohibited if such transfers run counter to Ukraine's international obligations, its national security interests, combating terrorism, and maintaining mutually beneficial cooperation with members of the international community, the principles and norms of international law, as well as cases wherein reliable end-use guarantees are absent." The recent decision to forego the export of gas turbines to the Iranian nuclear power station at Bushehr is an illustration of the catch-all clause in operation. Although the exports were legal in terms of national legislation and international obligations, the Ukrainian government, under considerable US pressure and cajoling, annulled said exports.
[74] Source: State Service on Export Controls, 1998.
[75] Author's interviews with SSEC officials, Kyiv, November 1997.
[76] For details, see the following Cabinet of Ministers Decrees: *Regulations on the Procedure for Controls on the Export, Import, and Transit of Commodities Which May Relate to Nuclear Activities and May Be Used to Develop Nuclear Weapons*, Decree No. 302 of March 12, 1996, Article 15; *Regulations on the Procedure for Controls on the Export, Import, and Transit of Missile Items, As Well As of Equipment, Materials and Technologies Which May be Used To Develop Missile Weapons*, Decree No. 563 of July 27, 1995, Article 14; *Regulations on the Procedure for Controls on the Export, Import, and Transit of Commodities Which May Be Used to Develop Chemical, Bacteriological (Biological) and Toxin Weapons*, Decree No. 384 of April 22, 1997, Article 16.
[77] Author's interviews with SSEC officials, Kyiv, November 1997.

[78] Margaret McClean and Deborah Palmieri, "Marketization through Defense Conversion: A Policy Prescriptive on the Ukrainian Case," in Deborah Palmieri, ed., *Russia and the NIS in the World Economy: East-West Investment, Financing, and Trade* (Westport, CT: Præger, 1996), pp. 149-60.

[79] See, C. Hummel, "Ukrainian Arms Makers Are Left on Their Own," *Radio Free Europe/Radio Liberty Research Report*, vol. 1, no. 32, pp. 33-41, 8 August 1992.

[80] The costs involved in developing and maintaining export controls are considerable. For an examination of the costs, see Kathleen Bailey, "Nonproliferation Export Controls: Problems and Alternatives," in Kathleen Bailey and Robert Rudney, eds., *Nonproliferation and Export Controls* (Lanham: University Press of America, 1993), pp. 50-61. Bailey notes: "Export controls divert resources of governments – particularly in countries that do not have large bureaucracies or budgets – that might be more profitably diverted to other government activities" (p. 52).

Chapter 5

Explaining Ukrainian Export Control Development

> And it ought to be remembered that there is nothing more difficult to take in hand, more perilous to conduct, or more uncertain in its success, than to take the lead in the introduction of a new order of things.
> Nicolo Machiavelli (1469-1527), *The Prince*

Based on the literature review in the preceding chapter concerning the rationales behind a state's decision to develop a nonproliferation export control system, one can expect various patterns of state behavior. This chapter examines the evidentiary history of the Ukrainian case and compares it to the behavioral expectations derived from various approaches to IR theory. Accordingly, this chapter is divided into five sections: four for each approach and related expectations and a final section comparing the findings of each section. At each section, the empirical data will be compared with the hypothetical expectations, thereby suggesting the relative strength and weakness of each approach in explaining the Ukrainian case. Here it is important to note that the approaches themselves are *not* being tested. The approaches, moreover, and derivative expectations are purely heuristic devices employed in order to explain in a systematic and rigorous fashion *why* Ukraine developed and continues to cooperate on an export control system.

5.1 Realism: Evolving Security Concepts

The Realist approach to international relations is of limited explanatory utility in accounting for Ukrainian export control developments. According to this approach, we would expect to see states develop export controls as a means of enhancing their security, of balancing the power of others, and/or of addressing external threats. Ukraine's geopolitical position is such that it sits astride a critical European juncture.[1] Ukrainian history is replete with periods of foreign occupation, the most recent being Russian, veiled under the veneer of Soviet social engineering. Moreover, pitted between a Russia wary of NATO expansion and a Europe and US ambivalent over extending full security guarantees, the resultant political-military pressures complicate Ukraine's avowed neutrality.[2] Furthermore, since independence, Russian-Ukrainian relations have been strained over such issues as border demarcation, energy arrears, nuclear weapons divestiture and indemnity, division of the Black Sea Fleet, and the political status of Crimea, conferred to Ukraine by Khrushchev in 1954. Generally speaking, Russia is seen as the only viable external threat to Ukrainian national security.[3]

With the exception of Russia, Ukraine has not articulated the presence of external threats to its physical security.[4] Ukraine enjoys generally good relations with its immediate and regional neighbors. For example, Ukraine and Romania recently signed a *Treaty on Friendship and Cooperation* that addressed issues such as border disputes and nationality questions. Furthermore, Ukraine interacts politically, economically, and militarily on a regular cooperative basis with Iran, a country the West deems a "rogue" and proliferant.

In 1996, the Ukrainian Parliament (Verkhovna Rada) approved the legislation of the *Ukrainian Security Concept*. This document sets out Ukraine's priorities as: ensuring state sovereignty, preserving its territorial integrity, and upholding the inviolability of borders. It also calls for overcoming the economic crisis, developing democratic institutions, and integration into the world and European community. Listed among the threats to Ukraine's security are interference in the country's internal affairs, territorial claims, instability and conflicts in neighboring states, separatism, and violations of the constitutional system. The document emphasizes acute and prolonged economic instability as being the primary threat to national security.[5] The Ukrainian economy is, owing to its structural inheritance, vulnerable to Russian and regional factors.[6] For example, Russian supplies of oil and gas have been used to pressure Ukraine on such issues as the division of the Black Sea Fleet.[7] Furthermore, a recent $500 million sale of 320 T-80 tanks to Pakistan prompted a Russian response threatening to deny Ukraine vital tank parts because Moscow believes Ukraine to be undercutting its arms market in South Asia.[8]

In contrast to the United States, Ukraine does not have extensive security interests in different parts of the world, nor does it have – with the exception of NATO Partnership for Peace (PfP) membership and imprecisely-defined participation in the GUUAM grouping (explained below) – an extensive network of military alliances. Generally speaking, Kyiv does not view the acquisition of long-range missiles, for example, by

Iran, Iraq, Libya, North Korea or Syria as directly affecting its military security interests. According to Alexander Negoda, director general of the Ukrainian National Space Agency: "For other countries, the transfer of their missile technologies means transfer of secrets and is a threat to their national security interests. For Ukraine, there is no direct threat to its national security from the sales of its missiles and related technologies. That makes Ukraine a unique country. In fact, having taken obligations on missile and nuclear nonproliferation, Ukraine contributes to the security of other countries more than it does for its own security."[9]

Ukraine regained its independence in December 1991 after some seventy years under Soviet rule.[10] The new Ukrainian state experienced many severe internal problems during its first eight years, including a catastrophic economic decline, occasional ethnic unrest in Crimea, and a growing political divide between the eastern and western portions of the country.[11] These difficulties inevitably took their toll on Ukrainian security strategy. Although most Ukrainians acknowledged that the gravest threats to Ukraine's survival as an independent state came from within, officials in Kyiv were also constantly mindful of the country's external situation, notably its proximity to Russia. Ukraine is contiguous with seven countries (Moldova, Romania, Hungary, Slovakia, Poland, Belarus, and Russia) at the crossroads between Europe and Asia, but the long border with Russia is by far the most important.[12]

Ukraine's continued dependence on Russia for vital energy supplies (which were sold at highly subsidized prices long after 1991), the extensive trade links between Russia and Ukraine, the presence of some 11.3 million ethnic Russians in Ukraine (out of a total population of 52 million), and the unsettled history of Russian-Ukrainian relations affected all aspects of Ukrainian strategy in the 1990s, including decisions about nuclear weapons.

5.1.1 Perceptions of External Threats: Relations with Russia ... then with Others

From the moment the Soviet Union disintegrated, Ukraine's relations with Russia were marked by periodic tensions and recriminations. Although most Ukrainian officials did not expect that Russia would try to re-conquer Ukraine through military force in the near future, they would not exclude the *possibility* of a large-scale conflict at some point in the future. Even in the near term, some Ukrainian officials were worried that a low-level military clash between the two former Soviet republics – perhaps over territorial issues – could escalate into something much larger than either side had anticipated.[13] Such a conflict, if it had transpired, would undoubtedly have worked to Ukraine's disadvantage. The Ukrainian army was one of the largest in Europe and was relatively well-equipped (primarily because sizable stocks of front-line weaponry were left on Ukrainian territory after the Soviet Union collapsed), but it would have been no match for the Russian army. Ukrainian officials were under no illusions that Ukraine's conventional forces could have repulsed a full-scale Russian attack.[14] The key problem for Ukrainian military officials, therefore, was how to make a prospective attack so costly that Russian leaders would not want to pay the price of "victory."[15]

As executed by the Kuchma administration, Ukrainian security policy has aimed to balance gradual but steady integration into Europe's political and economic structures with constructive, open relations with Russia. While many other Central European countries have declared their desire for admission into NATO, Ukraine has firmly committed itself to nonalignment. It has participated in NATO's Partnership for Peace (PfP) program – being the first former Soviet state to join – and now publicly seeks a special relationship with the alliance, parallel to that which Russia has demanded. The *Charter on a Distinctive Partnership between NATO and Ukraine* was signed in February 1998, thereby launching the NATO-Ukraine Joint Working Group on Defense Reform, which is designed to complement Ukraine's participation in PfP by addressing issues such as civil military relations, military reform and resource planning and management.[16]

Ukraine's positive, albeit modest, views about the expansion of NATO were greatly aided by Russia's brutal military intervention in Chechnya, which significantly eroded any domestic support for Ukraine's membership in the Tashkent Collective Security Treaty, even in Russian-speaking areas of eastern and southern Ukraine.[17] The public perception of one of the main reasons for the establishment of Ukrainian security forces was precisely to prevent Ukrainian troops dying in "in Russian imperialistic wars" in the former Soviet Union.[18] National Security and Defense Council secretary, Volodymyr Horbulin, outlined Ukraine's positive policy – as opposed to the Commonwealth of Independent States (CIS), for example – towards the expansion of NATO: "We view NATO as a *necessary* (author's emphasis) factor of stability and deterrence in Europe, though we never said this before."[19]

Ukraine's endorsement of the PfP program rested on a number of factors. First, Kyiv believed that it would increase Ukraine's international prestige. Secondly, such membership would provide "additional security guarantees" to those already obtained in the Trilateral Agreement and

Memorandum on Security Assurances.[20] Thirdly, "An important step [PfP membership] has been made in building a European security system, in bringing together Eastern and Western Europe," then President Kravchuk argued, hoping this would help to demilitarize the Black Sea region.[21] Fourthly, the PfP represented a reasonable and pragmatic alternative to partial or selective enlargement. Finally, Ukraine's PfP membership would allow it to balance its foreign and security policy *vis-à-vis* the CIS military bloc.[22] As the only country with potential territorial claims on Ukraine is Russia, it is not surprising that Ukraine always supported its participation within PfP because any potential territorial conflict would then be raised within NATO.

Under Kuchma, Ukraine's policies of neutrality, non-bloc status, opposition to political or military integration in the CIS, and joining a new confederation or Eurasian Union remains in place. For example, Ukraine has repeatedly refused to sign the 1992 CIS Tashkent Collective Security Agreement, much to the continuing dismay of Moscow.[23] In addition, Ukraine's more pragmatic involvement in economic questions within the CIS would not be at the expense of cooperation with the West, both for domestic and political reasons. Presidential chief of staff, Dmytro Tabachnyk, while preparing for President Kuchma's official 1994 visit to the United States, said that "Ukraine will not lean this way or that, Ukraine will stay where it is, according to its destiny, its history and geography."[24] In his 1996 independence day speech, President Kuchma outlined two main reasons for severely limited involvement in the CIS:

> Relations [with other states] via Moscow have no future, not only because Russia itself needs investment and technological and technical modernization. The main reason is that state and foreign structures can sense very well whether a country is truly independent. If the answer is negative, they will maintain contacts through a non-metropolis where real power is concentrated.[25]

Other perspectives, not only from the government, but from two thirds of the political spectrum (center-left to right) echo the same theme: not only does CIS integration represent the "accelerated integration of underdeveloped markets"[26] and hence a "guarantee of long-term economic and political backwardness"[27] but its supranational bodies are designed to promote the political and economic dominance of Russia. Nevertheless, relations with Russia are predicated upon Ukraine's fundamental economic vulnerability.

Internal economic weakness makes Ukraine susceptible to outside pressures and has complicated its security policy.[28] The prime example of this vulnerability is Ukraine's dependence on Russia for energy.[29] Russia supplies 80 percent of Ukraine's natural gas, and Ukraine has accumulated an energy debt of $4 billion, making energy Russia's most effective lever over the country. Gazprom, Russia's gas monopoly and a powerful lobby, has periodically threatened to close the pipeline to Ukraine unless it pays its bill. At one point, in exchange for debt relief, Gazprom unsuccessfully maneuvered for stakes of between 35 and 50 percent in 15 of Ukraine's most profitable and strategic national enterprises. In February 1997, for instance, Ukraine found itself on the edge of an energy collapse: coal miners' strikes coincided with Gazprom's decision to stop dealing with Ukraine's commercial gas importers and with Moscow's decision to disconnect Ukraine from its electricity system. Until the energy problem is addressed, Ukraine will remain a fragile state, vulnerable to Russian pressure. Export controls do nothing to address this liability. Reducing this dependence on Moscow, therefore, has become one of Ukraine's top security priorities.[30]

Some progress toward this goal has been made by commercializing its oil import business, restructuring its debt, and using IMF standby loans to pay its gas bills.[31] But the energy problem still awaits a comprehensive solution, and Russia has objected to some of Ukraine's stop-gap measures.[32] Policy solutions to this situation can be seen in the administration's attempt to discover and cultivate alternative energy relations. For example, Ukrainian and Azerbaijani participation in the construction of an Europe-Caucasus-Asia energy transport corridor and bilateral cooperation in the area of supplying Caspian energy resources to Ukraine and to the world markets has increased in recent years.[33] During an October 1999 visit to Kyiv, Azeri President Aliyev held talks with Ukrainian President Kuchma, Prime Minister Valery Pustovoitenko and parliament speaker Alexander Tkachenko on areas of energy cooperation. Specifically, the talks focused on Azerbaijani oil supplies to Ukraine and fuel payments. The two sides also considered prospects for increasing bilateral trade turnover. The two sides also discussed prospects for greater cooperation within the framework of the GUUAM alliance and measures to fight terrorism.[34]

Membership in the so-called GUUAM group is in keeping with Ukrainian attempts to realize a solution to its vulnerable position. The GUUAM alliance comprises Georgia, Ukraine and Uzbekistan, Azerbaijan, and Moldova. All are members of the CIS – founded by Russia to keep as much of the old Soviet empire together as possible. GUUAM is Westward-looking and independent-minded. The group has expanded the organization's remit from cooperation on trade to defense and security.[35]

GUUAM offices are in the process of being established in the capital cities of each member state. GUUAM members have also agreed that they would meet, on a bilateral basis, with NATO officials with the aim of increasing future cooperation. GUUAM countries have opted out of the Collective Security Treaty (Tashkent Treaty) in favor of pursuing closer ties with NATO. They were also seen by Russia – and Belarus, with whom Russia is now confederated – as the principal cause of disruption at the 4 June 1999 meeting of CIS foreign ministers in Minsk.[36] For Ukraine, GUUAM is viewed as a means by which to address energy sources concerns. For example, Volodomyr Horbulin, Secretary of the Ukrainian National Security and Defense Council, noted that GUUAM "will help Ukraine obtain fuel from several sources and make better use of Ukraine's geographic location."[37] Yet, until the energy problem is addressed, Ukraine will remain a weak state, especially susceptible to Russian pressure. Export controls do nothing to address this liability.

Besides the energy quandary, Russian-Ukrainian relations involve other issue areas. Initially, the chief points of contention between Ukraine and Russia were the division of the Black Sea Fleet (which both sides claimed), the status of Crimea (a peninsula in Ukraine inhabited mainly by ethnic Russians), and the deployment of nuclear weapons on Ukrainian territory. Although none of these disputes led to a military conflict, the series of disagreements reinforced Ukrainian leaders' suspicion that the large majority of Russians, whether government officials, military officers, or ordinary citizens, had not yet fully accepted the fact of Ukrainian independence.[38] Ukrainian leaders often expressed concern that ultra-nationalist and imperial-minded forces in Russia might yet succeed in roiling public sentiment in favor of an aggressive policy on behalf of the ethnic Russians living in the Crimea, Odessa, and the Donbass region. They feared that Russian hard-liners and security force personnel could manipulate domestic politics in Ukraine to provoke civil conflict that would create an opportunity and pretext for Russia to undertake more overt military intervention. Although the rebuff of the hardline revolt in Moscow in October 1993 briefly eased those concerns, the strong electoral showing of Zhirinovsky's ultranationalist forces in December 1993 caused many in Ukraine to fear that hardline elements in Moscow would eventually gain sway.[39]

Apprehension in Kyiv remained high in 1994 and 1995, as the tone of Russian politics veered in a more nationalist direction (symbolized by the war in Chechnya) and the Russian Communist party experienced a strong resurgence. Minatory statements by Russian military officers, including a remark about Ukraine's place "on the list of targets for Russian strategic nuclear forces," boosted tensions still further.[40] Nevertheless, Ukrainian relations with Russia began to improve after mid-1994, largely because of the election of Leonid Kuchma as president. Kuchma had made clear during the electoral campaign that he favored closer ties with Russia. His surprisingly wide victory in July 1994 – by a 52 to 45 margin – over the incumbent, Leonid Kravchuk, provided the impetus for a more conciliatory policy toward Russia. This new approach was not so drastic that it led to a full-scale rapprochement between Russia and Ukraine; on the contrary, most Ukrainian leaders remained highly suspicious of Russia's intentions, and bilateral disputes persisted over the Black Sea Fleet and other issues. Even so, the acrimonious and threatening atmosphere of 1992 and 1993 was at least partly alleviated. Ties between the two countries remained uneasy and tense after mid-1994, but the threat of armed conflict receded.[41]

A sign of how much the relationship had improved came in mid-1995 when a vote of independence by the Crimean parliament provoked a crackdown by the Ukrainian government. Had such a step been taken in 1992 or 1993, Russia undoubtedly would have responded very harshly and perhaps made some effort to provide direct aid to the Crimean government; but Kuchma's action provoked barely a murmur of protest from Moscow.[42]

Relations between the two countries continued to improve after 1995, despite periodic glitches and disruption. At a summit in Kyiv in late May 1997, Russian Prime Minister Viktor Chernomyrdin and Ukrainian Prime Minister Pavlo Lazarenko signed long-awaited agreements on the leasing of military facilities in Crimea and the division of the Black Sea Fleet. In terms of resolving the long-standing Black Sea Fleet issue, according to the Treaty, Russia will cede naval bays, that are to be leased to Russia, and half of the fleet rented by Russia from Ukraine, with the payments subtracted from Ukraine's enormous debt to Russia for gas and oil deliveries, estimated at the time of the treaty signing at $3–3.5 billion. At that same meeting, Kuchma and Russian president Boris Yeltsin signed a historic "Treaty on Friendship, Cooperation, and Partnership," which recast the bilateral relationship as a "strategic partnership."[43] The treaty marked the first time that Russia unequivocally affirmed the "territorial integrity" of Ukraine and the "inviolability of [its] existing borders." The Treaty was ratified by Russia in 1999.

Perhaps the greatest obstacle to the Russian recognition of Ukraine as a separate state was psychological: her unique place in Russia's historic memory and national conscience. Kyiv was the birthplace of the first Russian state and its first baptized city, from which Christianity spread throughout Russia. No other part of the non-Russian Soviet Union was so pivotal to Russian national identity as Ukraine.⁴⁴ For example, in commenting on the disintegration of the Soviet Union, then deputy speaker of the Russian State Duma, Mikhail Yuriyev, remarked:

> Ukraine and Belarus are not separate nations at all, they are Slavs, Russians [russkyie] in the broad sense of the term. I think, for example, that the Ukrainian language is a hundred times more poetic than the contemporary Russian language, but nonetheless is a dialect of the Russian language, just like, say, the Moscow accent or Siberian dialect. The questions should not be posed in terms of integration or consolidation, but rather in terms of returning these lands to the Russian Federation on conditions to those of, say, Tataria. This should be the cornerstone of our foreign policy.⁴⁵

In no other instance was the tempering of Russia's imperial tradition and instinct put to a harsher, more sobering test than by an independent Ukraine.

Despite this general improvement of relations, most Ukrainian officials still harbored little doubt that the only serious external threat to Ukraine over the long term would come from Russia. Ukraine's military planning and deployments remained geared toward deterrence of a Russian attack.⁴⁶ Ukrainian leaders realized that the limited détente between the two countries could easily be reversed, particularly if Communist and ultranationalist forces regained a dominant position in Russia.

At the same time, one key factor – the awareness, on both sides, of how disastrous a conflict would be even if no nuclear weapons were used – helped keep the relationship free of hostilities. Large-scale fighting would almost certainly have disrupted the flow of oil and natural gas through the pipelines extending from Russia to Ukraine and into Central Europe, causing vast economic upheaval throughout Europe. Hostilities between Russia and Ukraine might also have caused an accident at one of the five nuclear power stations in western and southern Ukraine, scattering highly radioactive debris all around the region on a scale far eclipsing even the 1986 Chernobyl disaster.⁴⁷ Because the potential consequences of a Russian-Ukrainian military confrontation would have been so inimical and long-lasting, it was hardly surprising that officials in both countries sought to avoid a direct clash. Nevertheless, Ukrainian leaders were well aware that a militant backlash in Russia could have ominous consequences for their own country. Although they acknowledged that internal problems posed the greatest threat to Ukrainian security in the near term, they would not completely rule out the prospect of a serious external danger in the future.⁴⁸

Despite the potential menace of Russian economic and political hegemony, external threats, however, do not explain Ukraine's relatively advanced export control system.[49] Russia and the NIS, once being a coherent political-economic unit, represent parts of a military-technological whole. Consequently, many sensitive items, technologies, and equipment are still, perforce, exchanged, sold and transferred between former republics, thereby resuming erstwhile division of labor patterns. For example, Ukraine's advanced missile and rocket industry is deeply integrated into the Russian space and missile program, as evidenced by an agreement to work on jointly modernizing SS-18 ballistic missiles so they can carry satellites.[50] Consequently, both Ukraine and Russia, are dependent on the comparative expertise of the other, thus highlighting the need for continual technological and material exchange.[51] Export controls, therefore, could hardly be expected to assuage Ukrainian security concerns in seeking to balance the power of others, Russia specifically. Furthermore, confronting decision makers is the sheer novelty of the nonproliferation issue. Unaccustomed to *global* security issues, nonproliferation export controls have not been conceptually linked by Ukrainian officials with national security.[52]

Aside from the Russian Federation, Ukraine has not identified the presence of regional threats.[53] Treaties recognizing inter-state frontiers and national minority rights have been signed by Ukraine with Hungary, Moldova, Poland and Slovakia.[54] Initially, a treaty with Romania languished for the same reasons that one was delayed between Romania and Moldova. Romania's insistence that any treaty denounce the Molov-Ribbentrop Pact was perceived by Ukraine as tantamount to demands for territorial revisions (Ukraine acquired territories from Romania, Czechoslavakia, and Poland as a result of the Soviet-Nazi treaty).[55] Nevertheless, relations with the regional states are positive and growing increasingly so.[56]

Because Ukraine's security concerns incorporate Russia, already substantially endowed with advanced sensitive materials and technologies, then any attempt to preclude Russia from strategic trade would be both ludicrous and self-defeating. Nonetheless, if not a regional concern, Ukrainian leaders maintain that WMD proliferation is a *global* security issue, and Ukrainian export control development as a means by which to address the *international* proliferation threat.[57] That proliferation concerns are addressed at all is testament to the perseverance of the international community, the US specifically, and Ukraine's cooperative response.

The *Ukrainian Security Concept* articulates internal threats as being the foremost obstacle to achieving Ukrainian security. Economic and political instability are real and immediate threats to Ukrainian sovereignty. Regional and ethnic frictions threaten to undermine the overall coherence of the territorial state.[58] For example, separatist pressures in Crimea and ethnic tensions in the ethnically Russian-dominated Donbas could be future points of conflict and instability.[59] Export controls, costly and ostensibly unrelated to the immediate dictates of economic and political perils, seem ill-suited to addressing Ukrainian security concerns, such as they are.

According to the Realist approach, state behavior is best explained in terms of its respective security concerns. As such, security issues occupy the highest priority on a state's political agenda. Were export controls seen as a viable and effective means by which to decrease security threats, then we would expect to see export controls figured prominently in the affairs of state, explicitly wedded to security policy. This is not the case in Ukraine.[60] In fact, concepts such as the dangers arising from nuclear proliferation were noticeably absent from the Ukrainian nuclear debate.[61] Ukrainian government officials clearly recognize the value of more effective export controls. However, while they recognize the importance of improving their current capabilities, they also acknowledge that export controls are only one among many political and economic priorities.[62] As, at best, second tier concerns, export controls are not seen as redressing security imbalances or minimizing security threats. Furthermore, Ukraine has sought Western security guarantees and the strengthening of its own military – and not export controls – as the primary vehicles by which to address its security concerns.[63] Thus, the Realist approach offers little explanatory power in accounting for the evolution of Ukrainian nonproliferation export controls.

5.2 Domestic Politics: Executive Action

> Someone once said: "Everything is within our power if all people in power are ours!" This is about Leonid Kuchma's presidential team! For instance, on a single day in Ukraine, the president bestowed the rank of general on 137 people by virtue of his edict. You know, even during the world wars, following brilliant strategic victories, satraps of totalitarian states did not take such liberties! The Kuchma-planned invasion of dilettantes in the entire executive branch is a serious threat to Ukrainian democracy and statehood.
>
> Yevhen Marchuk, former prime minister and 1999 presidential hopeful. Quoted in *Nezavisimaya Gazeta*, 21 September 1999

Domestic Politics expectations regarding export control behavior offer only marginal – save for one crucial expectation – assistance in explaining the Ukrainian case. The domestic political environment in Ukraine conforms to a pattern similar amongst the majority of the successor states governments: liberalizing executive pitted against a reactionary and leftist legislature.[64] As such, the political situation is fractious and highly variable. Legislation, executive action, and bureaucratic initiatives have been uncoordinated and, as a result, often inconsistent and contradictory. Consequently, the government is in a state of irresolution, a condition wherein the divisions of power and formal relations within the central government and between Kyiv and the regional governments has yet to be firmly established.[65] The decentralized trajectory of government reforms has complicated the overall political and economic climate. Nevertheless, as a consequence of a weak civil society and entrenched Soviet-era political culture, the Ukrainian state remains highly centralized.[66]

Owing to governmental immaturity and the uncertain political environment, the Ukrainian export control system has developed largely without the influence of interest groups or firmly established institutional structures outside of the government.[67] Interest groups cannot, at this time, be said to exist as viable political forces in Ukraine because there is no institutional pattern by which extra-government groups come to influence policy.[68] As noted above, export controls do not figure prominently in overall state policy making priorities. Save for well-publicized issues, such as talks over MTCR membership criteria, export controls are not an issue area around which a clearly identifiable interest group or public organization has coalesced. Moreover, civil society is still weak, leaving politics to a narrow circle of regional and central elites.[69] As all sensitive and military industries are state-owned, export control activities transpire solely within the government. Although attempting to decentralize, political power is still vested largely in the central government – specifically in the executive, which happens to be the locus of export control development initiatives. Therefore, we see that as a centralized state, Ukraine is better equipped to develop and coordinate export control activities. However, were export controls subject to the full range of the Ukrainian political process (i.e., Parliamentary vetting), then, despite its centralized structure, one would expect less export control development.[70]

To better illustrate the unilateral role played by the executive in export control policy, a brief examination of the separation and relations of powers in the Ukrainian government is in order.

5.2.1 Domestic Politics: A Brief Constitutional History

When Ukraine became independent in 1991, a key decision was made that set the framework within which the power struggle over the constitutional design would take place. The decision was to amend the existing [Soviet] Republic Constitution to create the office of president. While the Communists dominated the parliament and were strongly opposed to the addition of a presidency to the institutional mix, democratic reformers and nationalists succeeded in creating the institution of the presidency. They succeeded by arguing that a strong unified political institution was necessary as a means of ensuring Ukraine's sovereignty and independence. Even though they were in the minority, reformers and nationalists succeeded in large part because they were far more active in the policy making process than the Communists. The result of the interactions between key political forces were the three primary governing institutions: the president, the parliament, and the government composed of a prime minister and cabinet, both appointed, at that time, by the parliament. While the authority to govern these three entities was ill-defined, conflict among the branches was initially fairly low.[71]

Motyl (1995) argues that Ukraine's first president, Leonid Kravchuk, perceived his role less as a policy maker and more as a statesman, working to ensure that Ukraine became an independent state in the eyes of the international community.[72] Even in the midst of a nationwide economic crisis, Kravchuk did not pursue an economic reform agenda, lest, in the fragile political environment, he provoke the left-dominated parliament. Instead, Kravchuk maintained his distance, leaving domestic governance concerns largely to the prime minister – who at the time was Leonid Kuchma (1992-1993) – and government. The economic situation continued to worsen and the government failed to respond with consistent or coherent reform policies. However, while the existence of three institutions of national governance created the opportunity for a destabilizing interbranch conflict, it did not materialize. This was the case because neither the president, the prime minister and the government, nor the parliament pursued divisive policy objectives.[73] Nevertheless, relative interbranch peace was purchased at the expense of policy effectiveness, accompanied by decreasing popular legitimacy of the government.

Presidential elections in 1994 dramatically changed the dynamic between national political institutions, as Kravchuk lost to former Prime Minister, Leonid Kuchma. Kuchma came to power determined to initiate a radical program of political reform which he regarded as inseparable from economic reform and democratic change.[74] Specifically, Kuchma sought to: establish law and order; liberalize the economy; and reform the government. The latter two objectives set him at immediate odds with the parliament. Undoubtedly, his experience as prime minister colored his policies, when he found his best efforts at implementing policies frustrated at every level, as well as the legal and administrative chaos that reigned under his predecessor.[75] The election of a president bent on reform prevented the Communist block from dominating the government. Key elements of his political and economic reforms policy included the adoption of a "mini-constitution" (the "Law on Power") and Ukraine's first post-Soviet constitution, adopted in June 1995 and July 1996 respectively.[76]

In the mid-1990s, the dominant agenda item was how to respond to the economic crisis, and there were fundamentally opposing forces at play in that question. Certain economic sectors, although not unified, viewed economic reform and restructuring and gaining access to Western technology and capital as the only salvation for the stranded and decaying industries.[77] Kuchma's economic program fundamentally represented the "restructuring" forces. The administration's attempt to liberalize the economy, restructure the tax system, and reorganize agriculture and industry were repeatedly blocked by the Communist-Socialist-Agrarian block in parliament.[78] Since the nationalist and reformist groups in parliament remained fairly disaggregated, Kuchma began resorting to executive decrees, turning the presidency into a law-making institution. Consequently, policy battles between Kuchma and the Communists in parliament over reforming the economy, privatization, the intergovernmental system, and the reorganization of the agricultural and energy sectors, broadened to include conflict over which branch of government had the authority to rule over key policy areas and in what way.[79]

In June 1996 Ukraine adopted a new constitution, resulting in the accumulation of formal powers in the hands of the presidency.[80] This constitution allows the president to appoint judges for their first term (except to the Constitutional Court, where he only appoints six of eighteen); appoints the prime minister (with parliamentary consent), who in turn chooses the Cabinet of Ministers with the president; and can unilaterally revoke decisions of the Cabinet of Ministers. The president can also dismiss ministers, create or dissolve ministries, and call national referenda,[81] and he was granted three years in which to issue unilateral (i.e., *de facto*) decrees on economic reform.

While the new constitution enumerated the powers of the president and the parliament, it did not exhaustively discuss the structure or formation of the government. The question of the nature of the relationship between the presidential administration and the Cabinet of Ministers – nor to whom the prime minister and cabinet were subordinate – was not decisively resolved.[82] To resolve this issue in the administration's favor, the president passed a decree in December 1996 which stipulated that the ministries of the interior, foreign relations, information, and defense (the so-called "power ministries") were directly subordinate to the president. With increasing control over the Cabinet of Ministers came greater authority over export control policy.[83]

5.2.2 Elite Activism: Kuchma and Export Control Development

The Ukrainian export control system presently exists solely on the basis of presidential and government decrees. As such, the elite approach offers a rich explanatory means as to how and why the present system emerged and continues to develop. For example, a December 1996 Presidential decree established the creation of a new Ministry (SSEC) dealing exclusively with implementing export control policy. By conferring ministerial status to the state export control organ, President Kuchma enabled export control officials to solidify and rationalize their power base. Prior to this decree, the export control agency operated under the Cabinet of Ministers and was frequently beset by interagency conflicts.[84]

Various ministries – primarily the Ministry for Foreign Economic Relations; the Ministry of Defense; the Ministry of Machine Building, the Military-Industrial Complex, and Conversion; and the Ministry of Foreign Affairs – have vied for control over sensitive exports, mostly in the conventional weapons area.[85] Because the Ukrainian government structure is an amalgam of Soviet-era and liberalizing institutions, departmental or agency interests have not articulated a clear, consistent position on export control development. Parliamentary involvement is minimal with only desultory, *ad hoc* involvement by two Rada committees nominally addressing export control issues: Commission on Defense and State Security and the Commission on Foreign Affairs. In terms of the Domestic Politics approach, the Rada is dominated by "inward looking coalitions."[86] However, the Rada has demonstrably little involvement in export control policy. The "liberalizing coalitions," moreover, are to be found in the executive.

In 1994, then Prime Minister Leonid Kuchma, was elected the second president of Ukraine. Under the Kuchma administration, Ukraine increased its reformist pace by radical privatization plans and by a demonstrably Western bias in its foreign and economic policies. Indeed, since his 1994 election, a discernible Western-centric complexion has emerged in Kyiv.[87] Former director of the Yuzhnoye aerospace complex, President Kuchma built his early career in Dnipropetrovsk and drew its leaders to his administration.

President Kuchma has overcome a series of political obstacles to enact his liberalizing reform policies.[88] Packing the administration and government with allies has been a difficult and exacting struggle.[89] Nevertheless, since the passage of the post-Soviet constitution in June 1996, Kuchma continues to strengthen economic and political ties with the West while seeking to minimize Ukraine's involvement in the Commonwealth of Independent States (CIS).[90] Furthermore, Western assistance in general, the US in particular, has influenced the policy choices made by the Kuchma administration. For example, donor stipulations have shaped presidential economic reforms.[91]

Under the direction of the Kuchma government, the export control system structure has undergone a series of reorganizations which have involved removing export promoting agencies from issuing licenses.[92] The reorganization is meant to establish strict control over international transfers of arms and military technology as well as raw materials and skills that may be used for the production of weapons and other military technology. In fact, the Constitution stipulates the creation of a state export control organ and includes brief references to the necessity of export controls – albeit in generalist terms.[93] The presidential efforts to strengthen export controls are also seen in the recent decision to narrow controls over conventional arms exports.

The three main arms-export firms in Ukraine – Progress, Ukrinmash, and Ukroboronservice – were merged into one new company, Ukrspetsexport, to increase state control of weapons sales abroad.[94] Previously, the State Security Service, Ministry of Defense, and the Ministry of Foreign Economic Relations, respectively, independently managed the three firms.[95] These Ministries sought to retain exclusive control over exports, particularly the Ministry of Defense, which, with its surplus armaments and direct links to the military industry, views arms exports as a viable means of generating revenues for conversion efforts, equipment upgrades, and salaries.[96] The Ministry of Defense was also, for example, quite vocal with its concerns over sales disclosure protocols in the Wassenaar Arrangement, but were nevertheless persuaded by the Ministry of Foreign Affairs that Ukraine's membership was crucial to the legitimacy of future military sales.[97]

As part of his military and government reorganization plan, President Kuchma appointed the first civilian defense minister in the FSU,

Valery Shmarov, shortly after gaining office. Shmarov, a Kuchma colleague from the military industry, was also deputy prime minister for the military-industrial complex. As deputy prime minister, he headed the Governmental Commission on Export Controls (GCEC) and, as such, with the President, had the final say on all sensitive exports. Shmarov, moreover, was actively involved in promoting Ukrainian non-nuclear status and closer ties with NATO. Shmarov was eventually replaced by a young general, Olexander Kuzmuk. Many believe that Kuzmuk's appointment was Kuchma's attempt to consolidate his military reform programs by circumventing older, established elements in the Ministry of Defense.[98]

Coupled with the recent export control system reorganizations, the ability of export control opponents to influence the direction of export control developments has been substantially curtailed. The State Export Control Service (SSEC), the lead export control agency, has expanded in powers and responsibility under the Kuchma administration. However, its ability to *effectively* implement export control laws and procedures, is hampered by insufficient funding and inexperience. SSEC has received substantial US financial and technical assistance, thereby instilling an awareness of export control issues and international obligations that are otherwise lacking in other Ministries. The export control agencies are, however, limited in their autonomy given that much of the political elite hails from the military-industrial complex. For example, the former and present directors of SSEC are former military procurement specialists with close ties to the Ministry of Defense. Thus, the evidence attesting to the influence of the export control agencies is mixed.

5.3 Liberal Identity: Forging National Interests

> The West has often been critical of the pace of economic and political reform. It is clear that the West will not keep helping Ukraine if Ukraine doesn't move faster on these reforms. However, I would like to hear an example from anywhere else in the world about the possibility of carrying out reforms in two and a half years – take any country from South Korea to our East European neighbors. Ukraine had never been a state. We are truly a new state. We embarked on independence with no elite, no economists, no banking system, no financiers. Forty percent of Ukraine's capital assets were in the military-industrial complex. All of our best stuff was pumped out of Ukraine and sent to Moscow. We started to write our history, in fact, from zero.[99]

> We [the government] do not make a single move without the IMF and the World Bank.
> President Leonid Kuchma, 6 September 1999, quoted in *Nedelii Vedmosti*

> Whosoever desires constant success must change his conduct with the times.
> Nicolo Machiavelli, Chapter VI: Concerning New Principalities Which Are Acquired by One's Own Arms and Ability, *The Prince*

Explaining export control development as a function of identity dynamics, expectations derived from the Liberal Identity approach partially accounts for the Ukrainian case. This approach posits that states will develop export controls as a consequence of increased interaction and institutional and normative affinities with the Western,[100] liberal[101] community of states, and those states that have acknowledged a "sense of community" in export control matters and are interested in targeting the control of sensitive materials toward illiberal states. As such, interacting states come to regard themselves as intrinsic parts to the liberal whole, of which export controls are part of a larger battery of expected (i.e., legitimate, proper) behaviors. Ukraine, however, poses significant challenges to the derived expectations concerning export control development. These challenges arise from the difficulty in determining the overall political disposition of Ukraine, a country without, arguably, a definitive sense of a uniform political-national identity outside of the government. Nevertheless, the Ukrainian government clearly evinces a "liberal" predilection in both its political rhetoric and state building efforts. This section explores the identity issue and how the liberal community of states has influenced export control development in Ukraine.

The history of the Ukrainian people and of the Ukrainian territory does not abound with continuity and constant lines of development throughout the centuries. The dominant characteristic in the history of Ukraine is precisely the absence of an independent political entity. One Ukrainian scholar, for example, contends that "Ukraine is a nation without a politically usable past."[102] Ukrainian history thus deviates from the European pattern of state building.[103] Furthermore, Ukraine itself is internally divided. Galicia, or western Ukraine, tends to be more nationalistic than the south and east of the country. The latter, the regions of the Donbas and Crimea, are composed primarily of ethnic Russians. These regions clearly differ in demographic, economic, and religious-denominational terms. This informal dividing line is the source of chronic political tensions, thereby making consensus on political identity complex and laborious.[104]

Ukrainian political identity is further confounded by its shared political, cultural, religious and linguistic history with Russia. From the days of the Kyivan-Rus, Ukrainian and Russian histories have been inseparably linked.[105] In 1654, control over the Ukrainian region was formally ceded to the Russian Tsar. Both the Russian and Soviet yoke enfeebled any latent national aspirations. Until independence, Ukraine therefore existed as a Russian province.[106] Subsequently, both Ukraine and Russia have sought to determine the nature of their relationship, and, perforce, Ukraine has sought to differentiate itself from Russia as befits its new found sovereignty.

Ukrainian national and political identity has been, at best, a problematic issue arising fundamentally from the difficulties attendant to the creation of a new state.[107] However, Ukraine, under the direction of the president, evinces a decidedly Western disposition in its domestic and international policies. Economic liberalization efforts, democratic political reforms and courting the Western security communities have been clear indications of the pro-Western political complexion holding sway in Kyiv.[108] According to one Ukrainian export control official, regular interaction with Western states specifically addressing export control issues has resulted in palpable advances in export control development and the emergence of an export control "culture."[109]

Relations with the West have gradually evolved into the current state of positive engagement. After Ukraine undertook its nuclear divestiture, the West ostensibly lost interest in continued engagement. However, the inchoate economic and political reform efforts, waning relations with Russia, and the continued proliferation threat quickly refocused Western attention on this country of 51 million. To this end, the Kuchma administration and government actively courted Western sources of financial and security assistance. On continued economic and political cooperation with the West, Foreign Minister Hennady Udovenko remarked, "Integration with the West is the main direction of our foreign policy."[110]

An increased sense of community with the West is evinced by Ukraine's engagement with the liberal commons.[111] In a thorough sociological study of the Ukrainian political elite, Jeffery Checkel notes: "In Ukraine, one sees more evidence of social learning and a greater role played by Western hegemonic-power-coercion (than in Russia). Western norms have mattered most at the elite/state level, where the demand for new principles and norms has been high. Learning, from interaction, is significant because in the top-heavy Ukrainian state, the presidential administration – even more so than post-Soviet Russia – plays a *dominant role in policy making.*"[112] A key question remains, however: what motivated agents like Kuchma and his administration to 'learn'? One factor, readily admitted in interviews, was a simple combination of Western (primarily US) and Ukrainian strategic interests. Given its large and unpredictable neighbor to the east (Russia), Ukraine had a clear interest in joining "Euro-Atlantic structures," as Ukrainian policy makers never tire of declaring.[113] Furthermore, the contrast with post-Soviet Russia is also instructive in answering this question.

For Russia, many of the "new" elites are holdovers from the Soviet era, a fact explained by the massive size of the Soviet/Russian political-economic apparatus. In comparison, the USSR bequeathed Ukraine a vastly smaller personnel inheritance, as most key decisions during the Soviet period were taken in Moscow.[114] Thus, in relative terms, Ukraine was forced to recruit more outsiders for positions, which, in turn, has increased the probability of agent learning.[115] Checkel's avowedly norm-based study of Ukraine suggests that, at the political level, "normative socialization in Ukraine is expedited, as is the case in the Russian political establishment, by the lack of cognitive filters to such socialization and learning."[116] Put differently, the learning effects attendant to interaction with the West were promoted not just by strategic interests, but also by the absence of domestic norms acting as "cognitive filters." Indeed, a central legacy of the Soviet period is the country's *lack* of a developed sense of national identity.

Operating in a relatively indeterminate political environment, Ukraine's increased and routinized interactions with the West – on a variety of topical matters – influenced the institutional and ideational shape of Ukrainian policy makers, their perceptions and interests. Consistent throughout the Ukraine-West relationship are the recurring norms of democracy, liberal economics, and nonproliferation.[117] In the construction and articulation of a political identity, interests cannot be postulated *as prior* to identities and that identities themselves are not fixed in time but are *relationally* constructed.[118] The "dynamic density" of US-Ukrainian relations has increased the influence of US policies in Kyiv.[119] Thus, the formal incorporation of such norms are not merely identical with an antecedent hierarchy of interests, but constitutive of them – and with them, the figuring of identity.

The vehicle of norm transmission in the case of Ukraine has been through bi- and multilateral relations over time. For example, Ukraine is a member of the Council of Europe and was a charter member of the Wassenaar Arrangement. In the area of nonproliferation, Ukraine is a full member in the nonproliferation supplier regimes, all of which necessitate a commitment to development of national export controls. Furthermore, increased interaction continues to guarantee Ukraine's international commitments. For example, the US-Ukrainian Binational Commission, or the Gore-Kuchma Commission, was created 19 September 1996. The Commission explores economic, political, and security concerns shared by both governments.[120] Specifically, the Commission addresses nonproliferation and security issues.

Ukraine's decision to renounce nuclear weapons and adhere to export control norms was strongly affected by questions of international credibility.[121] From 1990 to 1992, the Ukrainian government repeatedly pledged to adopt a non-nuclear status. Later on, amidst growing tensions with Russia and the vigorous lobbying of pro-nuclear groups in Ukraine, Ukrainian leaders came under pressure to renege on their earlier commitments. The implications of such a move, however, would have been so grave that Kravchuk and Kuchma were able to fend off the lobbyists' pressure. Despite growing tensions with Russia, the vast majority of Ukrainian officials did not want their country to be branded a "pariah."[122] Even many of the pro-nuclear advocates said that Ukraine should keep its nuclear weapons only on a "temporary basis."[123] President Kravchuk never disavowed the earlier non-nuclear pledges, and Kuchma was determined to uphold them in deeds as well as words. The link between export control, as part of the overall nonproliferation effort, and international community condoned behavior is evident in various policy statements. For example, Anatoly Golubchenko, First Vice Prime Minister of Ukraine, Head of the Governmental Commission on Export Control Policy, noted (emphasis added):

> Ukraine's independence has brought about a number of problems, which need to be solved so that Ukraine can join the *community of civilized nations* as an equal partner. Among these problems is the export of military-related and dual-use goods and technologies. Ukraine has steadfastly declared its devotion to the international nonproliferation objectives, and through practical steps has been contributing to the strengthening of global and regional security. The national system of export control is an integral part of any state, which has obligations regarding the nonproliferation of weapons of mass destruction and their delivery means in order to secure peace and military-political stability in the world. After independence, Ukraine has been able to develop a well-structured, effective export control system, which ensures its national interests, the execution of its international obligations in the area of nonproliferation of weapons of mass destruction, and ensures the strict control over transfers of conventional arms.[124]

These inhibitions on Ukrainian policy suggested that the non-nuclear norm embodied in the NPT (and in the broader nuclear nonproliferation regime) had taken on a life of its own.[125] The stigma attached in recent years to aspiring nuclear states like Iran, Iraq, Libya, and North Korea is indicative of the growing weight of the non-nuclear norm. Had the NPT, for example, never existed, it is doubtful that Ukrainian officials would have felt the need to offer a non-nuclear pledge in the first place.[126] It is also doubtful that, in the absence of the NPT and the nonproliferation regime, Ukrainian leaders would have been so loath to renege on their country's non-nuclear promises and limit the exports of a heavily militarized economy. Realists have tended to downplay or even dismiss the role of norms in shaping state behavior, but the importance of the non-nuclear norm in the Ukrainian case indicates that a reassessment is in order.[127] Ukrainian leaders, even those who were wary of adopting a non-nuclear posture, were cognizant of the benefits they could gain by acting in accordance with the norm of nonproliferation.[128]

The dynamic of "norm legitimation" results from the realization (or creation) of a common interest or common aversion resulting from an intersubjective sense of appropriateness. The operative process in legitimation is the internalization by the actor of an external standard. The sense of legitimacy of a particular norm (e.g., nonproliferation) does not result solely from exogenous considerations, but does so through interaction with others.

> Norm internalization takes place when the actor's sense of its own interests is partly constituted by a force outside itself, that is, by standards, laws, rules, and norms present in the community, existing in the community, existing at the intersubjective level. A rule will become legitimate to a specific individual, and therefore become behaviorally significant, when the individual internalizes its content and reconceives his or her interests according to the rule. The norm affects the actor's own definition of its interests, not just the value of the payoffs of different options. Thus the actor does not perceive a conflict between its interests and obligations.[129]

Evidence exists in Ukraine to suggest that the nonproliferation norm is being "internalized." For example, Ukrainian Security Service chief, General Volodymyr Radchenko, observed: "Ukraine has and will never sell weapons of mass destruction or their technologies to anybody. The idea of selling such things is counter to Ukrainian interests and [her] international obligations. We are a member of the responsible community of states. This idea is ridiculous."[130]

The "Charter on a Distinctive Partnership between the North Atlantic Treaty Organization and Ukraine" was signed 8 July 1997. The agreement parallels the agreement signed between NATO and Russia in May. After the signing ceremony, President Kuchma explained that the most important item in the charter, in his opinion, is NATO's explicit recognition of Ukraine as an European nation. "This is a key issue of the document," he said. The charter wording reads: "Noting NATO's positive role in maintaining peace ... and its openness for cooperation with the new democracies of Central and Eastern Europe, an inseparable part of which is Ukraine." President Kuchma also expounded on what such recognition meant: "As President Jacques Chirac told me," he said, "'We cannot allow anything to happen to Ukraine. We will defend it both by political and economic methods.'"[131] Although not a full NATO member, Ukraine has inched closer to the prospect.[132] However, considerable parliamentary opposition – primarily communist – exists to the agreement or to continued interaction with NATO to the exclusion of Russia.

Specifically in the export control field, training and information exchange seminars on various aspects of export control implementation and development are regularly conducted between the US and Ukraine. For example, the Department of Energy's Lab-to-Lab program, the Department of Commerce's Symposium and export control working level training exchanges, US Customs and State Department training programs have been on-going since 1993. Exchanges of working and high-level Ukrainian export control officials host or visit the US for training, seminars, and symposia. For example, the Department of Defense and Federal Bureau of Investigation have established the DOD/FBI Counterproliferation Program. The Program has three major objectives: a) to assist in the establishment of a professional cadre of law enforcement personnel within participating nations who are trained and equipped to prevent, deter, and investigate crimes related to export control violations; b) to assist participating nations, upon their request, in developing appropriate laws, regulations and enforcement mechanisms in accordance with international standards; and c) to build a solid and long-lasting bureaucratic framework reinforced by political commitment the would enable participating governments to address the proliferation problem.[133] The nongovernmental community has also been actively involved in exchanges and training of Ukrainian officials. For instance the Center for Nonproliferation Studies at the Monterey Institute for International Studies and the Center for International Trade and Security at the University of Georgia have hosted, in both the US and Ukraine, numerous export control seminars and workshops since 1994.[134] The routine and multi-level exchanges between US and Ukrainian government and academic personnel on export control matters expedites the transmission of the nonproliferation export control norm in an environment from which it was previously an unknown, helping to create what many in the government and nongovernment community refer to as a "nonproliferation culture."[135]

In early 1992, the US government established programs of bilateral cooperation in control of exports of proliferation concern with Russia, Ukraine, Belarus, and Kazakhstan. The stated overall objective of this "nonproliferation program of cooperation" is as follows:

> ... to identify a cadre of like-minded individuals in the target countries and to work with them in order to transform the general political will for nonproliferation efforts into new laws, regulations, organizations, and procedures and the competent administrative officers required to build an infrastructure in all functional areas of export control systems.[136]

The US government views the following as an important indicator of the success of its programs:

> To have confidence that the country of concern has the capability and willingness to cooperate, on a multilateral and bilateral basis, in the coordination of export control policy, the investigation of suspect transactions, and the prosecution of export control policy violations.

> This would allow us to classify the country as a close trading partner and to liberalize the flow of trade between our two countries.[137]

It is entirely evident that US export control assistance programs in general, and with Ukraine in particular, were carefully and deliberately designed not only to provide the physical and infrastructural control system prerequisites, but also to instill an intellectual appreciation of export control policy and cooperation. Furthermore, the creation of a "cadre of like-minded individuals" was explicitly linked to a country's ability to trade with the US and wider Western community. According to Wendt:

> Repeated acts of cooperation will tend to have two effects on identities and interests. First, the symbolic interactionist concept of "reflected appraisals" suggests that actors form identities by learning, through interaction, to see themselves as others do. The more significant these others are, as measured by material and/or intersubjective dependency of the self upon them, the faster and deeper this process works. By showing others through cooperative acts that one expects them to be cooperators too, one change the intersubjective knowledge in which identities are defined. Second, by teaching others and themselves to cooperate, actors are simultaneously learning to identify with each other -- to see themselves as a "we" bound by certain norms.[138]

Clearly, even at this early stage in Ukraine's political development, we can associate export control development with the formation of a liberal identity.[139] Increased interaction with the West and a growing sense of community with Europe and the US are evident in Ukrainian foreign policy. For example, in addition to financial assistance, President Kuchma and the export control community are directly influenced, by Western involvement in the export control field. Nonproliferation regime membership and export control assistance have both directly and indirectly influenced Ukraine's sense of interest and identity as the state building process continues.[140] Export controls, well-developed in the Western states, are part and parcel of the structure of liberal states. However, the political, regional, and cultural differences in Ukraine combined with the lack of a coherent and uniform sense of political or national selfhood, suggest that Ukraine has yet to establish a universal foundation upon which to construct the overall political trajectory of its independence.[141] Despite peaceful transfers of power, universal suffrage, and a new, liberal-minded constitution, the emerging liberal order is, by and large, confined to sections of the government and to certain regions.[142]

The national government is still a mixture of Soviet-era and democratizing institutions and norms. Democracy and the rule of law are not universally practiced.[143] The emerging sense of community with the West is beginning, generally speaking, reach beyond the elite level. In this respect, export controls may merely represent an attempt to conform to expectations thereby assuring continued material and financial assistance. Furthermore, Ukraine has indicated its willingness to trade in sensitive items with illiberal states. For example, the 1996 sale of 320 T-80 tanks to Pakistan suggests that Ukraine may be adopting a more pragmatic approach to export controls in practice.[144] Multi-million dollar technology and trade agreements have been signed between Ukraine and Iran. Ukraine's largest non-CIS trading partner is China. In 1995, trade to China netted over $830 million. One economist notes: "A vast market exists in China for Ukraine's select scientific and technology exports."[145] Additionally, during Wassenaar negotiations, Ukraine hesitated to yield to the US request to take an obligation proscribing armaments and dual-use exports to Iran, Iraq, Libya and North Korea. Disputes centered primarily on exports to Iran. However, US-Ukrainian negotiations resulted in compromise, the terms of which both countries agreed not to make public.[146]

Ukraine's present membership in the nonproliferation regime and other security communities and its proposed, albeit distant, intention to join the European Union (EU) will most likely further integrate the emerging political identity with that of Western, liberal states. The recent 1999 reelection of President Kuchma suggests the further development of a political culture more receptive to Western-style governance. Further political, economic and security contacts ensure a long-term influence on the shape and scope of Ukrainian domestic and international policies generally, and export control policies specifically.

5.4 Rational Institutionalism: The Success of Incentives

Of the approaches examined in this study thus far, the Rational Institutional approach most reasonably explains the continued development of export controls in Ukraine. According to Rational Institutional expectations, a state will develop a nonproliferation export control system if it values future interactions with nonproliferation regime member states, is interested in engendering reciprocity and reducing transaction costs and uncertainty, receives side-payments, and otherwise calculates the associated costs and benefits.

Ukraine, with advanced missile/space and nuclear industries, believes its economic salvation lies in Western markets and through increased foreign direct investment.[147] Ukrainian political leaders recognize the link between international nonproliferation norms compliance and access to Western technology and markets.[148] For example, in August 1996, the US removed Ukraine from the International Traffic in Arms Regulations (ITAR) list. This means that US policy no longer prevents the issuance of licenses for the sale or purchase of military equipment or services to and from Ukraine.[149] The change in policy is contingent upon assurances that an adequate export control system is in place. Furthermore, nonproliferation regime membership (e.g., Nuclear Suppliers Group) and/or adherence (Australia Group) suggests that Ukraine realizes the long-term economic benefits accruing to compliance with the international nonproliferation regime.[150] Furthermore, Ukraine also realizes that high technology trade to and from Western states is contingent upon regime membership and full compliance. For example, after formally acceding to the MTCR, several Ukrainian firms and the FSU's largest nuclear missile producer, Yuzmash, have formed a consortium to promote Ukrainian space technologies to Western markets. Eduard Kuznetsov, deputy head of Ukraine's National Space Agency, remarked that "There is an urgent need to form a powerful structure which could become an important player on the world space market. Our already existing structures have demonstrated their inefficiency amid the current severe financial crisis. Such activities would not have been possible in the recent past [because of difficulties in entering the MTCR]."[151]

The Rational Institutional approach contends that states will have more developed export control systems when they perceive that transaction costs and uncertainty in their future interactions with others are reduced by joining or adhering to the international nonproliferation regime. Having joined or adhered to the supplier regimes, Ukraine cooperates on a regular basis with other states, thereby stabilizing and giving structure to subsequent interactions in an increasingly expanded array of issue areas.[152] Gradually, a wider representation of Ukrainian policy makers has been included in export control technical and working exchanges on a bilateral and multilateral basis, thus insuring broader support and understanding of export control norms and initiatives amongst state officials. As most Ukrainian government officials are unfamiliar with export control norms – as all export control issues were formerly handled in Moscow – nonproliferation regime norms and rules are conveyed via routine interactions between a widening representation of Ukrainian government officials and regime members. In this capacity, for example, stereotypes about the supplier "cartels" are disabused and, consequently, uncertainty between states reduced.[153] Nevertheless, it remains to be seen how effectively regime norms will constrain future export behavior, as *pro forma* adherence does not guarantee compliance.[154]

All things being equal, the costs of non-compliance with its international export control commitments would be considerable. Because Ukrainian economic reformation depends upon access to Western markets and aid disbursements, uncooperative behavior could jeopardize long-term economic and political objectives. For example, allegations were made against Kyiv involving Ukrainian arms and missile transfers and technology exports to Libya.[155] According to a 2 October 1996 CIA report, two Ukrainian "entities" concluded separate agreements, estimated to be worth $510 million, with the regime of Libyan leader Moammar Gadhafi. Congressional restrictions require a halt on US aid to Ukraine if that nation is found to be trading military goods to Libya. The allegations, if proven, could have affected $225 million earmarked for Ukraine in FY1997 and up to $900 million already appropriated. An initial payment of $3 million was allegedly made to "Ukrainian officials" in July 1996 for what the CIA report said were SS-21 or Scud B missiles that will be dismantled before delivery to Libya.[156] When completed, the transfer will be worth $500 million, the report said. A second deal, concluded in May 1996 between another Ukrainian firm and Libya, called for Ukraine to provide maintenance services and spare parts for Libya's four Soviet-era Foxtrot submarines and other surface ships. The service agreement grew out of a visit to Tripoli in May 1996 by a group of Ukrainians, an estimated $10 million if completed. A third agreement outlined in the report involves Iran's purchase in August of a large shipment of unspecified Ukrainian weapons "with the intention of transferring them to Libya."[157]

The military sales would violate UN sanctions imposed on Libya for its failure to turn over two Libyan agents wanted in the 1988 bombing of Pan Am Flight 103 over Lockerbie, Scotland. If the missiles are Scud-Bs, the transfer would violate the MTCR, which bans exports of missiles with ranges greater than 300 miles. The SS-21s would be illegal under the MTCR even if not fitted with chemical or biological warheads, government experts noted. Defense Department officials said Libya is believed to have the capability to produce chemical warheads.[158]

In response, the administration (specifically, the National Security and Defense Council) established a Parliamentary Commission to investigate charges of a strategic partnership between Tripoli and Kyiv. Secretary of the National Security and Defense Council, Volodymyr Horbulin, said the Ukrainian investigation confirmed that the charges were groundless. Nevertheless, in a meeting with US State Department director for CIS affairs, James Collins, Horbulin confided that he "hoped the affair would not affect the US Congress in dispensing aid to Ukraine."[159] The US Senate passed the foreign aid bill on 17 July 1997. The Senate's version of the bill maintained a $225 million earmark for Ukraine, for Fiscal Year 1998. Included were several subearmarks for specific programs needed in Ukraine: Chernobyl-related safety assistance, commercial law and legal reform, democratic initiatives, and law enforcement procedures. As he introduced the bill on the Senate floor on 16 July 1997, Foreign Operations Subcommittee Chairman Mitch McConnell (R-Ky.) stated: "We must use foreign aid to promote American values as well as American interests."[160] However, the bill contained language that "held" half of the earmarked funds until the Secretary of State certified that economic and political progress would continue in Ukraine (including continued nonproliferation cooperation), corruption was being dealt with appropriately, and American investor-business problems were being resolved.[161]

Ukraine has received broad side-payments, both for export control development specifically and in the form of general material and financial assistance.[162] Thus, Ukraine recognizes lesser costs in conforming to nonproliferation norms for its attendant benefits (e.g., access to Western markets and technologies).[163] The amounts and types of side-payments, both assisting specific export control efforts and general assistance rendered under the auspices of Ukrainian compliance (e.g., US Freedom for Russia and the Emerging Eurasian Democracies and Open Markets (FREEDOM) Support Act), correlate strongly to Ukraine's relatively advanced export control development among the NIS. Furthermore, Ukraine has received export control system material assistance in the form of computer hardware and software, enforcement and licensing training, and numerous US, EU and internationally sponsored nonproliferation export control workshops and seminars.[164] Thus, Western material and financial assistance offsets many of the costs associated with the erection and maintenance of the export control system.[165]

5.4.1 Overview of US Governmental Assistance: General and Export Control-Related

While other states have contributed general financial and material assistance to Ukraine, none have contributed the equal to that of the United States.[166] Since independence, Ukraine has figured prominently in US foreign assistance programs. For example, in FY 1998, the US government (USG) provided $372.3 million – the second largest amount of per country foreign assistance, behind Israel – worth of assistance to Ukraine, consisting of $225 million in FREEDOM Support Act funds, over $107 million in other USG general funds, and $39.25 million in Defense Department excess and privately donated humanitarian commodities.[167] United States Agency for International Development (USAID) assistance totaled $119 million in 1998, of which technical assistance represented 67 percent, and partnership activities 32 percent, and humanitarian assistance almost 1 percent (approximately $1 million). Under US laws, assistance is made contingent upon the certification of the Secretary of State that "significant progress" has been made on select political and economic reforms.[168]

The US economic assistance program for Ukraine, administered by the US Agency for International Development (AID), in 1995 became the third largest American aid program in the world. Funds granted through the Nunn-Lugar Program, targeted to assist Ukrainian nuclear disarmament efforts, are also supporting efforts to build an export control system and protect proliferation. In 1996, some $1.2 billion was pledged to support Ukraine's efforts with nuclear disarmament and economic transformation.

The United States has also played a pivotal role in supporting Ukrainian efforts with international organizations and international financial institutions. The US has provided technical assistance for Ukrainian efforts to accede to the World Trade Organization (WTO), which has been instrumental in helping Ukraine meet the conditionality placed on IMF and World Bank lending. In the commercial arena, the US has been working to establish a proper legal-commercial framework in which US companies can operate. The May 1993 US-Ukrainian Trade Agreement extended MFN status to Ukraine and provided a legal starting point for a number of subsequent agreements, such as the Bilateral Investment Treaty (BIT) and the Treaty to Avoid Dual Taxation. The Joint Commission on Trade and Investment (JCTI), a US-Ukrainian consultative group, was formed in March 1994 to promote bilateral investment and to confer on a range of issues affecting trade and investment in the US and Ukraine. Former US Secretary of Commerce Ronald Brown and Ukrainian Minister for Foreign Economic Relations and Trade Serhiy Osyka chaired the first meeting of the JCTI in November 1994, both stressing the need for US investment to support Ukrainian reform efforts. In Spring 1995, a joint Business Facilitation Working Group was established to address specific company problems faced in both countries.[169] The appointment of US and Ukrainian "ombudsmen" to troubleshoot issues of bilateral trade and investment was another example of joint governmental efforts to expand commercial ties. In 1996, the JCTI was superseded by the Committee on

Trade and Investment (CTI), under the auspices of the Gore-Kuchma Binational Commission.[170]

USG assistance priorities for Ukraine included enterprise development, deregulation, macro-economic reform, and community-based programs. Security assistance programs concentrated on the elimination of strategic nuclear arms, on military conversion, export controls, and on strengthening Ukraine's capability to operate jointly with NATO forces.[171] Assistance for export control development is part of an overall nonproliferation facilitation policy: the Cooperative Threat Reduction program (CTR).

In 1991, Congress directed the Department of Defense to help secure former Soviet weapons of mass destruction. Since 1991, Congress has provided $2.3 billion to support CTR efforts. Based on this congressional direction, CTR's mission is to provide assistance to eligible states of the former Soviet Union (FSU) in order to dismantle WMD and to reduce the threat of proliferation. The stated mission supports core US national security priorities.[172] In his May 1997 *National Security Strategy for a New Century*, President Clinton stressed that protecting the security of American citizens, territory, and way of life is the nation's "number one priority." Toward this end, the US security strategy identifies combating the spread and use of WMD, promoting arms control, and securing regional stability in the FSU as essential tasks. CTR is seen to play a critical role in accomplishing each task.

As originally designed, the CTR Program provided the Department of Defense (DOD) with the authority to fund assistance to the Soviet Union (and subsequently, to eligible post-Soviet states) to dismantle and destroy WMD; to strengthen the security of nuclear weapons and fissile materials in connection with dismantlement; to prevent proliferation; and to help demilitarize the industrial and scientific infrastructure that supported WMD in the successor states. Specific program objectives, as established by Congress, were to cooperate with NIS republics on a wide variety of arms control, nonproliferation and demilitarization programs.[173] Summarizing the purpose of the Program he co-sponsored with Senator Richard Lugar, Senator Sam Nunn observed in 1992: "I know of no more urgent national security challenge confronting our nation. Nor do I know of any greater opportunity to reduce the dangers confronting us."[174]

The CTR "mission" also supports other related US foreign policy goals. CTR plays an important role in the USG's policy of engagement with the FSU.[175] In conjunction with the Gore-Chernomyrdin Commission and Gore-Kuchma Commission and other bilateral initiatives, CTR was designed to advance joint US, Russian and Ukrainian security objectives, development of a free market economy in the FSU, as well as stability and democracy throughout the FSU.

Of the four nuclear successor states to the USSR – Russia, Belarus, Kazakhstan, and Ukraine – Ukraine has received the largest amount of export control assistance, both in financial and intellectual (e.g., exchanges and training seminars) terms. Approximately, $13.26 million has been devoted to export control development (see Table 5.1).

Table 5.1 CTR Funding: Ukraine Congressional Notifications and Corresponding Obligations

Data Current as of 31 January 1999 (Figures are rounded to the nearest thousand)

UKRAINE		
PROJECT TITLE	Notification (in US dollars)	Obligation (in US dollars)
Strategic Nuclear Arms Elimination SS-19 Liquid Propellant Disposition SS-19 Neutralization and Dismantlement Facility SS-19 Integrating Contract SS-19 Housing SS-24 Early Deactivation (FAST AID) SS-24 Silo Launcher and Missile Elimination Heavy Bomber & ALCM Elimination Non-Deployed ICBM & ALCM Elimination	366,400,000	327,083,000
Weapons of Mass Destruction Infrastructure Elimination	23,400,000	8,051,000
Material Control & Accounting	22,500,000	22,216,000
Science and Technology Center[176]	15,000,000	15,000,000
Export Control	**13,890,000**	**13,254,000**
Multilateral Nuclear Safety Initiative	11,000,000	11,000,000
Defense and Military Contacts	7,500,000	5,192,000
Emergency Response Training/Equipment	3,400,000	3,110,000
Government-to Government Communications Link	2,222,000	2,004,000
Defense Conversion[177]	55,730,000	54,918,000
TOTAL	521,042,000	461,828,000

This $13.26 million project assists in the building of export control institutions and infrastructure.[178] Assistance in Export Control has two objectives. The first objective is to assist Ukraine in developing and implementing an export control system which conforms to the Common Standard Level of Effective Protection, the former COCOM standard. The second is to assist Ukraine in achieving adherence to the multilateral regimes, such as Missile Technology Control Regime, which control transfer of weapons of mass destruction, related technologies, and other sensitive goods and technologies.

Export control assistance is divided into four interrelated, mutually reinforcing areas with an emphasis on procurement of networked automation equipment for administration and enforcement. Policy consultations between high-level US and Ukrainian officials help to develop and further the Ukrainian government's political will to engage in export controls and other nonproliferation initiatives. Technical interaction in seminars and conferences introduces Ukrainian officials directly involved in development and implementation to the international export control community. Training and technical assistance aids in developing and implementing a system based upon law, rather than decree, administered by well trained personnel. Equipment for networking the administration of export licenses and customs enforcement is provided to ensure that Ukraine has an effective and upgradeable tracking system.

The Defense Special Weapons Agency (DSWA) has been designated to assist the Assistant to the Secretary of Defense for Nuclear and Chemical and Biological Defense Programs for execution of duties under the CTR Program. The Department of State Office of Political-Military Affairs Export Controls, has been designated the policy lead in implementing export control assistance under CTR. The Department of Commerce, Bureau of Export Administration, assists in technical interaction and training efforts in establishing legislation, business outreach, and enforcement. The US Customs Service, International Affairs Bureau, assists Ukraine in enforcement and interdiction training and equipment assessments. The Department of Energy, Nuclear Proliferation Division, assists in training on nuclear materials detection, nonproliferation, and control lists. Equipment procurements are made by the selection of private business and through the General Services Administration (see Table 5.2).

Table 5.2 US Interagency Export Control Coordination Group

Agency	Legal Foundation & Regulatory Development	Control Lists & Licensing Procedures	Enforcement	Industry-Government Relations	Automation & System Management
DOC	X	X	X	X	X
Customs	X		X		X
DOD	X	X			X
DOE		X		X	X
Justice			X		
DOS	X	X			

Material and infrastructural procurements have been under way since 1993. The first material delivery, copying machines, arrived in Ukraine in June 1994. Contracts were awarded for the US Customs laboratory equipment and licensing and enforcement automation local-area-network procurements. The Customs lab equipment was delivered in October 1995. The local area network for the then Expert and Technical Committee and the automation and enforcement equipment for the Customs Committee were delivered in April 1996. Contracts award for the two x-ray vans occurred in September 1995. Vans were delivered in July 1996. An interagency technical working group met in Kyiv in October 1995 to discuss how the additional $6 million would be applied to this program. As a result of this meeting, procurements have been initiated for additional x-ray vans, baggage x-ray machines, and contraband detectors.[179] A contract was awarded for the contraband detectors and baggage x-ray machines in July 1996. The contraband detectors and seven baggage x-ray machines were delivered in January 1997. Six more baggage x-ray machines will be delivered in February 1997. A contract has been awarded for the x-ray vans with expected delivery in August 1997. The US Interagency working group has funded a proposal to use DSWA money for the automation of Ukrainian border posts, linking 125 posts with the Customs Data Center in Kyiv.

A Ukrainian delegation traveled to Washington, DC in February 1996 to further discuss the finalization of the project plan and the disposition of the remaining $6 million "plus-up."[180] Agreement in principle was reached on a series of working level technical exchanges to occur throughout 1996. A US interagency technical team traveled to Kyiv in May 1996 to discuss equipment requirements and perform a site assessment at the SSEC's new office facilities. During the May visit, the US and SSEC agreed on the following: the financial status of the CTR Program and the Ukrainian Automated System of Export Control (ASEC);[181] the office automation equipment and operating software were found to be properly stored and secured; the existing SSEC building was entirely unsuitable for the installation of $2 million of automation equipment, and as a result the US has funded a 150 square meter addition to the SSEC[182] building and performed repairs to the existing SSEC building (roof, waterproofing, electrical wiring, communications cabling, and other minor improvements); the Departments of Commerce and Energy technical exchange schedule was updated; and, the scope of the US support through December 1999 was also defined.

The following projects were completed by the end of FY 1996: the delivery of the remaining equipment for the Ukraine Customs Committee; monitoring the renovation and addition to the SSEC building, installed and provided support for all equipment provided under this assistance project; ordered spare parts and additional equipment with remaining funding; and turned the project completely over to the Department of State.

The Bureau of Nonproliferation of the Department of State was charged with administering the new funding mechanism: the NDF. The Nonproliferation and Disarmament Fund (NDF) was established pursuant to section 504 of the FREEDOM Support Act and established a broader mandate for CTR activities. Recently, US nonproliferation assistance efforts have been subsumed into a universal program: the Nonproliferation, Antiterrorism, Demining and Related (NADR) Program. NADR is a new account construction which combines of several previously separate sub-accounts into a single account. Congress appropriated items within a NADR account in FY 1997 and FY 1998. The grouped programs are: Nonproliferation and Disarmament Fund, Export Control Assistance (CTR),[183] Science Centers, IAEA Voluntary Contribution, CTBT Preparatory Commission Korean Peninsula Energy Development Organization (KEDO), Antiterrorism Assistance, Israel Emergency CT Assistance, and Demining. Export control assistance Ukraine continues under NADR.[184]

Plainly, the amounts and types of nonproliferation, in general, and export control assistance specifically has been considerable. Physically, the Ukrainian export control system is clearly a US-sponsored product. Assessing the intellectual aspect of export control assistance, its impact, is demonstrably more difficult. Nevertheless, the empirical record suggests a strong correlation between financial and nonmaterial assistance and

Ukrainian compliance and cooperation on nonproliferation. There is some evidence to suggest that international nonproliferation norms have constrained Ukrainian export control behavior. For example, under direct US pressure, Ukraine reneged on its plans to assist the Russian reactor project in Bushehr, Iran.[185]

The Ukrainian state-owned "Turboatom," working as subcontractor for the Russian Ministry of Atomic Energy (MINATOM), was to provide generator turbines. Believing the reactor to be part of the Iranian nuclear weapons program, officials in Washington said that such an arrangement would preclude the possibility of US-Ukrainian nuclear cooperation on commercial nuclear technology, and would threaten the increasingly warm US-Ukrainian relationship. Pressure from Israel and Germany also influenced Kyiv's decision not to participate in the Bushehr project.[186] Nevertheless, some US government officials contend that Ukraine regularly ignores international norms with its exports.[187]

Given the acute economic crisis currently plaguing Ukraine, we would expect any obstacle to selling readily marketable goods and technologies would be summarily removed. Regarding the development of export controls, such is not the case in Ukraine. Through regime membership, foreign financial and material export control assistance and training, enhanced access to much needed previously restricted technologies, and increased interactions with Western security and economic organizations, Ukraine has developed a capable export control system. Therefore, the Rational Institutional approach indicates that Ukrainian officials in fact derive greater benefits by conforming to international nonproliferation norms and rules than they would by ignoring them. Although Ukraine may not share the exact battery of security concerns as the West (e.g., "rogue"[188] states such as Iran), export controls are viewed by many in Kyiv as a means for insuring continued security and economic interaction.[189]

The Ukrainian government officials responsible for implementing and developing the export control system are also those attempting to reform the economy and government. The political and economic reform effort is avowedly modeled and dependent on the West.[190] As such, nonproliferation norms and rules violations would jeopardize this relationship.[191] Therefore, compliance with international standards is crucial to the Ukrainian economic stabilization and government reform effort. For example, the recent debate over Ukrainian MTCR membership illustrates the complexities involved in determining a state's weighing of the respective costs and benefits inherent in balancing international cooperation with the requisites of national interest. The MTCR case reveals how the cost-benefit process operates in Ukraine.

Being a critical and integral part of the former Soviet missile, space and satellite industry, Ukraine is rich in material, manufacturing and technological expertise. Furthermore, Ukraine is having limited success in its arms sales abroad.[192] As such, Ukraine hopes to compete in the global space launch market. However, owing to stringent – some would argue discriminatory – membership requirements enacted by the United States, Ukraine had, until recently, balked at full MTCR membership.[193]

In a memorandum of understanding (MOU) dated 13 May 1994, Ukraine agreed to conduct its missile-related exports according to MTCR criteria and standards. Under the MOU terms, Ukraine was to develop a control list in compliance with MTCR requirements. To this end, the Cabinet of Ministers approved the "Regulation Guiding the Control Over Export, Import, and Transit of Missile Technology Items, As Well As of Equipment, Materials and Technology used in the Manufacture of Missile Weapons" on 27 July 1995.

At that time, the prospects of Ukraine's full-membership in the regime were still unclear due to US criteria. Nevertheless, Ukraine has enacted a control list in complete compliance with MTCR standards. Additionally, Ukraine has professed not to have engaged in illicit missile trade with proliferant countries.[194] Lucrative trade with the West via a highly capable indigenous space industry necessitates full export control compliance.[195] Despite the strict criteria applied to MTCR membership, seen by many in Ukraine as economic discrimination, Ukraine and the US signed, during a state visit by President Kuchma, a Commercial Space Launch Agreement in February 1996. This agreement, operating on the assumption that Ukrainian export controls are in full compliance with international nonproliferation norms, allows Ukrainian access to the potentially lucrative US space and satellite market.

Control of missile-related exports is of particular concern to the President and his administration, as President Kuchma was the former director of the Yuzhnoye aerospace complex in Dnipropetrovsk.[196] The Kuchma administration has been indispensable in brokering aerospace business deals with foreign firms and governments. For example, the Sea Launch project – an international joint-venture between Boeing Commercial Space Company (US), Energia (Russia), Kvaerner Maritime (Norway), and Yuzhnoye (Ukraine) – formed to launch commercial satellites, represents the type of space activities in which Ukraine can prosper. The World Bank recently approved two partial risk guarantees of $100 million each in support of commercial bank loans to Sea Launch. The

Sea Launch Project will foster substantial economic benefits for Russia and Ukraine by generating close to an estimated $2 billion of incremental exports for Russia and Ukraine over the life of the project, thereby helping to maintain 20,000-30,000 high-wage, high-skilled jobs in Energia (Russia), Yuzhnoye, and their subcontractors throughout Russia and Ukraine. Other benefits for Ukraine include: enhancing the development of a high-tech sector in which Yuzhnoye has a clear comparative advantage; introducing local, high-tech firms to the international market place; teaching local firms how to structure international joint-ventures by exposing them to international business and financial practices; promoting cooperative ventures between Ukrainian and other international firms; and promoting additional guarantee operations for other high priority investment projects in Ukraine.[197] All manufacturing agreements and launches will be licensed, regulated and monitored by the US government.

The MTCR issue illustrates Ukrainian awareness of the rewards accruing to compliant behavior – most recently evidenced in Kyiv's response to the Libyan affair and regime cooperation in deciding not to supply key parts to the Russian Bushehr project. Thus, the powerful Dnipropetrovsk political clique, manning much of the government and presidential administration, is certain to continue pursuing commercial space projects as a means by which of revitalizing the reforming economy, thereby necessitating an export control system cognate with those in the West. As understood through the Rational Institutional approach, Ukrainian export control behavior makes clear why export control developments continue: cost and uncertainty reduction through cooperation with the nonproliferation regimes, on-going engagement with Western security and economic organizations, recognition that the benefits accruing to export control development outweighs the costs of developing such a system, and receipt of material incentives. These developments, moreover, are the result of a pro-active president and government – the primary political source enacting export control development in Ukraine.

Conclusion

When considering the economic and political difficulties confronting a state in the midst of creating itself anew, the developments of and consistent international cooperation on Ukrainian export control policy are all the more remarkable. Since 1992, Ukraine has joined or adheres to the all treaties in the international nonproliferation regime and has shown marked progress in developing the elements of an internationally compatible export control system. The theoretical examination accounting for these developments reveals interesting details about the Ukrainian case.

Table 5.3 summarizes the results of the Ukrainian case study. We see that, apart from Rational Institutionalism, no one particular theory dominates. Instead, the results indicate a compounding effect, wherein expectations of some approaches tend to buttress the others. For example, we see that the primary political actors in Ukraine, the elites, are leading the developments in export control. As such, they are realizing the benefits of steady interaction with the West (i.e., the "liberal community") through market access and direct financial material inducements. The evidence suggests that the liberalizing elites, primarily President Kuchma and his administration, have managed through constitutional and indirect political means to be the primary actors in governmental decision making regarding export control policy. However, the Kuchma administration is acting in, by and large, contradistinction to the political and economic preferences of the legislature, which is dominated by leftists steadfastly opposed to market economic and political reforms. Despite executive-legislative antagonism, export control policy has not been a subject of parliamentary concern. This situation is due to the government's ability to isolate export control policy from the full political process.

Table 5.3 Explanations of Export Control Development: Ukraine Theory and Evidence

	Positive	Negative	Mixed
Realism			
• External security threats		-	
• Balance power of others		-	
• Prevent gain of others		-	
• Controls as security enhancement		-	
Domestic Politics			
• Interest group pressures		-	
• Elite perceptions of national interest	+		
• Centralized state/society relations		-	
• Export control agencies influential			+/-
Liberal Identity			
• *Sense of community with liberal states*	+		
• *Interaction with liberal community*	+		
• Liberal, democratic government			+/-
• Target illiberal states			+/-
Rational Institutionalism			
• Explicit cost/benefit analysis	+		
• Regimes rules/norms constrain behavior	+		
• Reduce transaction costs/uncertainty	+		
• Material side-payments	+		

Foreign assistance is, in most instances, linked to issue areas of concern to donor countries and organizations. In this respect, export control developments are the direct and indisputable result of international financial and material assistance. Furthermore, we see that US assistance, both general and export control-specific, was crucial to the creation and further development of the Ukrainian system, establishing a "positive-reinforcement"[198] dynamic: export control development and cooperation made contingent upon and reinforced through inducements and incentives.[199] The continuance of aid is often made contingent upon compliance and further cooperation. For example, the prompt Ukrainian response on the Libya scandal, the decision not to supply power turbines to the Iranian Bushehr reactor, and Kuchma's recent avowal – prompted to do so in working sessions of the Gore-Kuchma Commission – to decommission its stock of SS-24 missiles are all policy moves that suggests Kyiv is weighing its options in such a way commensurate with US foreign policy objectives. For example, outlining the position of President Kuchma on the decision to forgo the Iran nuclear reactor deal, Presidential Press Secretary, Oleksander Mdidannyk said: "The position of the President is simple. Those political benefits that will occur because Ukraine declined the deal will be much more than the real money from selling the turbines."[200]

President Kuchma's strong relationship with the West (primarily the United States) has ensured continued financial and material support despite the poor record on economic reform. Since independence, consistent interaction with the US and other western governments, NGOs, and international financial and security organizations has fostered a recognizably liberal cadre of policy makers in the Kuchma government.[201] In terms of export control interaction and the ability to link material side-payments to a course of cooperative behavior, US export control assistance has provided both the material and intellectual substance of the Ukrainian export control system. US assistance and exchanges were successful largely because Ukrainian policy makers came to form their interests in light of and relation to bilateral cooperation. It is precisely through these processes of interaction that identities and interests are formed:

> The mechanism here is reinforcements; interactions reward actors for holding certain ideas about each other and discourages them from holding others. If repeated long enough, these "reciprocal typifications" will create relatively stable concepts of self and other regarding the issue at stake in the interaction. It is through reciprocal interaction, in other words, that we create and instantiate the relatively enduring social structures in terms of which define our *identities* and *interests*.[202]

The process, albeit very subtle, of interest and identity formation is born out of and through interaction in which continued aid is made contingent upon conditioned compliance and further cooperation. In other words, following Wendt, the "reciprocal typifications" in export control cooperation "will create relatively stable concepts of self and other regarding the issue at stake in the interaction." This dynamic is graphically depicted in Table 5.4.

Table 5.4 Two-Level Interaction and Policy Formulation[203]

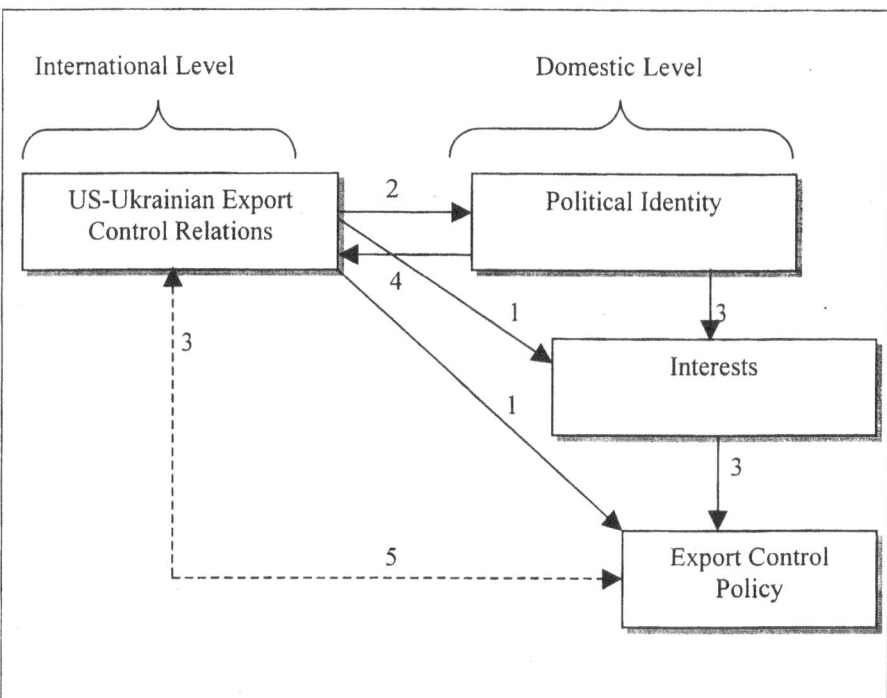

The chart outlines the process of incentive/norm interaction, appraisal of interest (which assumes that identity is also part of the interaction process and not an *a priori* given), and resultant policy:

1) Effects of Norms & Incentives (I) US incentives/norms influence interests and policy.
2) Effects of Norms & Incentives (II) US incentives/norms influence identity.
3) Effects of Identity (I) variation in state identity affect preferences of states and resultant policies.
4) Effects of Identity (II) configurations of state identity affect interstate relations.
5) Recursivity: state policies both reproduce and reconstruct institutional (and cultural) structures over time.[204]

As the evidence suggests, Ukraine's interests in cooperating on export control issues developed in reaction with and to US incentives.[205] Further, the Kuchma administration came to construe its position in Ukraine and the world as a state whose interests are served by adopting nonproliferation norms,[206] realized through such policies as nuclear weapons divestiture and export control development.[207] Why Ukraine was so receptive to US suggestion is cogently expressed by Chafetz, *et al*.:

> Consistent with identity theory, change [of identity] was relatively easy for Ukraine compared to other more established states because it was still searching for an [political] identity rather than defending long-cherished roles and sense of political self.[208]

In other words, states sharing a "transnational identity" act in the context of organized patterns by recognizing each other as occupants of certain roles. Actors tend to adhere to their roles when a positive relationship to its reference others depends on its being a particular type of actor. Under these circumstances its ability to maintain a positive transnational identity, as well as its "membership" in the transnational social group, is tied to willingness to act in a certain manner. Roles proscribe a *range* of behaviors that are consistent with a particular identity Thus, there is often conflict and/or disagreement as to what a particular identity entails, for example, what it means to "act like a great power" or "act like a European." However there are limits to how far a state can deviate from accepted group norms and still be considered part of the group. For example, democratic states are expected to conduct their foreign relations according to the "rule of law," at least in their dealings with each other, and the community of democratic states often pressures its members to do so.[209] So, as US pressure, coupled with and made contingent upon further assistance, on Ukraine to cooperate on and develop export control policies increased over time, changes in the perception of its role – and therefore interest – conception conformed increasingly to a tendency toward nonproliferation.

Nonproliferation and export control relations with Ukraine, like Russia, have occupied prominent positions in the foreign policy agendas of both the Bush and Clinton Administrations. Moreover, while in many cases problematizing US-Russian relations, the nonproliferation emphasis of US-Ukrainian relations is one of the primary areas of constant and increasing interaction and mutual cooperation. In brief, Ukraine is developing an export control system because of US financial and material assistance. Also, and in relation to the incentives represented in this assistance, the effects of routine interaction – what Buzan (1993) refers to as "dynamic density" – with the US and other Western states on export control matters have influenced Ukraine's sense of identity *and*, therefore, interests. In other words, regular "interactions reward actors for holding certain ideas about each other and discourages them from holding others" (Wendt 1987: 405). Thus, Ukraine developed an export control system because the United States, primarily, financed its construction while linking continued export control cooperation to further overall US assistance. Furthermore, US incentives deeply influenced the preference structure of the Kuchma administration in such a way that Ukraine wedded its understanding of its interests with further cooperation.

Clearly, in the case of Ukraine, there is a mutually reinforcing link between incentives and behavioral outcome. This link warrants further examination. In the following chapter, this connection will be examined in light of the Bushehr nuclear reactor deal, thereby illustrating in detail this dynamic of incentive and behavior.

Notes

[1] See, John Mroz and Oleksandr Pavliuk, "Ukraine: Europe's Linchpin," *Foreign Affairs*, vol. 75, no. 3, pp. 52-63, May/June 1996; and A. Karatnycky, "The Ukraine Factor," *Foreign Affairs*, 71/3 (Summer 1992), pp. 90-107.

[2] A. Karatnycky, "Ukraine at the Crossroads," *Journal of Democracy*, 6/1 (January 1995), pp. 117-30; and "Between East and West: Ukraine," *The Economist*, 28 September 1996, vol. 340, no. 7985, pp. 58-59.

[3] It should be noted, however, that Russian-Ukrainian relations are complicated by a substantial ethnic Russian presence in the southern and eastern regions. The western region, Galicia, traditionally nationalist and ultimately distrustful of Moscow, tends to see Russian regional activities as a threat to Ukrainian sovereignty. See, John Morrison, "Pereiaslav and After: the Russian-Ukrainian Relationship," *International Affairs*, vol. 64, no. 9, October 1993, pp. 677-704. See also, Julian Birch, "Ukraine - A Nation-State or a State of Nations?" *Journal of Ukrainian Studies*, 21/1-2 (Summer-Winter 1996), pp. 109-124; and Chrystyna Lapychak, "Ukraine's Troubled Rebirth," *Current History*, 92/576 (October 1993), pp. 337-341.

[4] Ukraine has generally good relations with its neighbors, as evidenced in the number of bilateral political and economic accords enacted between such states as Poland, Romania, Iran, Iraq, Turkey, and the Czech Republic. A scholar of Ukrainian security issues notes: "On the whole, external military threats from neighboring nations other than Russia are a distant security priority." N.S. Krawciw, "Ukrainian Security and Military Doctrine," in Bruce Parrott, ed., *State Building and Military Power in Russia and the New States of Eurasia* (New York: M.E. Sharp, 1995), p. 138. See also, Leonid Kistersky "General Theory of Ukrainian Security," in Leonid Kistersky, ed., *Security in Eastern Europe: The Case of Ukraine* (Providence: Brown University Press, 1994), pp. 7-17.

[5] Ustina Markus, "Ukrainian Parliament Confirms Security Concept," *OMRI Daily Digest*, 25 May 1996.

[6] The degree of economic interdependence became abundantly clear during the August 1998 collapse of the Russian economy. See, Paul Goble, "Ukraine Feels Russian Aftershocks," *RFE/RL Weekday*, 29 October 1998; and Erik Whitlock, "Ukrainian-Russian Trade: the Economics of Dependency," *RFE/RL Research Report*, vol. 2, no. 43, pp. 38-42, 29 October 1999.

[7] On 9 July 1993, the Russian Duma passed a resolution claiming that Sevastopol was a Russian city. Coupled with the Duma's attempt to pass legislation negating the dissolution of the Soviet Union, tensions between Moscow and Kyiv have been chronic; see, "Kommjunike o Vstrece Prezidentov Rossii i Ukrainy," *Rossijskaja Gazeta*, 18 July 1995. However, the long-awaited *Basic Treaty on Friendship and Cooperation* between Russian and Ukraine, in which Ukrainian territorial integrity is observed, has been signed, as has a formal and final agreement on the division of the Black Sea Fleet.

[8] "Russia's Bid to Stop Ukraine Arms to Pakistan," *The Hindu*, 3 December 1996. Increasing competition between Russian and Ukrainian arms manufacturers in the Middle Eastern and South Asian markets have served to exacerbate relations between the two. See also, Paul Goble, "Arms Races and Cash Flows: Russian-Ukrainian Arms Competition Increases," *RFE/RL Research Report*, 4 April 1997.

[9] Quoted in Gary K. Bertsch and Victor Zaborsky, "Bringing Ukraine into the MTCR: Can US Policy Succeed?" *Arms Control Today* 27, no. 2, April 1997, pp. 9-14. This view is common amongst high-ranking government officials.

[10] Ukraine experienced three brief years as an independent nation-state from 1919-1922, after which it became the Ukrainian Soviet Socialist Republic. A historical examination of this period is found in Anna Rice, *Borderland: A Journey Through the History of Ukraine* (London: Weidenfeld & Nicolson, 1997).

[11] On political and economic developments in independent Ukraine, see Taras Kuzio, *Ukraine Under Kuchma: Political Reform, Economic Transformation, and Security Policy* (Basingstoke: Macmillan, 1997); Adrian Karatnycky, "Ukraine at the Crossroads," *Journal of Democracy* 6 (1) (January 1995): 117–30; Peter Hole et al., *Ukraine*, IMF Economic Review Series (Washington, DC: International Monetary Fund, November 1995); Gerhard Simon, "Probleme der ukrainischen Staatsbildung," *Aussenpolitik*, no. 1 (1994): 67–78; V.S. Nebozhenko, *Sotsial'na napruzhenist' i konflikty v Ukrainskomu suspil'stvi* (Kyiv: Abrys, 1994); Oleksandr Kovalenko, *Ukraina: Sotsial'na sfera u perekhidnyi period* (Kyiv: Osnovy, 1994); Chrystyna Lapychak, "Ukraine's Troubled Rebirth," *Current History* 92 (10) (October 1993): 337–41; Alexander Duleba, "Povolebna Ukrajina: Najdiskutovanejsie otazky vnutropolitickeho vyvoja a zahranicna politika," *Medzinarodne otazky* (Bratislava) 3 (4) (1994): 69–80; Ilya Prizel, "Ukraine Between Proto-Democracy and 'Soft' Authoritarianism," in Karen Dawisha and Bruce Parrott, eds., *Democratic Changes and Authoritarian Reactions in Russia, Ukraine, Belarus, and Moldova* (New York: Cambridge University Press, 1995), 330–69; Roman Solchanyk, "The Politics of State-Building: Centre-Periphery

Relations in Post-Soviet Ukraine," *Europe-Asia Studies* 46/1 (January 1994), pp. 47-68; and "A Survey of Ukraine," 18-page supplement to *The Economist*, 7 May, 1994.

[12] For two brief but very useful assessments of Ukraine's strategic situation, see Sherman W. Garnett, *Keystone in the Arch: Ukraine in the Emerging Security Environment of Central and Eastern Europe* (Washington, DC: Carnegie Endowment for International Peace, 1997); and Taras Kuzio, *Ukrainian Security Policy*, Washington Paper No. 167 (Westport, CT: Praeger, 1996). Ukraine had latent disputes with Moldova and Romania over the status of northern Bukovina and southern Odessa oblast, but these differences remained submerged and were greatly overshadowed by the frictions with Russia. Ukraine and Romania signed an agreement in early June 1997 that largely resolved their remaining territorial differences. See also, Margarita Balmaceda, "The Role of Central Europe in Ukrainian Security," *East European Quarterly* 32, no. 3 (Fall 1998), pp. 335-351; and Andrej Kreutz, "Polish-Ukrainian dilemmas: A Difficult Partnership," *Canadian Slavonic Papers* 39, nos.1/2 (March 1997), pp. 209-221.

[13] Interviews with government officials and scholars in Moscow and Kyiv suggest that the tension between Russia and Ukraine was more rhetorical than real. Generally speaking, neither side viewed the current disputes as warranting full-scale hostilities.

[14] See, for example, "Vystup Ministra oborony Ukrainy generala armii Ukrainy VOL. G. Radetskogo," *Narodna armiya* (Kyiv), December 6, 1993, 1-2.

[15] Taras Kuzio, "Ukraine – Past, Present and Future," *The World in Conflict – Jane's Intelligence Review Yearbook*, 1994/95, pp. 49-53.

[16] Kyiv's involvement in and with NATO, while always a source of concern in Moscow, was recently strained over NATO actions in Kosovo and the commitment of Ukrainian peacekeepers under NATO auspices.

[17] See, Taras Kuzio, *Ukraine Under Kuchma: Political Reform, Economic Transformation, and Security Policy* (Basingstoke: Macmillan, 1997), p. 189.

[18] See, Taras Kuzio, "Civil-Military Relations in Ukraine: 1989-1991," *Armed Forces and Society* 22, no. 1 (Fall 1995), pp. 25-49.

[19] "Ukraine's Horbulin on NATO," *Reuters*, 3 May 1996.

[20] See, Tor Bukvoll, "Ukraine and NATO: The Politics of Soft Cooperation," *Security Dialogue* 28, no. 3 (September 1997), pp. 363-374.

[21] "Kravchuk Supports Ukraine's Place in NATO," *Reuters*, 8 February 1994.

[22] See, Paul D'Anieri, "Dilemmas of Interdependence: Autonomy, Prosperity, and Sovereignty in Ukraine's Russia Policy," *Problems of Post-Communism* (January-February 1997), pp. 16-25. Quoting President Kuchma, D'Anieri notes: Ukraine's involvement in PfP was perceived as a means to buttress its security because "NATO consults with any active PfP member if it feels a direct threat to its territorial integrity, independence or security."

[23] Ukraine has also refused to join the CIS Customs Union (March 1992), the CIS Interparliamentary Assembly, or to sign the CIS Charter (January 1993). The priority, in sum, lies in resisting Russian attempts to transform the CIS from an

interstate association into a supranational structure. See, Bohdan Lupiy, *Ukraine and European Security: International Mechanisms as Non-Military Security Options for Ukraine* (London: Peter Lang Publishing, 1997), pp. 45-62.

[24] *The Ukrainian Weekly*, 9 October 1994.

[25] Kuchma, in *Uradovyi Kurier*, 29 August 1996.

[26] Volodymyr Horbulin, "Ukraine's Place in Today's Europe" (*Summary of World Broadcasts*, 19 July 1996). On numerous occasions, Horbulin, secretary of the Ukrainian National and Security Council, has articulated the view that Ukraine's principal security threat is economic instability and continuing energy dependence on Russia. See also, "Horbulin on Ukrainian Security and Relations," *Interfax*, Moscow, 30 December 1998.

[27] Anton Filepenko, "The CIS Economic Union: Pros and Cons," *Politics and the Times*, October-December 1995, p. 60.

[28] For example, Ukraine is facing the distinct possibility of a sovereign debt default in 2000 as foreign debt payments exceed the government's ability to service the debt. Recently, President Kuchma warned: "In 2000 Ukraine will have to pay more than $3 billion which can not be found in our budget. There is no doubt we are in for a default." Further, Kuchma said if a left-wing candidate was elected at the 31 October 1999 presidential election, creditors would not agree to restructure the debt. In recent years, Ukraine has been struggling to shift a crushing load of debt into longer-term maturities since August 1998, but many analysts say the cash-strapped country will have a very difficult job meeting all its obligations. "Kuchma: Ukraine May Default On 2000 Foreign Debt," *Reuters*, 31 August 1999.

[29] An excellent study of this situation is Paul J. D'Anieri, *Economic Interdependence in Ukrainian-Russian Relations* (Albany: State University of New York Press, 1999).

[30] As noted earlier, energy dependence on Russia is a pressing security concern for Kyiv. The Russian-Ukrainian energy interdependence is intricately complex. Ukraine is a major consumer of Russian energy and has been and will be somewhat vulnerable to Russian political-economic pressure. However, in addition to pursuing foreign energy sources, Ukraine controls a large share of the energy transportation system between Russia and lucrative markets in Western Europe. For example, the Druzhba pipeline carries Russian oil to Western European consumers. The oil that flows through the Druzhba accounts for some 40 percent of Russia's total oil exports – thereby limiting, to some extent, Russia's ability to manipulate Ukraine. See, John E. Tedstrom, Ukraine's Economy: Strategic Issues for Successful Recovery, in Taras Kuzio, ed., *Contemporary Ukraine: Dynamics of Post-Soviet Transformation* (New York: M.E. Sharpe, 1998), pp. 201-217 (208).

[31] A recent initiative to address energy arrears to Moscow and reduce military stockpiles is the Ukrainian proposal to pay some of its multi-million dollar energy debts by handing over 11 – eight Tupolev-160 strategic bombers and three Tupolev-95 long-range bombers – strategic bombers that once carried Soviet

nuclear weapons. As of this writing, Moscow agreed to the proposal. See, "Russia to Swap Ukraine Energy Debt for Bombers," *Reuters*, 4 September 1999.

[32] See, "Ukraine's Debt to Russia," *Nuclear Engineering International*, 30 September 1999, p. 7.

[33] For example, see Jolyon Naegele, "Georgia, Azerbaijan and Ukraine Inaugurate Oil Pipeline," *RFE/RL Weekday Magazine*, 20 April 1999.

[34] "Aliyev, Kuchma Discuss Construction of Transport Corridor," *Itar-Tass*, 14 October 1999.

[35] "Commando Force to Guard New Caspian Pipeline," *Reuters*, 16 April 1999.

[36] Recently, Ukraine has reconfirmed its previous stance to stay away from the union of the three Slavic republics of the former Soviet Union: Russia, Ukraine, and Belarus. For example, Ukrainian Foreign Ministry spokesman Igor Grushko noted after the Kuchma's reelection to a second presidential term, "Ukraine is interested in deepening cooperation with all the neighboring countries, but that does not mean the Ukrainian state has an intention to join any unions." "Ukraine Confirms Intention to Stay Away from Slavic Union," *Itar-Tass*, 16 November 1999.

[37] See, "The Eastern Outsiders' Club," *Foreign Report*, Jane's Information Group, July 15, 1999.

[38] Nikolai Churilov and Tatyana Koshechkina, "Public Attitudes in Ukraine," and Leonid Kistersky and Serhii Pirozhkov, "Ukraine: Policy Analysis and Options," both in Richard Smoke, ed., *Perceptions of Security: Public Opinion and Expert Assessments in Europe's New Democracies* (Manchester: Manchester University Press, 1996), esp. pp. 192-94 and 216-18, respectively. See also Roman Solchanyk, "Russia, Ukraine, and the Imperial Legacy," *Post-Soviet Affairs* 9 (4) (October–December 1993): 358-62; and Jeremy Lester, "Russian Political Attitudes to Ukrainian Independence," *Journal of Communist Studies and Transition Politics* 10 (3) (June 1994): 193-233.

[39] "Perspektyvy Ukrainy pisla vyborov u Rosii," *Holos Ukrainy* (Kyiv), December 28, 1993, 2.

[40] Comment by General Gennadii Dmitriev, cited in Zhilin, "Voennaya politika i voina politikov," 10.

[41] In the final analysis, Ukrainian-Russian relations do not portend military conflict. Elite-level, cultural, and historical relations hedge against it. For example, Russia is to base Su-24 *Fencer* bombers in Ukraine; Russia will base 20 Su-24 tactical bombers at Gvardeyskoye air base near Simferopol on the Crimean Peninsula, Ukraine, following the conclusion of two years of negotiations between the two countries. *Jane's Defence Weekly* 32, no. 16, October 1999.

[42] Chrystyna Lapychak, "Crackdown on Crimean Separatism," *Transition* 1 (8) (May 26, 1995): 2-5. Moscow's restraint may have been partly intended to reciprocate for Kuchma's low-key and muted statements about Russia's intervention in Chechnya earlier in that year, but the chief reasons for Russia's discretion were the general improvement in bilateral relations and a recognition in

Moscow that the Crimean leader, Yurii Meshkov, had lost almost all of his popularity.

[43] "Dogovor o druzhbe, sotrudnichestve i partnerstve mezhdu Rossiiskoi Federatsiei i Ukrainoi," May 31, 1997, in *Diplomaticheskii vestnik* (Moscow), No. 7 (July 1997): 35-41. For the various agreements on Crimea and the Black Sea Fleet signed by Russian prime minister Viktor Chernomyrdin and Ukrainian prime minister Pavlo Lazarenko, see "Rossiya-Ukraina: Dokumenty o rossiisko-ukrainskom sotrudnichestve," *Diplomaticheskii vestnik* (Moscow), No. 8 (August 1997): 29–41.

[44] See, Roman Szporluk, "Ukraine: From an Imperial Periphery to a Sovereign State," *Daedalus*, no. 3 (Summer 1997), pp. 85-119.

[45] "Vcyeuo Narodnii," *Nezavisimaia Gazeta*, 30 March 1996.

[46] Ustina Markus, "Recent Defense Developments in Ukraine," *RFE/RL Research Report* 3 (4) (28 January 1994): 26-32. The assessment here is also based on four lengthy interviews by the author with General Konstyantin Morozov, the former Ukrainian defense minister, in Cambridge, MA, May-June 1994.

[47] A. Kachinsky, *Kontseptsiya riziku u svitli ekolohichnoi bezpeky Ukrainy*, Working Paper No. 14 (Kyiv: Ukrainian National Institute for Strategic Studies, November 1993), esp. 21-25.

[48] Safeguarding positive relations with Russia, despite the existing military and economic asymmetry and periodic revanchist threats, President Kuchma maintains: "You know my stand of principle regarding Ukraine's foreign policy: Ukraine's European choice should not be interpreted simplistically only as alignment with the West. The strengthening of confidence-building and cooperation with Russia is among Ukraine's main international priorities. Our ability to ensure the existence of a sovereign, independent and undivided Ukraine which has every opportunity to become a sub-regional state in the critically important part of Europe depends on the consistency of our political course which is neither pro-Western nor pro-Eastern, but pro-Ukrainian, depends on the quality of strategic forecast and awareness of possible external threats and ways to avoid them." Kuchma contends that Ukraine's staying outside blocs while avoiding the prospects of becoming a buffer zone, a "gray zone" between NATO and Russia, is among the main purposes of its foreign and security policy. "Cooperation with Russia among Ukraine's Priorities, Kuchma," *Itar-Tass*, 23 August 1997. Similarly, Ilya Prizel notes: "The economic failure of Ukrainian independence has made a profound impression on Ukraine's political landscape. While there is no visible external threat to the country's security, there are some indications that internal stability may be in jeopardy." Ilya Prizel, "Ukraine Between Proto-Democracy and 'Soft' Authoritarianism," in Karen Dawisha and Bruce Parrott, eds., *Democratic Changes and Authoritarian Reactions in Russia, Ukraine, Belarus, and Moldova* (New York: Cambridge University Press, 1995), pp. 330-69 (363).

[49] A useful examination of Ukrainian-Russian strategic relations is Sherman W. Garnett, *Keystone in the Arch: Ukraine in the Emerging Security Environment of*

Central and Eastern Europe (Washington, DC: Carnegie Endowment for International Peace, 1997). See especially pp. 41-82.

[50] See, Yevgenii Sharov, "Ukraine and the MTCR," *The Monitor: Nonproliferation, Demilitarization and Arms Control*, vol. 1, no. 2, Spring 1995; and "Missiles to Get New Mission," *Asia Times*, 18 July 1997.

[51] For example, the former Soviet missile and space infrastructure is now split between Ukraine and Russia. Consequently, commercial space launch activities engaged in by either necessitates involvement of the other. See, "Ukraine's Space Launch Industry: Interview with Yuzhnoye Plant Director," *Space News*, 29 November 1993, pp. 1, 20.

[52] Author's interview with Ukrainian Ministry of Foreign Affairs and National Security and Defense Council officials, Washington, DC, July 1999.

[53] Mroz and Pavliuk, p. 59.

[54] For example, see Bogdan Turek, "Poland/Ukraine: Presidents Discuss Visa-Free Travel," *RFE/RL Weekday Magazine*, 24 June 1999.

[55] See, William Kincade, "Unneighborly Neighbors," *Foreign Policy* 94 (Spring 1994), pp. 84-104.

[56] For example, see, Ian Brzezinski, "Polish-Ukrainian Relations: Europe's Neglected Strategic Axis," *Survival* 35, no. 3 (Autumn 1995), pp. 26-37.

[57] See, Vladimir Tsimbalyk, "The Ukrainian Export Control System. *The Monitor: Nonproliferation, Demilitarization and Arms Control*, vol. 1, no. 4, Fall 1995, p. 1; and Victor Vaschilin, "State Export Controls in Ukraine," *The Monitor: Nonproliferation, Demilitarization and Arms Control*, vol. 3, no. 3, Summer 1997, pp. 12-15. Tsimbaluk, a former Red Army General, was the first Director of the Expert and Technical Committee, the governmental body charged with licensing exports. Tsimbaluk, in an open interview with the author, noted the sheer novelty of nonproliferation and export controls as policy issues. He remarked: "Most government officials and industry heads have little to no understanding about export controls, let alone Ukraine's system" (24 April 1997, Athens, GA).

[58] Kuzio, pp. 25-30.

[59] The author would like to thank Dr. Volodymyr Chumak for his insight on the origins and the potential and actual political challenge posed by the "Donbas Russians."

[60] Interviews with Ministry of Foreign Affair and export control officials, July 1996, Los Alamos National Laboratory.

[61] Kuzio (1995), *op. cit.*, p. 54.

[62] Author interviews with Ukrainian government officials, June 1995, Kyiv.

[63] Contingent upon enacting the Lisbon Protocol, the 1994 Trilateral Agreement, and the NPT, Ukraine predicated nuclear disarmament on Western Security guarantees as the primary means by which to address its security concerns. See, Taras Kuzio, *Ukrainian Security Policy* (Westport: Præger, 1995). The resultant guarantees were formally declared at a 1995 Budapest Organization for Security and Cooperation in Europe (OSCE) conference. For a succinct study on the

Ukrainian effort to augment its military structure, see James Joung-Jun Na, "Non-Nuclear Military Security of Ukraine," in Leonid Kistersky, ed., *Security in Eastern Europe: The Case of Ukraine* (Providence: Brown University, 1995), pp. 75-99. And, for an analysis of how Ukrainian security concerns apply to state-building, see Andrea Chandler, "Statebuilding and Political Priorities in Post-Soviet Ukraine: The Role of the Military," *Armed Forces and Society*, vol. 22, no. 4, Summer 1996, pp. 573-597.

[64] See, G. Rozman and S. Sato, *Dismantling Communism: Common Causes and Regional Variations* (Washington, DC: Woodrow Wilson Center Press: 1994).

[65] The post-Soviet constitution was ratified in June 1996. However, there is still considerable debate over the particulars of the division of political power as enumerated in the new constitution. The remaining friction continues between the Parliament and President Kuchma's reformist government. Furthermore, regional politics and players have complicated the national political landscape. Elite politicians and bureaucrats from economically and politically powerful regions, including the eastern city of Kharkiv, the Donetsk basin, and the port of Odessa, have challenged those from Dnepropetrovsk, a region heavy with military industry and President Kuchma's home district. See, James Rupert, "Regional Tensions Trip Up Ukraine's Quest of Stability," *The Washington Post*, 27 October 1996.

[66] See Alexander J. Motyl, *Dilemmas of Independence: Ukraine After Totalitarianism* (New York: The Council on Foreign Relations, 1994).

[67] For example, Prizel notes: "Ukraine lacks a political and cultural elite with roots stretching back for a significant period of the nation's history. Furthermore, Ukraine has no historical political parties and institutions to draw upon." See, Ilya Prizel, "Ukraine Between Proto-Democracy and 'Soft' Authoritarianism," in Karen Dawisha and Bruce Parrott, eds., p. 331.

[68] Interviews with US Embassy-Kyiv officials, August 1999. See also, United Nation Human Development Yearly Report: Ukraine 1995.

[69] Motyl (1994), pp. 107-125.

[70] Importantly, governmental centralization should not be confused with overall political power. While political power in contemporary Ukraine still resides at the center (i.e., little official regional or local autonomy), power within the center tends to be diffuse and imprecisely defined. See, M. Shugart, "Executive-Legislative Relations in Post-Communist Europe," *Transitions*, 13 December 1996, pp. 6-11. The author would like to thank Dr. Sergei Galaka for his insights on this issue.

[71] T. Brown and C. Wise, "Laying the Foundation for Institutionalization of Democratic Parliaments in the NIS: The Case of Ukraine," *Journal of Legislative Studies* 2, no. 3 (1996), pp. 216-244.

[72] Alexander Motyl, "The Conceptual President: Leonid Kravchuk and the Politics of Surrealism," in T. Colton and R. Tucker, eds., *Patterns in Post-Soviet Leadership* (Boulder: Westview Press, 1995), pp. 103-122.

[73] The early post-independence period has been referred to as "politically torpid." See, Taras Kuzio, "Ukraine: The Unfinished Revolution," *European Security Studies* 16 (London: Institute for European Defence and Strategic Studies, 1993).
[74] Kuzio, *Ukraine Under Kuchma*, p. 134.
[75] A. Agh, "The Experience of the First Democratic Parliaments in Eastern Europe," *Communist and Post-Communist Studies* 28, no. 2, March 1996, pp. 203-214 (207-210).
[76] Kuzio, *Ukraine: Nation and State Building*, pp. 65-66. The "mini-constitution" was an interim Constitutional arrangement in which the president, who drafted the document, was given exclusive authority to appoint the prime minister, the cabinet, and a handful of other key state officials *without* the parliamentary confirmation. He was also granted the power to reorganize the executive branch at will and in the absence of a functioning judiciary was given the authority to determine the constitutionality of laws.
[77] T. Brown and C. Wise, "The Separation of Powers in Ukraine," *Communist/Post-Communist Studies* 32 (1999), pp. 23-44 (32).
[78] While the Communist faction gained seats in the 1994 parliamentary elections, the cohesion of the faction quickly began to weaken. New parliamentary factions were formed by deputies departing the ranks of the Communist faction, notably the Socialist faction who served as the primary partner of the Communists in voting against Kuchma's reform proposals. A detailed study of the 1994 elections is found in T. Brown and C. Wise, "The Internal Development of the Ukrainian Parliament," *Public Administration and Development* 16, no. 3 (1996), pp. 265-279.
[79] Oliver Vorndran, *The Constitutional Process in Ukraine: Context and Structure, Research Papers in Russian and East European Studies, REES97/3*, Birmingham, December 1997.
[80] An excellent study of how Kuchma came to augment the office of the president in the new constitution is found in Kataryna Wolczuk, "The Politics of Constitution Making," in Taras Kuzio, *Contemporary Ukraine*, pp. 118-137 (135). Wolczuk contends that a "semi-presidential" system is not necessarily the most structurally sound – as evidenced in the 1993 shelling of the State Duma in Russia – but for fractured polities, it may be, in the short term, the more practical.
[81] The threat of a Constitutional referendum was the means by which Kuchma forced parliament's hand in adopting the 1996 Constitution.
[82] For example, President Kuchma recently signed a joint declaration with the Union of Regional and Local Authorities which initiated a national referendum to introduce amendments into the Constitution. Specifically, Kuchma is supporting the idea of creating a bicameral parliament in an effort to further dilute the Left's power. This initiative will be placed on the proposed referendum. The Constitution is also expected to be approved in a national vote, so that, according to Kuchma, "the politicians get no wish to raise the issue of constitutional changes at each parliamentary session." Kuchma contends that the present Constitution prevents him from actively and effectively carrying out reforms and that more power

should be devolved to the regions. "Kuchma, Local Authorities Initiate Constitutional Changes," *Itar-Tass*, 27 September 1999.

[83] As noted in chapter 3, export control policy exists solely on the basis of Cabinet of Ministers and Presidential decrees. As such it is insulated from what would otherwise most likely be parliamentary interference. See, "Kuchma Tightens Control Over Arms Control and Exports," *FBIS-SOV-1999*-0428, *Itar Tass World Service*, 28 April 1999. Furthermore, since 1995, author's interviews with governmental officials suggest that export control policy is simply not a well-known issue in government circles. As such, it is relatively easy for Kuchma et al. to consolidate political control over this policy area.

[84] Interview with Expert and Technical Committee official, University of Georgia, October 1995.

[85] For details regarding the structure of the post-Presidential December decree export control system, see S. Jones and V. Zaborsky, in Gary K. Bertsch, ed., pp. 17-30.

[86] Of the total occupied 414 seats in the Rada, 93 are held by the Communist Party of Ukraine. The Communist bloc holds a substantial amount of power in that there are no strong coalitions among the other parties to act as a counter. In practice, a communist-agrarian bloc dominates the legislature; centrist-reformist parties, including the Interregional Reform Bloc of Kuchma, did very poorly in 1994 Parliamentary elections. Opposition to Kuchma's economic reforms in Parliament is led by Oleksander O. Morov, chairman of the Socialist Party, who threatens to overturn Kuchma's decrees and oppose economic reforms. Morov proclaimed the socialists as "opposition to the presidential course."

[87] Mroz and Pavliuk, p. 60.

[88] For brief biographical sketches on President Kuchma and former Prime Minister Pavel Lazarenko, see "Khto ie Khto v Ukrains'kiy Politytsi," *Vypusk 2* (Kyiv: KIS, 1995).

[89] See, Konstantin Parishkura, "President Kuchma Revamps Cabinet," *The Current Digest of the Post-Soviet Press*, 2 August 1995, vol. 47, no. 27, p. 21 (3). President Kuchma is leading the changes in government since adoption of the post-Soviet constitution. On the political front, his goal of paring down the swollen Soviet-era bureaucracy has met with, predictably, considerable parliamentary and bureaucratic resistance. For example, on 19 December 1996 President Kuchma signed a decree fixing the number of ministers in the cabinet as well as the total number of ministries. The decree also directly subordinates the interior, foreign, information, and defense ministers to the president. The decree has sparked controversy among deputies, some of whom say it is unconstitutional and accuse the president of taking over some of parliament's prerogatives. Rada Deputy Volodymyr Chemerys said parliament may turn to the Constitutional Court to have the decree revoked. See also, Gwynne Oosterbaan, "Clan Based Politics in Ukraine and the Implications for Democratization," conference proceedings, East Europe Institute, March 1997 (www.ciao.org).

[90] See, Taras Kuzio, "A Friend in Need: Kyiv Woos Washington," *The World Today*, April 1996, vol. 52, no. 61, p. 96; and Ustina Markus "Ukrainian President on CIS," *OMRI Daily Digest*, 27 March 1996.

[91] For example, concerned over rampant official corruption and the pace and direction of economic reforms, the International Monetary Fund (IMF) decided not to extend a $2.5 billion credit until reforms are harmonized with IMF prerequisites. Shortly after the IMF decision, President Kuchma reshuffled his cabinet and upgraded the auditing powers of the newly created anti-corruption investigatory committee, the National Bureau of Investigation. See, Pavel Polityuk, "Ukrainian Leader Shuffles Cabinet," *The Washington Post*, 25 July 1997.

[92] For example, although providing input into license reviews, the Ministry of Defense no longer makes export decisions on its own.

[93] One such provision is the president's right to authorize top secret transfers and embargoes. Apparently, this clause was suggested to the final draft by the Kuchma administration. Author's interview with Ukrainian export control official, 4 August 1999, Kyiv.

[94] Ustina Markus, "Ukrainian President Increases Control over Arms Exports," *OMRI Daily Digest*, 3 January 1997.

[95] Taras Kuzio, "Ukraine Arms Sales," *Jane's Intelligence Review*, March 1997, pp. 100-11.

[96] Taras Kuzio (1995), *op. cit.*, pp. 45-47.

[97] Interview with SSEC official, Washington, DC, January 1997.

[98] Tor Bukkvoll, *Ukraine and European Security* (London: The Royal Institute of International Affairs, 1997), pp. 20-22.

[99] President Kuchma quoted in Pavel Ivanov, "Pace of Ukrainian Reform Questioned," *Asia Times*, 4 April 1994.

[100] The "West" is a generic historical, political, and economic term, seldom explicitly defined, used to designate an ostensibly distinct "civilization." This term is, needless to say, problematic at best. Nevertheless, for the sake of this study, the "West" is understood to be a political-economic community of similar states sharing the primary tenets of Western society. David Gress presents an apropos description of these central tenets: "With the end of the Cold War and the collapse of the Soviet empire, the *market economy* and *democracy* appear to have triumphed. Universally praised, these two central values of Western society have become the prerequisite for any nation seeking acceptance by the international community or assistance from international financial institutions." David Gress, "The Modern Western Identity: Its Fit in World Politics," *Current*, no. 398, December 1997, pp. 7-18. Recent studies of the "West" include: Samuel Huntington, *The Clash of Civilizations and the Remaking of World Order* (New York: Simon and Schuster, 1996); Thomas C. Patterson, *Inventing Western Civilization* (New York: Monthly Review Press, 1997); Jacques Attali, "The Crash of Western Civilization: The limits of the Market and Democracy," *Foreign Policy*, no. 107, Summer 1997, pp. 54-64.

[101] The term "liberal," like the "West" or "Western," is an assumed rather than questioned concept. Competing interpretations aside, "liberal," as used in this paper, follows that offered by Fukuyama: "[Political] liberalism can be defined simply as a rule of law that recognizes individual rights or freedoms from government control. Liberalism is also the recognition of the rights of free economic activity and economic exchange based on private property and markets." Francis Fukuyama, *The End of History and the Last Man* (New York: The Free Press, 1992), pp. 44-45. See also, Michael Doyle, "Kant, Liberal Legacies, and Foreign Affairs," *Philosophy and Public Affairs* 12 (Summer 1983), pp. 205-235.

[102] Ilya Prizel, "Ukraine Between Proto-Democracy and 'Soft' Authoritarianism," in Karen Dawisha and Bruce Parrott, eds., pp. 330-332.

[103] For accounts of the history of nation-state building in Europe and Eurasia, see Charles Tilly, *The Formation of National States in Western Europe* (Princeton: Princeton University Press, 1975) and Fernand Braudel, *A History of Civilizations* (London: Penguin Books, 1987). On the Ukrainian effort, see Taras Kuzio, with Marc Nordberg, "Nation and State Building, Historical Legacies and National Identities in Belarus and Ukraine: A Comparative Analysis," *Canadian Review of Studies in Nationalism*, 26/1-2 (1999); A. Motyl and B. Krawchenko, "Ukraine: from empire to statehood," in Ian Bremmer and Ray Taras, eds., *New States, New Politics: Building the Post-Soviet Nations* (Cambridge: Cambridge University Press, 1997), pp. 235-275; Roman Szporluk, "Nation-Building in Ukraine: Problems and Prospects," in J. Blaney, ed., *The Successor States to the USSR* (Washington: CSIS, 1995), pp. 173-183; Torbakov Igor, "Historiography and Modern Nation-Building," *Transition*, 2/18 (6 September 1996) and "Ukraine: From an Imperial Periphery to a Sovereign State," *Daedalus*, 126/3 (Summer 1997), pp. 85-120.

[104] Orest Subtelny, "Imperial Disintegration and Nation State Formation: The Case of Ukraine," in John Blaney, ed., *The Successor States to the USSR* (Washington: Congressional Quarterly, inc., 1996), pp. 184-96; and G. Simon, "Problems Facing the Formation of the Ukrainian State," *Aussenpolitik*, 45/1 (1994), pp. 61-67.

[105] Braudel (1987), pp. 530-72 and, R. Solchanyk, "Russia, Ukraine, and the Imperial Legacy," *Post-Soviet Affairs*, vol. 9, no. 4, Fall 1993, pp. 340-1.

[106] Ukraine has always been somewhat of an international anomaly: posturing as state, but lacking the trappings thereof. For example, while in the Soviet Union, Ukraine occupied a nominal seat at the United Nations.

[107] Bohdan Krawchenko, "Ukraine: the Politics of Independence," in Ian Bremmer and Ray Taras, eds., *Nationalism and Politics in the Soviet Successor States* (Cambridge: Cambridge University Press, 1993), pp. 99-115.

[108] Speaking of the leftist Parliamentary opposition, President Kuchma observed: "The only problem with the Communists today is that they want to build a Soviet Socialist Republic, while I want to build a civilized, democratic, and lawful state" (The Ukrainian Information Agency - *Unian*, 5 May 1996).

[109] Author's interview with SSEC official, Washington, DC, January 1997. Through CTR and NDF programs, for example, the United States has taken an active role in export control initiatives in Ukraine.

[110] Quoted in Pavel Ivanov, "And What About Ukraine?" *Asia Times*, 5 May 1997. Many in the executive administration have voiced similar sentiments with respect to political-economic integration with the West. For example, Volodomyr Horbulin, Secretary of the Ukrainian National Security and Defense Council, noted that "the relationship between Ukraine and the European Union is the nucleus of Ukraine's economic security. The scenarios of reforming the economy and joining the EU coincide. Relations between Ukraine and the EU are developing inadmissably slowly and are handicapped, first of all, by us being a backward country. Our relations with the United States are, some would say, most important. Our relations have been developing, with meetings of the Gore-Kuchma Commission being their core." "Horbulin on Ukrainian Security and Relations," *Interfax*, Moscow, 30 December 1998. The National Security and Defense Council is one of the primary bodies in the export control system, having been made so recently by Presidential decree. See, Mikhail Melnik, "Kuchma Tightens Control Over Arms Exports," *Itar-Tass*, *FBIS-SOV-1999-0428*, 12 May 1999.

[111] Broadly speaking, the "Constructivist" approach to IR contends that states are socialized to accept new norms, values, and perceptions of interest through interaction with other states and international organizations. Martha Finnemore maintains: "The fact that we live in an *international society* means that what we want and, in some ways, who we are are shaped by social norms, rules, understandings, and relationships we have with others. These social realities are as influential as material realities in determining behavior. Indeed, they are what endow material realities with meaning and purpose. Norms operate in more than a regulative way; they are constitutive in the sense that they constitute, create, or revise the actor's *interests* and *identity*." National Interests in International Society (Ithaca: Cornell University Press, 1996), pp. 128-130. See also, Jeffrey Checkel, "The Constructivist Turn in International Relations Theory," *World Politics*, 50 (2), 1998, pp. 324-48; Michael Desch, "Culture Clash: Assessing the Importance of Ideas in Security Studies," *International Security*, vol. 23, no. 1, 1998, pp. 141-170; Ted Hopf, "The Promise of Constructivism in International Relations Theory," *International Security*, vol. 23, no. 1, Summer 1998, pp. 171-200; John G. Ruggie, *Constructing the World Polity* (London: Routledge, 1997), pp. 1-39 J.S. Levy, "Learning and Foreign Policy: Sweeping a Conceptual Minefield, *International Organization*, 48, 1994, pp. 279-312; Alexander Wendt, "Collective Identity Formation and the International State," *American Political Science Review* 88(2), pp. 384-396.

[112] See, Jeffrey T. Checkel, "International Norms and Domestic Agents: Probing the Dynamics of Socialization," Columbia International Affairs Online, 15 May 1998, www.ciao.org/conf/ssr01.html, pp. 12-18.

[113] See, Taras Kuzio, *Ukraine Under Kuchma* (1997), pp. 220-221. Specifically, Kuzio notes that the "West has been far more forthcoming in supporting [than Russia] political reforms in Ukraine. Numerous financial bodies, both supranational, governmental, and private, are involved in providing technical expertise, training and financial support for democratic change in Ukraine. On the other side of this interaction process, Ukraine has sought to extract more specific concessions; for example, Ukraine's attempt to use its ratification of the NPT to exact more Western aid was largely successful. By 1996, when the last nuclear weapons had been removed from Ukraine, it had already become the third largest recipient of US aid (after Israel and Egypt, and, for the first time, ahead of Russia)." At a recent Parliamentary Assembly meeting of the North-Atlantic alliance, Ukrainian Foreign Minister Borys Tarasyuk stressed that "European and European-Atlantic integration remains Ukraine's top priority" ("Ukraine's Foreign Minister Looks West," *RFE/RL Daily Report*, 10 July 1999).

[114] Author's interview, officials from Ministry of Foreign Affairs, Ministry of Defense, National Security and Defense Council, and SSEC, Kyiv, February 1997 and August 1999.

[115] For example, Ukrainian scholar Taras Kuzio notes: "The scale of the problem facing Ukraine in the formation of a new elite could be seen by the fact that it was allegedly the largest country in the world without political elites." See, Kuzio, *Ukraine: State and Nation Building* (London: Routledge, 1998), p. 23. See also, Mark Bessinger, "Elites and Ethnic Identities in Soviet and Post-Soviet Politics," in Alexander Motyl, ed., *The Post-Soviet Nations: Perspectives on the Demise of the USSR* (New York: Columbia University Press, 1992), p. 157; and Alexander Motyl, "State, Nation, and Elites in Independent Ukraine," in Taras Kuzio, ed., *Contemporary Ukraine: Dynamics of Post-Soviet Transformation* (New York: M.E. Sharpe, 1998), pp. 3-17.

[116] Checkel, "International Norms and Domestic Agents: Probing the Dynamics of Socialization" (1998) p. 13.

[117] See, Yaroslav Hrytsak, "Shifting Identities in Western and Eastern Ukraine," *The East and Central Europe Program Bulletin*, vol. 5, no. 3 (February 1995), pp. 3-5; and Volodmymyr Zviglyanich, "Ukrainian Reforms: A Sociological Analysis," *The Ukrainian Weekly*, 14 July 1996.

[118] For an instructive study of how interests, relations, and identity are inextricably linked, see Iver Neumann, "Collective Identity Formation: Self and Other in International Relations," *European Journal of International Relations*, 2, pp. 139-174. It is important to note that 'Liberal Identity,' as an explanatory approach, seeks only to stress the importance of norms and identity formation. It does *not*, moreover, suggest that materialist accounts for behavior and identity are irrelevant.

[119] As noted earlier, "normative socialization in Ukraine is expedited by the lack of cognitive filters to such socialization and learning" (Checkel 1998: 13). This socialization process is especially responsive to outside influence. As explained by Wendt: "The changes in the context of interaction will sometimes affect only the

price of behavior, but they may also change identities and interests. Indeed, dependence, whether material or intersubjective, is a key determinant of the extent to which an actor's identity is shaped by interaction. . . . As interdependence arises, in other words, so will the potential for endogenous transformations of identity." A. Wendt, "Collective Identity Formation and the International State," pp. 389-390.

[120] Commenting on the Gore-Kuchma Commission, Secretary of the National Security and Defense Council, Volodymyr Horbulin remarked: "Relations with the US and Ukraine have been expanding, especially through the work of the Gore-Kuchma Binational Commission. For instance, Ukraine and Washington have made great progress in the area of nonproliferation and arms control." "Volodymyr Horbulin on Ukrainian Security," *Interfax-Ukraine*, 30 December 1997.

[121] Suzette Grillot, Explaining *Ukrainian Denuclearization: Identity Versus Interests*, Ph.D. Dissertation (Athens: University of Georgia, 1998).

[122] For example, see Hillel Abramson, Glenn Chafetz, Suzette Grillot, "Role Theory in Foreign Policy: Belarussian and Ukrainian Compliance with the Nuclear Nonproliferation Regime," *Political Psychology*, vol. 17, no. 4, 1996, pp. 727-757. Chafetz et al. note, "The individuals who make foreign policy in the name of states do so on the basis of their ideas about the roles of their state in the world and which roles will be acceptable to their constituents."

[123] For a detailed survey of the twists in the debate, see Bohdan Nahaylo, "The Shaping of Ukrainian Attitudes Toward Nuclear Arms," *RFE/RL Research Report* 2 (8) (February 19, 1993): 21-45.

[124] Anatoly Golubchenko, "Ukraine's Policy in the Area of Nonproliferation and Export Control," in *The 1998 Official Report on Ukrainian Export Controls*, compiled and edited by Victor L. Zaborsky, Gary K. Bertsch, and Scott A. Jones (Athens: Center for International Trade and Security at the University of Georgia, June 1998). In this report, see also, Victor Vaschilin, Head, State Service on Export Control of the Cabinet of Ministers of Ukraine, "Ukraine's Export Control System: Evolution and Current Status." Vaschilin contends that the main objective of the SSEC "is to support the national interests and security of Ukraine, not creating a threat by the sale or illegal export of weapons to regions where they would contribute to destabilization of the situation. The main efforts in this sphere have been concentrated on preventing the proliferation of weapons of mass destruction and their delivery systems. Overall, our objective is to avoid compromising Ukraine in the eyes of the world community as a violator of international treaties." "Official Explains Arms Export Control Procedures," *FBIS-SOV-1228-97, Kyiv Nezavisimost*, 24 September 1997.

[125] On the non-proliferation norm, see Roger K. Smith, "Explaining the Non-Proliferation Regime: Anomalies for Contemporary International Relations Theory," *International Organization* 41 (2) (Spring 1987): 252–81; Steven Lee, "Nuclear Proliferation and Nuclear Entitlement," *Ethics International Affairs*, 9 (1995): 101-31, esp. pp. 123-31; and John Simpson, "Nuclear Non-Proliferation in

the Post-Cold War Era," *International Affairs* 70 (1) (January 1994): 17-39, esp. pp. 18, 36; and Ethan Nadelmann, "Global Prohibition Regimes: the Evolution of Norms in International Society," *International Organization*, 44, 4, Autumn 1990, pp. 479-526. Nadelmann defines prohibition norms as "The norms that strictly circumscribe the conditions under which states can participate in and authorize various activities. Those who refuse or fail to conform are labeled deviants and condemned not just by states but by most communities as well as individuals. Both the substance of these norms and the processes by which they are enforced are institutionalized in global prohibition regimes" (479). For more general discussions of norms in world politics, see the essays in Volker Rittberger, ed., *Regime Theory and International Relations* (Oxford: Clarendon Press, 1993).

[126] Author's interview, Ukrainian Ministry of Foreign Affairs official. Los Alamos National Laboratory, July 1996.

[127] See, Suzette Grillot, *Ukrainian Denuclearization: Identity Versus Interests*, pp. 136-147. See also, Keith Krause, "Constructing Non-Proliferation and Arms Control: The Norms of Western Practice," in Keith Krause, ed., *Culture and Security: Multilateralism, Arms Control and Security Building* (New York: Frank Cass & Co., 1999).

[128] Ukrainian policy makers, at the time of the nuclear renunciation debates, were acutely aware of the ability to leverage preferences with the West's insistence on complete nuclear disarmament. For example, Taras Kuzio notes: "In the aftermath of parliamentary ratification of the NPT, Foreign Minister, Hennady Udovenko, came out with new demands for the West to increase its levels of foreign aid. Ukraine's attempt to use NPT ratification to exact more Western aid was largely successful. By 1996, when the last nuclear weapons had been removed from Ukraine, it had already become the third largest recipient of US aid (after Israel and Egypt, ahead of Russia)." Kuzio, *Ukraine Under Kuchma*, p. 219.

[129] Ian Hurd, "Legitimacy and Authority in International Politics," *International Organization* 53, no. 2, pp. 387-388.

[130] Yuliya Mostova, "SBU Chief on Arms Trade, Domestic Issues," *FBIS-TAC-97-007, Kyiv Zerkalo Nedeli*, 7 February 1999. See also, Keith Krause, "Constructing Non-Proliferation and Arms Control: The Norms of Western Practice," in Keith Krause, ed., *Culture and Security: Multilateralism, Arms Control and Security Building* (New York: Frank Cass & Co., 1999).

[131] Roman Woronowycz, "Ukraine and NATO Sign Partnership Charter," *Interfax-Ukraine*, 9 July 1997. On a visit to Kyiv shortly after the Madrid signing, US Secretary of Defense, William Cohen praised the Ukrainian president in his efforts to reform the Ukrainain state: "We appreciate the courageous stands that President Kuchma has taken in trying to develop a free market and a prosperous economy, the courageous steps that he has taken to get rid of nuclear weapons on Ukraine's soil, and that he intends to lead Ukraine into a very stable, democratic and prosperous 21st century."

[132] At the opening of a special alliance meeting on furthering Ukraine-NATO relations NATO in Washington, DC, NATO General Secretary Javier Solana

commented on the state of deepening NATO-Ukrainian relations: "NATO gains from [the relationship] by having a strong cooperation partner for enhancing European security together. And Ukraine gains from it by finding a NATO that is a strong supporter of its independence, and a far-reaching program of political, economic and defense reform. The distinctive partnership between NATO and Ukraine provides all of us with a new model of cooperation. A model worthy of a new Europe we are building together." See, Julie Moffett, "Ukraine: Kosovo Creates Defining Moment In NATO Relationship," *RFE/RL Weekday Magazine*, 26 April 1999.

[133] Author's interview notes, Department of Defense, Defense Special Weapons Agency, December 1996.

[134] The author has been involved in – and in some cases organized – many such export control training and workshop exchanges, both as an employee of the US government and as an associate at the Center for International Trade and Security at the University of Georgia. As noted, these exchanges involve a wide range of US and Ukrainian government and non-government personnel. The overriding theme of said exchanges is the emphasis placed on the connection between export control compliance and proper state decorum. In other words, states that do not comply are marginalized both politically and economically.

[135] For example, on 13-17 January 1997, in Washington, DC, a technical exchange forum – "Ukraine Technical Exchange on Control Lists, Licensing Procedure and Law Development" – between the US Departments of Commerce, Customs, Defense, Energy, and State with a Ukrainian delegation from the State Service on Export Control, the Ukraine Parliament, and the Office of the Prime Minister. Sessions covered the elements necessary for an effective national control list, licensing procedures, obligations under the various international licensing control regimes, and legal issue. Funding for this and other exchanges was provided by CTR, as channeled through the NDF. The author helped organize and participated in this forum. See, *Bureau of Export Administration: 1998 Annual Report* (Washington, DC: US Department of Commerce), pp. 119-135.

[136] Provided by the US Department of State, September 1996. See also, National Research Council, *Proliferation Concerns: Assessing US Efforts to Help Contain Nuclear and Other Dangerous Materials and Technologies in the Former Soviet Union* (Washington, DC, National Academy Press, 1997), see especially pp. 97-102 for a complete itemization of all US government export control assistance programs and exchanges.

[137] *Ibid.*

[138] Wendt, "Collective Identity Formation and the International State," *American Political Science Review* 88 (2), p. 390. This concept is also captured in Ruggie's "embedded liberalism." See Ruggie, "International Regimes, Transactions, and Change: Embedded Liberalism in Post-War Economic Order," in Stephen Krasner, ed., *International Regimes* (Ithaca: Cornell University Press, 1983).

[139] For more information on the subject of the emerging Ukrainian political identity see Taras Kuzio, *Ukraine: From Perestroika to Independence* (New York:

St. Martin's Press, 1994) and Roman Szporluk, "Nation Building in Ukraine: Problems and Prospects," in John Blaney, ed., *The Successor States to the USSR* (Washington, DC: Congressional Quarterly, Inc., 1995), pp. 173-84.

[140] Recently, in a telling remark, President Kuchma said of the decision to abandon nuclear assistance to Iran: "In light of the concern surrounding the possibility of nuclear weapons proliferation, it would be irresponsible for our state [Ukraine] to continue the deal with Iran." Pavel Polityuk, "US Pressures Ukraine on Iran Deal," *Kyiv Post*, 20 March 1998.

[141] Ukraine has a considerable political and economic distance to go before we can confidently refer to Ukraine as manifesting a "liberal identity." See, *Human Development Report 1996: Ukraine*, chapter 3: Civil Society and Political Participation (New York: United Nations, 1996). Some would argue that Ukraine, or Russia, is incapable of adopting a liberal identity. For example, see Samuel Huntington, *The Clash of Civilizations and the Remaking of World Order* (New York: Simon and Schuster, 1996).

[142] For a comprehensive study of Ukraine's relative democratic development, see Roger Kaplan, ed., *Freedom in the World: The Annual Survey of Political Rights and Civil Liberties 1996-1997* (New York: The Freedom House, 1997) and Adrian Karatnycky, Alexander Motyl, and Boris Shor, eds., *Nations in Transit: Civil Society, Democracy and Markets in Eastern and Central Europe and the Newly Independent States* (New York: The Freedom House, 1997). Both works have lengthy sections exploring the Ukrainian case in terms of civil rights, political participation, and economic freedoms. See also, Taras Kuzio, "The Sultan and the Hetman: Democracy Building in Belarus and Ukraine in a Grey Security Zone," in Jan Zielonka Jan, ed., *Democratic Consolidation in Eastern Europe: International and Transnational Factors* (Florence, 1999).

[143] For example, the US State Department Human Rights Report for Ukraine 1996 noted the following: "the persistence of unreformed legal and prison systems, occasional government attempts to control the press, beatings by police and prison officials, limits on freedom of association, restrictions on foreign religious organizations, societal anti-Semitism, some discrimination against women, and ethnic tensions in Crimea."

[144] "Ukraine Signs Tank Deal with Pakistan," *OMRI Daily Digest*, 1 August 1996. Pakistan is seen by many in the West as nuclear proliferant and irresponsible exporter. The US stopped all military supplies to Pakistan in 1990.

[145] Raphael Shen, *Ukraine's Economic Reform: Obstacles, Errors, Lessons* (Westport: Praeger Press, 1996), p. 145. See also, "Ukraine: Nuclear Agreement Signed with PRC," FBIS-SOV-96-064, *Interfax* (Moscow) 4 January 1996.

[146] Jones and Zaborsky, in Bertsch, ed., pp. 27-8.

[147] See, for example, Aslund Ånders, "Eurasia Letter: Ukraine's Turnaround," *Foreign Policy*, 100 (Fall 1995), pp. 125-143; and "Ukraine's Resurrection," *American Foreign Policy Interests*, 17/3 (June 1995), pp. 12-17; Ustina Markus, "Ukraine Seeks Investment," *OMRI Daily Digest*, 19 February 1996; and Paula

Dobriansky, "Ukraine: A Question of Survival," *The National Interest*, 36 (Summer 1994), pp. 65-72.

[148] Ukrainian government officials and Western economists maintain that access to Western markets is necessary for successful economic transition. The dissolution of COCOM in March 1994 signaled a new era in East-West trade, thereby allowing for vital transfers of advanced technologies and goods to occur. Contingent, however, upon these changes were assurances that export controls would be implemented by FSU states.

[149] Nikolai Novichkov, "Ukraine Starts Selling Weapons to NATO," *Jane's Defence Weekly*, 19 August 1998.

[150] Interview with Ukrainian export control official, Washington, DC, February 1997.

[151] "Ukraine Forms New Unit to Sell Space Technologies," *Reuters*, 20 January 1999.

[152] For example, MTCR accession talks between the US and Ukraine have resulted in the creation of cooperative space projects.

[153] According to one Ministry of Foreign Affairs official, regime membership has "indicated to Ukraine that the US is not using the supplier regimes as an economic tool against the less developed world, but that Washington simply has legitimate security concerns." Author's interview, Los Alamos National Laboratory, June 1996.

[154] See, Grillot, Beck, and Wolfe, "FSU Export Control Development: The Factors that Matter," in Bertsch and Grillot, eds., *Arms on the Market*, pp. 226-228.

[155] Bill Gertz, "Kyiv Imperils US Aid with Libya Arms Deal," *The Washington Times*, 9 December 1996, pp. A1, A12.

[156] Author's interview, US Department of Defense, Washington, DC, November 1996.

[157] Jones and Zaborsky, in Bertsch, ed., p. 26; and Bill Gertz "Kyiv Imperils US Aid with Libya Arms Deal," *The Washington Times*, 9 December 1996, A1, A12.

[158] Author's interviews, Washington, DC, January 1997.

[159] Ustina Markus, "Ukraine to Set Up Commission on Libyan Arms Deal," *OMRI Daily Digest*, 13 December 1996. The release of 1996 US aid for Ukraine was contingent upon the findings of a US presidential investigatory committee.

[160] In Kyiv, the Congressional hearing were closely observed. For example, Ukrainian Security Chief, Volodymyr Radchenko observed: "There is a decision by the US Congress saying that if the US President obtained trustworthy data of intergovernmental relations between Ukraine and Libya in the area of military-technical cooperation, he would have the right to halt financial aid. This would be extremely serious for Ukraine. We need the support." Yuliya Mostova, "SBU Chief on Arms Trade, Domestic Issues," *FBIS-TAC-97-007, Kyiv Zerkalo Nedeli*, 7 February 1999.

[161] Michael Sawkiw, "Senate Approved Foreign Aid Bill with Earmarks, Conditions for Ukraine," Ukrainian National Information Service (*Unian*), 20 July 1997.

[162] Ukraine has received export control assistance from the US Cooperative Threat Reduction Program (CTR) – from which $13.26 million is budgeted for export control development – and the Nonproliferation and Disarmament Fund (NDF). Export control assistance from Norway, Japan, and Germany and coordinated multilateral efforts from the International Atomic Energy Agency (IAEA) have augmented Ukraine's export control system development activities. In addition, Ukraine is the third largest, behind Israel and Egypt, recipient of US direct aid. Receipt of aid is frequently contingent upon compliance with donor concerns.

[163] See, Anthony Gadzey, *The Political Economy of Power: Hegemony and Economic Liberalism* (New York: St. Martin's Press, 1994). US nonproliferation activism can be seen, arguably, as part of its role as post Cold War hegemon: "Hegemony rests on the subjective awareness by elites in secondary states that they are benefiting, as well as on the willingness of the hegemon itself to sacrifice tangible short-term benefits for long term gains." in Robert Keohane, *After Hegemony: Cooperation and Discord in the World Political Economy* (Princeton: Princeton University Press, 1984), p. 88.

[164] Under CTR and NDF funds, Ukraine received and continues to receive US material assistance thereby significantly reducing the costs incurred to Kyiv in constructing a system from scratch. European and Japanese material and financial assistance has also been significant. The latter contributions are coordinated through the European Union and the IAEA. Kuchma cited the EU's contribution of 85 million ecus during a press conference after his return from the CSCE summit; see "Ukraina mae stati mostom mizh Skhodom i zakhodom," *Holos Ukrainy* (Kyiv), 9 December 1994, 2.

[165] A Ministry of Foreign Affairs official noted that export controls were not high political priorities in Kyiv. He asserted that Western material and financial assistance were therefore crucial to export control development in Ukraine. Author's interview, Los Alamos National Laboratory, July 1996. Several export control agency officials later confirmed this assertion.

[166] John E. Tedstrom, Ukraine's Economy: Strategic Issues for Successful Recovery, in Taras Kuzio, ed., *Contemporary Ukraine: Dynamics of Post-Soviet Transformation*, p. 211.

[167] US Department of State, *Summary and Highlights FY 1999 International Affairs* (Function 150) Budget Request Resources, Plans & Policy, Office of the Secretary of State, 2 February 1998; and *US Government Assistance to and Cooperative Activities with the New Independent States of the Former Soviet Union: FY 1998 Annual Report* (Washington, DC: US Department of State, 1999).

[168] Security assistance, however, is exempt from certification. See also, Robert Lyle, "US Aid to Kyiv to Await Albright's Ruling," *RFE/RL Daily Report*, 2 February 1999.

[169] R.S. Kravchuk, *Ukrainian Politics, Economics and Governance*, 1991-96 (New York, 1999); and John Tedstrom, *Ukraine's Economy at Risk*, MR-752.0-RC (Santa Monica: RAND Corporation, 1996), pp. 25-29.

[170] Mohammed Ishaq, "Foreign Direct Investment in Ukraine Since Transition," *Communist & Post-Communist Studies* 32, no. 1 (March 1999), pp. 91-109.
[171] *Ibid.*, p. 61.
[172] US Department of Defense, *CTR Handbook* (Washington, DC, 1998).
[173] Activities included: the destruction of chemical, nuclear, and biological weapons; transporting, storing, disabling and safeguarding weapons in connection with their destruction; establishing verifiable safeguards against the proliferation of such weapons; preventing diversion of weapons-related expertise; facilitating the demilitarization of defense industries and the conversion of military technologies and capabilities; expanding defense and military contacts between the US and NIS; converting defense industrial facilities to commercial applications; and facilitating environmental cleanup of nuclear contamination in the Arctic Ocean. The scale and sheer fact of the program itself (i.e., one state assisting another in its demilitarization efforts) is, in the history of international relations, truly unprecedented.
[174] William Potter and John Shields, "Assessing the Dismantlement Process," in Potter and Shields, eds., *Dismantling the Cold War: US and NIS Perspectives on the Nunn-Lugar Cooperative Threat Reduction Program* (Cambridge: MIT Press, 1997), pp. 3-4.
[175] Senator Sam Nunn, "Foreward: Changing Threats in the Post-Cold War World," in William Potter and John Shields, eds., *Dismantling the Cold War*.
[176] The Scientific and Technology Center of Ukraine (STCU) provides "peaceful and economically productive" employment for scientists formerly employed in weapons of mass destruction activities. To date, there have been 42 projects funded and 4,500 scientists employed under International Scientific and Technology Center in Moscow.
[177] Congressional notification for these items do not specify individual project notifications.
[178] Signed on 5 December 1993, the "Agreement between the Expert and Technical Committee of the Cabinet of Ministers of Ukraine and the United States Department of Defense on the Provisions of Assistance to Ukraine Related to the Establishment of an Export Control System to Prevent the Proliferation of Weapons of Mass Destruction" is the legal basis upon which assistance rests.
[179] Author's interviews, US Departments of Defense, Energy, Customs, and State, October-December 1996.
[180] The author participated in these meetings as a DOE contractor.
[181] The nuclear version of this system – the Nuclear Export License Review System (NELRS) – was developed in Los Alamos, the agreement for which was signed 18 July 1996. The author was present for and participated in the exchange between lab and Ukrainian government officials.
[182] One SSEC official noted: "Nunn and Lugar literally built our new building." Author's interview notes, 3 August 1999, Kyiv.
[183] Recently, the USG and Ukraine exchanged diplomatic notes extending the agreement to continue the CTR program in Ukraine through December 2006.

Through FY 1999, the USG has provided a total of $2.7 billion for CTR programs. Of that amount, $569 million has been dedicated to efforts in Ukraine. "US Ukraine Extend CTR," *News Release*, Office of Assistant Secretary of Defense, 5 August 1999.

[184] US Department of State, Summary and Highlights FY 1999 International Affairs (Function 150) Budget Request Resources, Plans & Policy, Office of the Secretary of State, 2 February 1998.

[185] The Bushehr case will be examined at greater length in the subsequent chapter.

[186] Michael Gordon, "Ukraine Decides Not to Supply Key Parts for Iranian Reactor," *New York Times*, 14 April 1997. More recently, however, Ukraine has expressed its intention of reviewing the earlier Presidential decision against supplying the Iranian reactor. Speaking in the city of Kharkiv, home of the turbine plant, Foreign Minister Hennady Udovenko on 18 August said he would study a draft contract under which Turboatom would supply a 1,000-megawatt turbine for the plant in the Iranian city of Busehr. Udovenko admitted that "fulfillment of the contract could complicate relations with our partners." The US and Israel have argued that the plant could help Iran develop nuclear weapons. See, "Ukraine May Supply Turbine to Iran," *RFE/RL Daily Report*, 19 August 1997.

[187] Author's interviews with US government officials, Washington, DC, Fall 1996. See also, Jeffrey Smith, "Iraq Buying Missile Parts Covertly," *The Washington Post*, 16 October 1995.

[188] For more on the concept of "rogue" states, see Michael Klare, *Rogue States and Nuclear Outlaws: America's Search for a New Foreign Policy* (New York: Hill and Wang, 1995).

[189] An Ukrainian export control agency official likened export controls to nuclear divestiture: as a means of insuring Western confidence in and support for the Ukrainian state building effort. Author's interview, Washington DC, January 1997. Furthermore, financial inducements to cooperate on export controls influence policy makers in Kyiv. For example, as part of the bilateral nuclear agreement (resulting from reneging on the Bushehr deal), Ukraine immediately received technical assistance by the US estimated at $30 million to develop documentation for launching a nuclear fuel production cycle for VVER-100 reactors. Ukrainian Foreign Minister Boris Tarasyuk said that "the next stage of realization of this agreement is that large-scale projects are to be launched and investment opportunities are to be aimed at creating Ukraine's own nuclear fuel production cycle." He further stressed that "Ukraine would continue cooperation with Russia in the field of nuclear power engineering. At the same time, the signed agreement will make it possible to realize a number of scientific-technological projects which in the future will lay the foundations for production of Ukraine's own nuclear fuel." Natalia Kozlova, "US To Give Ukraine $30 Million for Nuclear Research," *FBIS-SOV-98-126, Itar-Tass*, 6 May 1998.

[190] Taras Kuzio, Paul D'Anieri, and R. Kravchuk, *Politics and Society in Ukraine* (Boulder: Westview Press, 1999).

[191] See, Khristina Lew, "Kuchma, Gore Convene First Session of US-Ukraine Commission," *The Ukrainian Weekly*, no. 21, 25 May 1997. During his May 1997 visit to Washington, President Kuchma assured US officials that market-oriented economic and democratic political reforms would continue.

[192] Potentially the most lucrative arms sale Kyiv has made to date (an estimated $500 million controversial tank deal with Pakistan), was recently canceled by Islamabad. After receiving 32 out of a proposed 320 T-80 UD tanks, Pakistan claimed the tanks were not built to specifications and suffered from manufacturing flaws. See, Pavel Ivanov, "Ukraine Tries to Elbow its Way into Global Arms Market," *Asia Times*, 2 July 1997.

[193] The Ukrainian Ministry of Foreign Affairs continues to express concerns that the US is attempting to limit Ukrainian access to the commercial space launch market. For an informative account of the complicated debate between the US and Ukraine on MTCR compliance and membership, see Victor Zaborsky, "Ukraine's Missile Industry and National Space Program: MTCR Compliance or Proliferation Threat?" *The Monitor: Nonproliferation, Demilitarization and Arms Control*, vol. 1, no. 3, Summer 1995; and, Victor Zaborsky, "Ukraine's Niche in the US Launch Market: Will Kyiv's Hopes Come True," *World Affairs*, vol. 159, no. 2, Fall 1996, pp. 55-63.

[194] This assertion is somewhat suspect. For example, in late 1993, Iran reportedly purchased eight SS-N-22 'Sunburn' supersonic anti-ship missiles from Ukraine for $600,000 each. See *Defense News*, 4 October 1993, pp. 25-26.

[195] Regarding Ukrainian prospects on the world space market, see John Baker, *Nonproliferation Incentives for Russia and Ukraine*, Adelphi Paper 309 (London: International Institute for Strategic Studies, 1997), pp. 31-52.

[196] President Kuchma, through his association with the Kuchma-Gore Commission, acknowledged the necessity of an effective export control system to the future of the Ukrainian space and missile industry. See "Ukrainian President in US Congress" *RFE/RL Daily Report*, 16 May 1997. Also, other CTR programs, such as the Industrial Partnership Project, seek to augment a state's technical expertise via viable defense conversion. For example, approximately $5 million has been awarded to a US company to form a joint stock company with Ukraine's Monolit to convert a manufacturer of spacecraft and missile electrical, control and guidance systems into a producer of digital instrumentation and control systems for nuclear power plants. See, "US Assists in Developing Key Ukrainian Industries," *News Release*, Office of Assistant Secretary of Defense, 20 November 1996.

[197] World Bank News Release No. 97/1369 ECA, "World Bank Supports International Aerospace Joint-Venture," 30 May 1997.

[198] Behaviorists (including experimental behavior analysts and applied behavior analysts) study overt behavior and its observable environmental, social, and physiological determinants. Specifically, they suggest that positive feedback at each stage of development will reinforce a particular behavior. See, R. Uttal, *Toward a New Behaviorism: The Case Against Perceptual Reductionism*

(Mahwah, NJ: Lawrence Erlbaum Associates, 1998) and A. Catania and S. Harnad, eds., *The Selection of Behavior: The Operant Behaviorism of B.F. Skinner: Comments and Consequences* (New York: Verso Press, 1989).

[199] Although other states – such as Finland, Germany, and the United Kingdom – have provided export control assistance, when compared with US efforts, they are statistically insignificant. See, *International Atomic Energy Agency Annual Report: Export Control Assistance to the NIS 1997* (Vienna: IAEA, 1997).

[200] Pavel Polityuk, "Ukraine and US Sign Agreement on Peaceful Nuclear Cooperation," *The Ukrainian Weekly*, 7 May 1998.

[201] This pattern – liberalizing executive versus a leftist-dominated legislature – is common throughout the FSU states. See, Ghia Nodia, "How Different Are Post-Communist Transitions?" *Journal of Democracy* 7, no. 4 (October 1996), pp. 15-17, 22-24. On the situation in Ukraine, see Kuzio, *Ukraine Under Kuchma*, pp. 63-65; and Alexander Motyl, "State, Nation and Elites in Independent Ukraine," in Kuzio, *Contemporary Ukraine*, pp. 3-16 (13).

[202] Alexander Wendt, "Anarchy is What States Make of It: The Social Construction of Power Politics," *International Organization*, vol. 46, no. 2, pp. 391-425, pp. 405-06.

[203] This table is modified from a similar model in Ronald Jepperson, Alexander Wendt, and Peter Katzenstein, "Norms, Identity, and Culture in National Security," in Peter Katzenstein, ed., *The Culture of National Security*, p. 53.

[204] The term "recursiveness" is not familiar in the field of International Relations. Yet it is now making its way into the literature. Onuf defines recursion as "the propensity of knowledgeable agents to refer to their own or others' past and anticipated actions in deciding how to act" (1989:62). Giddens, who has discussed the idea and implications of recursion extensively, refers to the phenomenon as "reflexive self-regulation" (1979:78). But, in fact, this graphic phrase simply provides a more vivid way of expressing Schelling's more mundane reference to "interdependent decision making" which lies at the root of his conception of strategy (Schelling 1960: ch. 4). The concept takes on a new dimension when social theorists like Giddens have extended the idea of a recursive process to describe the mutual constitution of agents and structures. Giddens insists that although the activities associated with any habitual social practice will not have been introduced by any given agent, nevertheless, by engaging in the practice, the agent will "reproduce the conditions that make these activities possible" (Giddens 1984:2). The idea of recursion gives this process a social-political dimension. See, Anthony Giddens, *Central Problems in Social Theory* (London: Macmillan, 1979) and *The Constitution of Society: An Outline of the Theory of Structuration* (Cambridge: Polity Press, 1984); Nicholas Onuf, *World of Our Making: Rules and Rule in Social Theory and International Relations* (Columbia: University of South Carolina Press, 1989); and Thomas Schelling, *The Strategy of Conflict* (London: Oxford University Press: 1960).

[205] Author's note: this situation (viz., US involvement) represents one of the challenges of conducting social *science* research in the classic sense; namely, the

absence of a control case. For example, we cannot compare – in the sense of Mill's 'method of difference' – Ukraine *without* US involvement and Ukraine *with* US involvement, drawing inferences from the hypothesized differences of involvement. The historical record makes clear the palpable – indeed measurable (see chapter 4) – impact of US engagement in Ukraine's nonproliferation export control policy.

[206] Ukraine's compliance with the nonproliferation norm was decidedly evidenced in the decision to denuclearize. In other words, there was a basis in Ukraine upon which to draw reference in further nonproliferation behavior. See, Jane Dawson, *Eco-Nationalism. Anti-Nuclear Activism and National Identity in Russia, Lithuania and Ukraine* (Durham, Duke University Press, 1996). Further sensitizing Ukraine to the nonproliferation norm was the 1986 Chernobyl nuclear disaster. See, Kuzio, Ukrainian Security Policy, pp. 48-49. See also, David Marples, "The Legacy of Chernobyl in 1997: Impact on Ukraine and Belarus," *Post-Soviet Geography & Economics* 38, no. 3 (March 1997), pp. 163-170.

[207] See, Steven Flank, "Exploding the Black Box: The Historical Sociology of Nuclear Proliferation," *Security Studies* 3: 1994, pp. 259-294. Flack notes that questions of national interest were not independent of national identity regarding nuclearization. Further, national identity and the interest battery derived therefrom arose from a sense of the state as it stood in the world, through its interaction with other states as a key determinant to whether or not to nuclearize. Importantly, such assertions do not undercut a realist explanation of why states acquire nuclear weapons. A cognitive/constructivist approach complements the realist oversight regarding identity and interest change over time. See also, Chafetz, *et al.*, "Role Theory and Foreign Policy." Chafetz, *et al.*, notes: "Ukrainian leaders have never articulated a *consistent* role conception" (751).

[208] Chafetz, *et al.*, "Role Theory and Foreign Policy," p. 739. Similarly, Checkel asserts that the lack of "cognitive filters" amongst much of the political establishment is a necessary cause for norm receptivity. Checkel, "International Norms and Domestic Agents: Probing the Dynamics of Socialization."

[209] Anne-Marie Burley argues, for example, that liberal states tend to hold each other to a different standard than that for nonliberal regimes. Thus, for states to enter the club of liberal nations, they are expected to follow certain norms in choosing their governments and in their foreign relations. See her "Law Among Liberal States: Liberal Internationalism and the Act of State Doctrine," in *Columbia Law Review*, vol. 92, no. 8 (December 1992), p. 1913. On the concept of "transnational identity," see Bruce Cronin, *Community Under Anarchy: Transnational Identity and the Evolution of Cooperation* (New York: Columbia University Press, 1999), pp. 30-39.

Chapter 6

Incentives, Coop(t)eration, and Evolving Self-Interest in the Development of the Ukrainian Export Control System: The Bushehr Case

The findings of the previous chapter strongly suggest that expectation derived from Rational Institutionalism and Liberal Identity (hereafter RI and LI) bear the explanatory weight accounting for the continued development of and international (i.e., US) cooperation on Ukrainian export control policy, as made manifest in the creation, augmentation and exercise of a formal system of controls. In other words, state behavior – in this case – is best explained by the aforementioned two IR approaches; namely, that Ukraine developed a system of nonproliferation export controls for material *and* ideational reasons (see Table 6.1).

Table 6.1 Explanations of Export Control Development: Ukraine Theory and Evidence RI & LI

	Positive	Negative	Mixed
RI			
• Explicit cost/benefit analysis	+		
• Regimes rules/norms constrain behavior	+		
• Reduce transaction costs/uncertainty	+		
• Material side-payments	+		
LI			
• Sense of community with liberal states	+		
• Interaction with liberal community	+		
• Liberal, democratic government			+/-
• Target illiberal states			+/-

As noted earlier, the theoretical approaches and derivative hypotheses should in no way be viewed as mutually exclusive. Moreover, they are, in many respects, mutually reinforcing in general and in the Ukrainian case specifically. Indeed, the operative theoretical premise of this study is that IR theories are not "incommensurable paradigms."[1] Moreover, RI and LI, in the case of Ukraine, work in tandem to explicate state behavior. This chapter will highlight *how* RI and LI interact to produce a compelling explanation of *why* Ukraine developed an export control system and continues to cooperate on nonproliferation matters.

At this point, it is important to remind the reader that the object of this paper is *not* theory testing. Moreover, the goal of this chapter is merely to elaborate on the conclusions reached in the former chapter by portraying how primarily US economic and technology incentives shaped Ukraine's preferences and, consequently, its notions of self-interest. To do so, the Bushehr reactor case and subsequent Ukrainian decision will be examined in detail. Specifically, a number of factors become evident in this case: explicit cost-benefit calculation, normative constraint, side payments, targeting illiberal states, interaction with liberal states, and the continued development of a sense of community with the Western states. Further, these factors are mutually reinforcing insofar as the ideational aspects (LI) are interdependent and coextensive with the material (RI). This case also illustrates the simple fact of and degree to which the US profoundly influenced the development of Ukrainian export controls with the use of economic incentives and the corresponding evolution of Ukrainian interests.

6.1 The Power of Economic Incentives: Bilateral Relations and Policy Preferences

"Why did Ukraine develop, and continue to do so over time, an export control system?" The most genuinely parsimonious answer would be: "Because it was in its self-interest to do so. Its preference structure was such that development would optimize said self-interest." In explaining behavior in general, the risk of tautology is real.[2] Explaining *state* behavior is every bit as problematic. The problem is further exacerbated if one questions the nature of those interest; i.e., how did they develop and are they are an *a priori* given (irrespective of context) and do they change over time? Based on the previous chapter, we see that Ukraine's export control policy decisions neither originated or developed in isolation, but were in fact directly influenced by the United States – and to a lesser extent the broader international nonproliferation community.[3]

However measured, it is clear that the United States is the foremost *power* in the international system.[4] The reach and influence of US policies is extensive, especially when focused on particular regions, states, or issues. As such, its political and economic influence is considerable.[5] For example, Paul Kowert and Jeffrey Legro contend: "Norms backed by the United States are likely to become more widespread and effectual than otherwise similar norms originating in Luxembourg."[6] In the case of nonproliferation export controls, this is especially the case. US government technical, intellectual, and material assistance both in general and specifically for export control development influenced the export control development process in Ukraine, as made abundantly clear in the previous chapter. Furthermore, the international nonproliferation export control norm – arguably an international norm institutionalized and vigorously promoted by the United States[7] – also affected Ukrainian preferences in such a way that resulted in policy implementation.

It is also clear that the United States is meeting its security challenges through economic incentives and expanded commercial exchange.[8] Incentives have been prescribed for diverse problems including staunching the flow of weapons material, technology and expertise from the FSU; dissuading North Korea from developing nuclear weapons or convincing Ukraine to destroy them; encouraging nations to adopt less environmentally dangerous economic policies or coping with new security threats such as immigration and drug trafficking[9] With incentives the sender is offering new or additional gains from trade, technology transfer, or capital for a desired policy adjustment by the recipient.[10]

In Ukraine's decision to denuclearize, for example, western incentives played a key role. Under the 1994 Trilateral Agreement with Russia and the United States, Kyiv was obliged to relinquish some 1,900 nuclear weapons remaining on Ukrainian territory by sending them to Russia to be dismantled. In exchange, the United States and Russia made a series of security assurances to Ukraine. Moscow also agreed to provide Ukraine with nuclear reactor fuel as compensation for the highly enriched uranium lost in the dismantling of warheads. Washington pledged to give Kyiv both financial and technical assistance for denuclearization and defense conversion and economic reforms. The US government also raised the prospect of aerospace cooperation, including the possibility of eventually receiving commercial contracts for launching US satellites using Ukrainian space-launch vehicles. This package – combining security and economic and technical assistance – was a powerful incentive to Kyiv.[11]

In the case of Ukraine, trade and technology and outright financial incentives are a mode of "co-optive" (Nye 1990) power exercised through the promise or giving of an economic benefit to induce a state to develop or change its political behavior. The granting of a preferential trading arrangement, such as acquiescing to a commodity agreement, is another transfer of resources through trade.[12] Technological benefits can occur through government policies that permit or facilitate the exchange of scientists or engineers (e.g., Ukrainian Scientific and Technical Center), the export of turnkey plants (e.g., microchip production plants), or the transfer of disembodied technology (such as a computer code or other intellectual property). In capital transfer, incentives include not only foreign aid but also investment guarantees (e.g., Ex-Im Bank or OPIC), encouragement of public or private multilateral capital exports (e.g., Merril Lynch Inc. and the IMF), the creation and distribution of special drawing rights to developing countries, debt forgiveness or loan rescheduling, outright grants, and more.[13]

6.2 Bilateral Relations and Policy Preferences: Two Levels

This chapter seeks to examines how economic and political incentives affected the policy outcome reached by Kyiv regarding the proposed Ukrainian sale of gas turbines to the Iranian nuclear reactor project at Bushehr. This case is selected because it illustrates the overall findings of the previous chapter. Namely, that the Ukrainian decision to create, develop, and exercise a nonproliferation export control system is best explained by expectations derived from RI and LI. The Bushehr case – an export control issue of political and economic importance to Ukraine – elucidates in miniature the overall driving variables in Ukrainian export control policy: supporting its perception as a responsible member of the world community and indirect and direct economic incentives. The perception of a responsible state is directly and necessarily related to economic incentives. Thus, the connection between RI and LI are concrete and critical. However, the exact nature of this relationship is merely suggestive and therefore needs to be made plain.

In short, we are asking: How can economic incentives (trade and technology) offered over time induce bilateral cooperation, that is, shape preferences and actions of the recipient in a manner consistent with the sender's intent? This question is especially telling in that the very idea of export controls – and the attendant policies and structures – was foreign to newly independent Ukrainian policy makers. Further, those setting the policy agenda for export controls were removed from the otherwise fractious political process between the executive and parliament; therefore, in a relatively concentrated policy making milieu, the impact of export control norms coupled with economic incentives was direct and immediately evident.[14]

Because incentives influence both international behavior and domestic politics, it is necessary to include variables at the level of both the international structure and the agents (i.e., states) that comprise it. Alexander Wendt maintains that agents and social structures are, in one way or another, "theoretically interdependent or mutually implicating entities." He continues: "It is then a plausible step to believe that the properties of agents [states] and those of social structures are both relevant to explanations of social [political] behavior."[15] Similarly, in "Constructing International Politics," Wendt asserts that "the fundamental structures of international politics are social rather than strictly material, and that these structures shape actors' identities and interests, rather than just their behavior."[16] Consistent with Wendt's approach, there are both structural and agent-level dependent variables in this examination of the Ukrainian export control system – bilateral cooperation and domestic policy preferences – and these dependent variables are themselves interdependent. The advantage of this approach is that neither state agents nor the international structure in which they operate are treated as a given; they are *both* causally relevant. This distinction is important because theories at the level of structure and theories at the level of agents explain different things. As David Dessler argues, "Structures alone explains only the possibilities (and impossibilities) of action,"[17] that is, "Why did X happen rather than Y?"[18] Similarly, Robert Keohane writes that "asking why an actor behaved in a certain way is equivalent to asking what the incentives were: that is, what were the opportunity courses of action? Opportunity costs are determined by the nature of the environment as well as by the characteristics of the actor."[19] In explaining the impact of incentives on state action, therefore, this chapter will employ theoretical understandings of both system and agents.

As we are concerned with US-Ukrainian relations, at the level of the international system, the dependent variable is bilateral cooperation. The analysis focuses on how incentives affect the international environment for bilateral cooperation or non-cooperation. Cooperation, as defined by Keohane, means the existence of a degree of policy coordination where "actors adjust their behavior to the actual or anticipated preferences of others." Cooperation requires that a state adjust its policies to reduce the negative consequences on, or facilitate the goals of, another state.[20] Further, policy adjustment suggests some degree of legitimacy. In other words, the policy change (or the creation thereof) must be legitimated.[21] In this instance, the internalization of the nonproliferation norm in Ukraine represented costs for both the US and Ukrainian sides. Legitimacy as a device of social control affecting both levels has long-run efficiency advantages over coercion in reducing some kinds of enforcement costs and increasing the apparent "freedom" of subordinates, although it is more expensive in the short run.[22]

At the national or agent level, the dependent variable is state policy preference. Terry Moe presents an especially useful approach to defining actors' preferences. He rejects goals such as "utility maximization" or "security" as too unspecified and undirected. Rather, substantively defined actor preferences "are proximate to policy, and they are inevitably context-dependent."[23] In other words, state policy preference formation and change are central to interstate cooperation. Indeed, the definition of cooperation offered by Keohane incorporates this national-level variable within it. As Andrew Moravcsik explains: "Rationality suggests that parsimonious explanations of international conflict or cooperation can be constructed by employing two types of theory sequentially: a theory of national preference formation *and* a theory of interstate strategic interaction."[24] Similarly, Jeffrey Legro notes:

> International cooperation can be conceptualized as part of a two-step process. One part involved the formation of preferences of actors, the second interaction among the preferences of actors that lead to an outcome. An understanding of both is necessary to explain behavior, as both are causally related.[25]

In short, explaining how incentives form or alter behavior requires an understanding of their impact on strategic interaction *and* how such interactions alter national preferences.

In terms of assessing how incentives may influence state preferences and shape – in this case, bilateral relations – it is necessary to note where state preferences come from and how they are altered. This project is suggesting that economic incentives (specifically trade and technology) can in some instances and in some measure, help explain the origin and evolution of state interest and behavior. Hypothetically, trade and technology incentives can alter a state's calculation of self-interest by changing its perceptions, attitudes, perceived opportunities, and preferences. These changes could, in turn, alter the actions a state chooses to pursue. In short, economic incentives can affect a state's definition of its preferences by changing its external payoff environment *and* its domestic politics.[26]

The remaining sections of the chapter will present an analysis of the Ukrainian decision to forego nuclear exports to Iran. Specifically, such an examination seeks to clarify the causal factors involved in US success and Ukrainian compliance. Further, in this case, we see how self-interest and incentives combine to result in mutually positive outcomes.

6.3 Bushehr: US Incentives and the Political Evolution of a New State

> This decision took great statesmanship. By carrying it out [the Bushehr decision], Ukraine will cement its place in the international coalition to halt the proliferation of weapons of mass destruction.
> Secretary of State Madeline Albright, highlighting Ukraine's decision not to provide turbines to the Iranian "Bushehr Project," Mariinsky Palace, Kyiv, Ukraine, 6 March 1998

> One way or another, this is the price [reneging on the Bushehr deal] one has to pay for strategic partnership with the world's sole superpower."
> Ukrainian government official commenting on the March 1998 US-Ukrainian decision

> Ukraine will not go back on its pledges to refrain from deals that could help Iran, Iraq or Libya develop nuclear weapons.
> Ukrainian Foreign Minister, Gennady Udovenko, commenting on proliferation concerns by visiting UN Ambassador Bill Richardson, Kyiv, April 1997

In 1976 the German contractor Siemens began the construction of two 1300 megawatt-electric light-water reactors (LWRs) near Bushehr about 750 kilometers south of Tehran. The *Bushehr I* reactor was 85 percent complete and the *Bushehr II* reactor was partially complete prior to the 1979 Iranian Revolution, after which construction of both reactors halted. During the Iran-Iraq War, Iraqi strike aircraft partially damaged both reactors, one quite extensively. Iran was subsequently unable to persuade Siemens to continue work on the reactors, due in large part to pronounced diplomatic pressure applied from the United States.[27]

After several years of negotiation, in January 1995 Russia and Iran signed an agreement under which Russia would provide two VVER-1000 MW (electrical) light water reactors at Bushehr for payments totalling nearly one billion dollars. Ukraine's AOA Turboatom of Kharkiv was expected to provide a custom-built $45 million gas turbine for the $850 million light-water reactor project. Russia began work on the project in May 1995 with 150 Russian technicians at the site, and as many as 3,000 Russian workers would be dispatched to assist the proposed 2000-2001 completion date.[28]

Despite intense US diplomatic efforts to halt Russian-Iranian nuclear cooperation, construction work has begun under a Russian-Iranian contract to finish building one of two partially completed nuclear reactors at the Bushehr complex. The Clinton administration has repeatedly asked the government of Russian President Boris Yeltsin to cancel the January 1995 deal. In tandem with its overall nonproliferation policy, the United States opposes all nuclear cooperation with Iran on the grounds that it would enhance Tehran's ability to build nuclear weapons. In an annual proliferation report, the Pentagon described Iran as "committed to acquiring nuclear weapons."[29]

Iran and Russia maintain that their nuclear cooperation is completely legal under the nuclear Nonproliferation Treaty (NPT). In fact, Iran is considered to be a member in good standing under the treaty.[30] Further, Tehran has promised to place all its Russian and proposed Ukrainian-supplied technology under international safeguards and in 1998 announced that it would return to Russia the plutonium-laden spent fuel from the reactor. Russia's Ministry of Atomic Energy (MINATOM) has promised to provide Iran with 20 years' worth of fresh fuel for the reactor.

Although MINATOM in the past expressed interest in completing construction of the second reactor at Bushehr and selling Iran two "turn-key" 440-megawatt reactors, MINATOM officials have not signed any other reactor contracts with Iran. However, Russia's Nuclear Physics Research Institute is reportedly negotiating a contract with Iran to train up to 500 technicians in the operation and maintenance of the WER-1000 reactor. Similar training proposals were made to Ukraine. The United States specifically opposes the training of Iranian technicians because of fears it would enhance Tehran's long-term ability to make weapon-grade nuclear material and eventually nuclear bombs.[31]

Formal US protest was lodged against both Russian and Ukrainian participation in the project the moment the deal was announced. In both cases, the apparent willingness of Russia and Ukraine to forgo the nuclear contract if compensated beyond the amount present in the deal suggests that reproach coupled with incentives can directly influence behavior.[32] However, unlike the Russian case, the US government linked export control cooperation with other assistance programs to Ukraine.[33] American officials were quoted as saying that Ukrainian participation in the Iranian nuclear project would "represent a major impediment to closer US-

Ukrainian relations and would preclude future American-Ukrainian cooperation on commercial nuclear technology and possibly other areas of technical cooperation."[34] The US position was conveyed formally via the US-Ukraine Binational (or Gore-Kuchma) Commission and other high-level diplomatic channels.

In May 1997, on a state visit to Kyiv, Israeli Trade and Industry Minister Natan Sharansky said President Kuchma had promised him that Ukraine would not provide Russia with turbines for the Bushehr project or "do anything to help Iran, Iraq or Libya create weapons of mass destruction." Later, however, Kyiv issued the Turboatom plant the document needed to allow it to go ahead with the deal.[35] When the deal was first made public and the US voiced its concern over Ukraine's participation, Kyiv responded that its supply of turbines to Russia did not contradict any international nuclear proliferation regimes because Turboatom would deal only with Russia and that Iran was a member in good standing of the IAEA and NPT.[36] At that time, Washington said Ukraine would be effectively compensated for the loss of the contracts, if US companies were permitted, as was planned, to work in Ukraine's nuclear energy market.[37]

Subsequent equivocal comments on Ukrainian intentions created further tensions between Washington and Kyiv. For example, Ukraine's Presidential Foreign Policy Directorate chief, Volodymyr Ohryzko, said that "[the] Ukrainian shipment of components for the construction of the Bushehr nuclear power plant will be decided on the basis of universally recognized norms.[38] Our cooperation with Tehran has thus far produced tangible results, and for that reason, we are still considering the deal."[39] Also, a top Ukrainian government official said that "Ukraine still has a chance to change its mind on not participating in the Russian-Iranian nuclear project. If we do not receive real compensation for our losses from the United States, we could lose more than we have already lost, and compensation means not just direct funds but new contracts and jobs for Turboatom, the main company involved."[40] Also at this time, Russia, Iran and Kharkiv regional officials pressured the Kuchma administration to complete the contract. Moscow maintained that the nature of the deal was in perfect legal standing, citing Iran's membership of the NPT and acceptance of full-scope safeguards. Thus, the Bushehr case represented the first major test of Ukrainian export control policy.

At a ceremony attended by Secretary of State Madeleine Albright, the United States and Ukraine signed a nuclear cooperation agreement on 6 March 1998, based on a new commitment by Kyiv to end its nuclear cooperation with Iran.[41] In addition, Secretary Albright announced that the

United States would support Ukraine's entry into the Missile Technology Control Regime (MTCR) *without* insisting that Kyiv give up all of its offensive missile programs, as Washington had previously demanded of all new members.[42]

Ukraine's insistence on maintaining the right to produce offensive missiles had been a sticking point in negotiations with Washington about bringing Kyiv into the MTCR.[43] As part of the March agreement, Ukraine will keep its hundreds of Scud missiles – the type of rocket MTCR was specifically designed to counter – through the end of their service lives, and will not forswear future production of short-range missiles should Kyiv find it necessary. When asked about Ukraine's Scuds, a State Department official said "We've discussed their plans, and we're content their plans are compatible with MTCR membership."[44] This arrangement constitutes a major change in US policy. To prevent the MTCR from becoming a missile technology "supermarket," the Clinton administration since 1993 had insisted that prospective member states give up their offensive missile programs – except for the five nuclear weapon states – as a condition for MTCR membership. As all MTCR decisions are made by consensus, Washington holds an effective veto over membership decisions. MTCR membership represent to Kyiv one of the chief means by which it proposes to strengthen its ailing economy: "Launching satellites is one of very few services Ukraine may offer to foreign customers, and is a major source of much-needed revenue."[45]

At the signing ceremony for the US-Ukrainian nuclear deal, Kuchma pointed out that the financial rewards of participation in international space launch projects such as *Sea Launch* and *Globalstar* would more than compensate for the loss of nuclear commerce with Iran. The two projects promise dozens of potential launch contracts for Ukraine's space industry, with each contract worth $40 million or more.[46] President Kuchma declared (emphasis added):

> The contract on the building of Bushehr project was signed by the Soviet Union. You must calculate how many years it lasts. And besides I can bring you up to date, that nothing besides (the) document was made in Kharkiv. And today nobody can be sure how many years will elapse until the construction is over. We estimate this construction to be something like $45 million for Ukraine. Owing to this decision, Ukraine's *accession to the MTCR removes all the limitations as to Ukraine in the space market.* In no case this is no balance (equivalent) to the issue of one turbine. Because it would mean the Sea Launch project, the Global Star launches projects and prospects for other

possibilities. So this *decision has been taken only in the national interests of Ukraine.*⁴⁷

US firms are also set to benefit from the agreements reached in Kyiv. In particular, General Electric has indicated its readiness to complete two Russian-origin nuclear reactors at Khmelnitskiy and Rivno. Finishing the two plants will cost $1.2 billion but would enable Ukraine to some day permanently close Chernobyl. Secretary Albright also pointed out that the nuclear cooperation agreement will open the way for Ukraine to diversify its options for purchasing nuclear reactor fuel (i.e., reduce energy dependence on Russia).⁴⁸ Pointedly, Washington made the nuclear bilateral accord contingent upon Ukraine's agreement to continue to improve its export control system. The Clinton administration had been concerned that Ukraine, without adequate export controls, could have sold Westinghouse equipment and technology to countries it considers "rogue" states. The deal also paves the way for constructing a closed nuclear fuel cycle.⁴⁹

Shortly after the Albright-Kuchma meeting, the Sea Launch program was restarted.⁵⁰ Furthermore, the Dnipropetrovs'k region is heavily dependent on the success of this program. President Kuchma, as was noted earlier, is the former director of the Yuzhnoye design bureau and Yuzhmash production plant. Furthermore, Kuchma and his allies have ensured the "packing" of senior level positions in the administration with Dnipropetrovsk allies.⁵¹ Thus, Kyiv's interest in continuing its space industry production and access to Western markets was keen.⁵²

To offset the resulting economic difficulties in the Kharkiv region, the US enacted the "Kharkiv Initiative" as part of its FY 1999 foreign assistance program to Ukraine.⁵³ The Kharkiv Initiative is a regional economic development effort to concentrate the resources of the Ukrainian national government, Kharkiv oblast and municipal governments, in order to create a "positive business climate and accelerate economic reform throughout the oblast, with the assistance of US and Ukrainian private investment."⁵⁴ The Kharkiv Initiative is one of the several US measures taken in the context of the US-Ukrainian agreement on nuclear nonproliferation and the decision to cancel participation in the Bushehr deal. In sum, the United States undertook the following additional commitments on the occasion of the visit of Secretary of State Albright to Kyiv in March 1998:

1) Assistance to Ukraine in the development of diversified sources of nuclear fuel, based on the *Agreement for Cooperation Between the United States and Ukraine Concerning Peaceful Uses of Nuclear*

Energy. The Agreement is an enabling document allowing a wide range cooperation in technology transfer and trade in commercial nuclear products. It was signed on 6 May 1998 and approved by the US Congress in October, entering into force as soon as it was ratified by the Verkhovna Rada. In the context of the Agreement, the US Government has already budgeted $8 million to fund qualification of an alternate fuel supplier, and further funds will be forthcoming;[55]

2) Convening a conference on nuclear trade and cooperation in Washington, DC to facilitate the exchange of information and ideas on commercial nuclear technologies and opportunities. The conference was held 9-10 November 1998 and served as a forum to promote Ukrainian nuclear technologies to US and Western industry;[56]

3) Support for immediate Ukrainian membership in the Missile Technology Control Regime (MTCR). Ukraine is now a full member of the MTCR, which permits an expansion of US-Ukraine space cooperation consistent with the countries' arms control and non-proliferation commitments;[57]

4) Provision of technical assistance, through the Department of Defense, in the areas of military base closings, privatization of services on military bases, and support for local economic adjustments in communities affected by military base or defense industry closings, and in establishing a Ukrainian program for economic adjustment;

5) Agreement to increase US funding of the Science and Technology Center in Ukraine, which provides professional opportunities for Ukrainian defense scientists and engineers. The US Government provided $6 million to the Center in the summer of 1999; and

6) Expansion of US aid to Ukraine's export control activities, in fulfillment of shared non-proliferation commitments, including the installation in Ukraine of an automated export licensing system.[58]

For Ukraine, US technology incentives were significant factors in their ultimate decision, especially when compared with the prospective gains accruing from a deal whose completion was far from certain. The connection between US incentives and Ukrainian compliance is robustly self-evident. Especially telling are the comments made by Ukrainian

Foreign Minister Hennady Udovenko, which are quoted here at some length (emphases added):

> In the course of negotiations with you, we discussed an extensive scope of issues related to the Ukrainian-US relations in particular political, trade, economic, non-proliferation, and security issues. Special attention was attached to the cooperation in the field of peaceful use of nuclear energy and space research. The agreement of cooperation in the field of peaceful use of nuclear energy that has been *initialed opens opportunities for attracting financial assistance and private investments from the US and reform programs and development of Ukraine's nuclear energy sector.*
>
> The documents concerning protection of satellite technologies pave the way for Ukraine's participation in international commercial space projects including such large ones as the "Sea Launch" and the "Global Star." The fact that the United States of America fully supports immediate accession of Ukraine to the Missile Technology Control Regime is considered by us as a very important step in the spirit of strategic partnership. In addition, the USA will insist on the support of Ukrainian membership in this regime by other MTCR members. So we can hope that in the nearest future, Ukraine will accede to the missile technology control regime and fully participate in international cooperation in this field where, as is known, we have a great scientific and industrial potential.
>
> I would like to stress that *this arrangement corresponds to Ukrainian national interests.* We have discussed with the Secretary of State issues of international security and cooperation, in particular, preventing the proliferation of weapons of mass destruction and related technologies and equipment. In this connection, Ukraine has decided to refrain from nuclear cooperation with Iran, including the supply of turbines to the "Bushehr Project."
>
> It was not an easy decision since our companies are having very substantial financial losses and, (but) we have our international commitments and therefore made this decision. In this connection, I would like to stress on the importance of the provision of the agreement we have just signed that we are going to send a group of experts to Kharkiv to work, to examine this issue.
>
> We have focused our attention on deepened integration of Ukraine into your Atlantic structures, including development of cooperation with NATO based on the charter of special partnership. During our meeting with the President, we have also discussed possibilities of improving

the investment climate in Ukraine and creation of favorable environment for business activities which finally should promote our economy and economic growth."[59]

Subsequent technology deals have materialized between US and Ukrainian companies as a result of Kyiv's decision on Bushehr. For example, the southern California-based Platforms International Corporation (PIC) and a consortium of Ukrainian aerospace firms plans to incrementally develop a family of airborne launch vehicles that will deliver 2,200-30,000 lb. of payload to low-Earth orbit (LEO). PIC has secured US and Ukrainian approval to purchase three supersonic Tu-160 Blackjack bombers for use as airborne launchers of commercial space vehicles, the first step of an ambitious multiphase launcher development program. The deal was approved in early December 1998 by President Kuchma, the Ukrainian National Security and Defense Council, and the US government. Initially, PIC expressed concern over the Tu-160s being quickly demilitarized so all START treaty-related issues were satisfied. Ukraine officials took the lead in this process, and a meeting at the UN in February 1999 successfully assured all parties that proper steps were being taken to convert the aircraft from bombers to commercial air-launch vehicles and did not violate export control regulations. A PIC spokesman noted: "This deal, which would have been impossible a new months ago, is in everybody's interest to bolster the Ukrainian economy and engage Ukrainian technological expertise in commercial projects."[60]

Conclusion

As the resolution of the Bushehr case suggest, the battery of US technology and economic incentives strongly influenced the payoff structure facing Ukrainian decision makers. Specifically, the Kuchma administration – the primary actor in export control policy making – underwent a series of overt calculations which included US incentives. Politically, Ukraine stood to gain from an enhanced reputation as a, according to President Kuchma, "a responsible member of the world community." Further, strengthened ties to the West could be used to off-set domestic political opposition. Economically, the gain took the form of increased access to technology – much needed for the current economic development program – and to outside markets, primarily in the aerospace and nuclear industries, which are critically important sectors in the Ukrainian economy.

Costs included exacerbating relations with Russia and, of lesser import, relations with Iran. In the former case, Russia was candidly empathetic, realizing that Ukraine's current economic and political position was such that a package of such incentives would be impossible to deny. Further, at the outset of the Iran reactor deal, *both* Russia and Ukraine were willing to cancel the deal should adequate compensation be made. The Russian media conveyed the Kremlin's sense of understanding and resignation (emphasis added):

> In making its decision the Ukrainian leadership faced a difficult choice between the interests of two strategic partners. The one who promised more has won, as usual. Financial aid in the amount of $224 million promised by the United States this year is attractive for Ukraine, but it is hardly the threat of being denied this sum, which is already included in the budget, that made Kyiv more compliant. Proving to be far more important were the prospects *of long-term investment and cooperation in the sphere of high technologies.* What has Kyiv got for such a concession? The Americans promised to compensate the loss of money involved in the Bushehr project, and to find an investor for [the turbine manufacturer] Turboatom. Furthermore, Kyiv and Washington initialed an intergovernmental agreement on cooperation in the sphere of the peaceful use of nuclear power. This enables Ukraine to hope for additional financial aid from the United States and private capital in completing the construction of two power-generating units at the Khmelnitskiy and Rivno nuclear plants, and in modernizing hydroelectric power and heat and power stations. Westinghouse Electric intends to invest more than $1 billion in the development of Ukrainian power engineering. It is a sin for Kyiv to neglect such sums since, during all its years of independence, Ukraine has got a little more than $2 billion in foreign investments, whereas Russia had $10 billion last year alone ($2.8 billion of this from America). Payment for Bushehr is, of course, the agreement on American support for Kyiv's accession to the Missile Technology Control Regime [MTCR]. Joining the 29 countries which ascribe to the MTCR (Russia among them) will enable Ukraine to make a serious entry into the world market with its carrier rockets, which are far from being the worst.[61]

Relations with Iran, while temporarily aggravated, quickly resumed normalcy, as is shown by continued trade talks and delegation visits between Teheran and Kyiv.[62]

This case was selected because it illustrates the overall findings of the previous chapter. Namely, that the Ukrainian decision to create, develop, and exercise a nonproliferation export control system is best explained by expectations derived from RI and LI. The Bushehr case – an export control issue of political and economic importance to Ukraine – elucidates in miniature the overall driving variables in Ukrainian export control policy: supporting its perception as a responsible member of the world community and indirect and direct economic incentives. The perception of a responsible state is directly and necessarily related to economic incentives. Thus, US incentives were an important factor in shaping the final decision on Bushehr – and on export control development in general – because the US conditioned receipt of technology and greater market access on export control cooperation. Failure to comply would mean the loss of necessary technology and markets. Cooperation was also shaped by its desire to adopt Western norms, as policy makers in Kyiv could use international standards and rules as a political tool for building domestic support for export controls. Internally, incentives shaped state preferences in a cooperative direction.[63]

Primarily US economic incentives (trade and technology) offered over time induced bilateral cooperation, that is, shaped preferences and actions of the recipient in a manner consistent with the sender's intent. As a politically and economically challenged state, Ukraine's ability to counter US incentives was also a deciding factor in this case. For example, regarding relative power positions and influence, Wendt asserts: "[Indeed] dependency, whether material or intersubjective, is a key determinant to the extent to which an actor's identity is shaped by interaction, which is why a child's development is normally far more influenced by its parents than by other actors."[64] Those setting the policy agenda for export controls were voluntarily isolated from the otherwise fractious political process between the executive and parliament; therefore, in a relatively concentrated policy making milieu, the impact of export control norms coupled with economic incentives was immediately evident in the steady development of the export control system.

The concluding chapter will canvass the policy and theoretical implications of the finding of chapters five and six.

Notes

[1] Ole Wæver notes: "The image of incommensurable paradigms is a block to scientific progress as well as to earnest, painful criticism and its 'theory of science' basis is at least contestable." See, Ole Wæver, "Rise and Fall of the Inter-Paradigm Debate," in Smith, Booth & Zalewski, eds., *International Theory: Positivism and Beyond* (Cambridge: Cambridge University Press, 1996), pp. 159-160.

[2] Indeed, the concept of (self-) interest is seldom analyzed in theories of international relations. Tracing the history of the term, Albert Hirschman observes:

"The idea of "pursuing one's interests" can cover – to the point of tautology – all of human action while explaining relatively little." A. Hirschman, "The Concept of Interest: From Euphemism to Tautology," in A. Hirschman, ed., *Rival Views of Market Society and Other Recent Essays* (New York; Viking Press, 1986), pp. 35-55 (35-36). Interestingly, a criticism of the tautological and thereby unavailing aspects of overly broad sense of the term comes from as far back as 1829, when T.B. Macaulay wrote the following as part of his response to James Mill's *Essay on Government*: "Certainly, the behavior of man is explained by self-interest. But, we pain nothing by knowing this, except the pleasure, if it be one, of multiplying useless words ... it is idle to attribute any importance to a proposition, which, when interpreted, means only that a man had rather do what he had rather do." T.B. Macaulay, "Mill's Essay on Government: Utilitarian Logic and Politics," in J. Lively and John Rees, eds., *The Debates between Macaulay and Mill* (Oxford: Oxford University Press, 1978), p. 125. Criticisms aside, this paper defines interest as goals and conditions *believed* to positively related to an actor's well-being. Similarly, "preferences" are the goals and things desired. See also, Jane Manbridge, ed., *Beyond Self-Interest* (Chicago: University of Chicago Press, 1990); see especially Robert Keohane, "Empathy and International Relations," p. 228.

[3] Some scholars have argued that the nonproliferation norm and US nonproliferation policy are identical. Specifically, like most norms at the international level, a leading power is needed to introduce, sponsor and institutionalize norms if they are to take root at the international level. The classic work is Robert Keohane, *After Hegemony: Cooperation and Discord in the World Political Economy* (Princeton: Princeton University Press, 1984). See also, Robert Axelrod, "An Evolutionary Approach to Norms," *American Political Science Review*, 80, 4, December 1986, pp. 1095-1110; Stuart MacDonald, *Technology and the Tyranny of Export Controls: Whisper Who Dares* (New York: St. Martins Press, 1990); Ann Florini, "The Evolution of International Norms," *International Studies Quarterly* (1996), 40, pp. 363-389; and Martha Finnemore and Kathryn Sikkink, "International Norm Dynamics and Political Change," *International Organization*, 52, 4, Autumn 1998, pp. 887-917. Finnemore and Sikkink maintain: "Many international norms began as domestic norms and became international through the efforts of entrepreneurs of various kinds, mostly through the sponsorship of powerful states."

[4] "Power," as defined by Nye (1990: 177) is the "ability to achieve one's purposes or goals." On US power, see Richard N. Haass, *The Reluctant Sheriff: The United States after the Cold War* (New York: Council on Foreign Relations, 1997); Fareed Zakaria, *From Wealth to Power: The Unusual Origins of America's World Role* (Princeton: Princeton University Press, 1998); Robert Gilpin, *US Power and the Multinational Corporation* (New York: Basic Books, 1975); G. John Ikenberry, "Rethinking the Origins of American Hegemony," *Political Science Quarterly*.

[5] Scholarly work on US 'hegemony' is extensive. For example, Joseph S. Nye, Jr., *Bound to Lead: The Changing Nature of American Power* (New York: Basic Books, 1990), Anthony Tuo-Kofi Gadzey, *International relations: The Political Economy of Power: Hegemony and Economic Liberalism* (New York: Free Press, 1996); Zbigniew K. Brzezinski, *The Grand Chessboard: American Primacy and Its Geostrategic Imperatives* (New York: Basic Books, 1998); Robert O. Keohane, "The Theory of Hegemonic Stability and Changes in International Economic Regimes, 1967–1977," in Ole R. Holsti, Randolph M. Siverson, and Alexander L. George, eds., *Changes in the International System* (Boulder, CO: Westview Press, 1980); Charles P. Kindleberger, *The World in Depression* (Berkeley: University of California Press, 1973); Kindleberger, "Dominance and Leadership in the International Economy: Exploitation, Public Goods, and Free Riders," *International Studies Quarterly* 25 (1981) pp. 242-54.

[6] P. Kowert and J. Legro, "Norms, Identity, and Their Limits: A Theoretical Reprise," in Peter J. Katzenstein, ed., *The Culture of National Security: Norms and Identity in World Politics* (New York: Columbia University Press, 1996), p. 491.

[7] See, Keohane, *After Hegemony*, p. 58. Finnemore notes the role and importance – although not necessity – of norm "entrepreneurs" in elevating or institutionalizing norms at the international level. Martha Finnemore, "The Evolution of International Norms," pp. 381-382.

[8] In explaining the ability to influence target states, Nye's concept of "soft power" is especially apropos. Nye explains: "Getting other states to change might be called the directive or commanding method of exercising power. Command power can rest on inducements ("carrots") or threats ("sticks"). But there is also an indirect way to exercise power. A country may achieve the outcomes it prefers in world politics because other countries want to follow it or have agreed to a system that produces such effects . . . Co-optive power can rest on the attraction of one's ideas or on the ability to set the political agenda in a way that shapes the preferences that others express . . . The ability to establish preferences tends to be associated with intangible power resources such as culture, ideology, and institutions. *Co-optive power is the ability to shape what others want.*" Joseph Nye, "The Changing Nature of World Power," *Political Science Quarterly* 105, no. 2 (1990), pp. 180-182. See also, John Ikenberry and Charles Kupchan, "Socialization and Hegemonic Power," *International Organization* 44 (Winter 1990), pp. 283-315.

[9] David Baldwin, *Economic Statecraft*, pp. 75-81. See also, William Long, *Economic Incentives and Bilateral Relations* (Ann Arbor: University of Michigan Press, 1996), p. 1.

[10] On the nature of coercive or non-coercive power, see David A. Baldwin, "Power and Social Exchange," American Political Science Review 72, no. 4 (December 1978). In that article, Baldwin argues that all exchange relationships can be described in terms of conventional power concepts. Baldwin maintains: "To describe a power relationship in terms of A getting B to do something against his

will is to obscure the heart of the power process, i.e., A's manipulation of the incentives (or opportunity costs) that B associates with various courses of action."

[11] John Baker, *Nonproliferation Incentives for Russia and Ukraine*, Adelphi Paper 309 (London: Institute for International and Strategic Studies, 1997), p. 21.

[12] See, David Dyker, *Foreign Direct Investment and Technology Transfer in the Former Soviet Union* (London: Edward Elgar Publishers, 1999); and Malcolm Hill and Caroline M. Hay, Trade, *Industrial Cooperation and Technology Transfer: Continuity and Change in a New Era of East-West Relations* (Aldershot: Avebury, 1993).

[13] See, David Baldwin, *Economic Statecraft* (Princeton: Princeton University Press, 1985) pp. 40-50. To further illustrate the point, limits on high technology transfer, a common US policy instrument during the Cold War, now serve as bases for trade and technology incentives. Thus, as the denial of trade benefits grew as a foreign economic policy weapon, so grew the opportunity to relax or remove such restrictions as a means of influence. Baldwin further notes: "Today's reward may lay the groundwork for tomorrow's threat, and tomorrow's threat may lay the groundwork for a promise the day after tomorrow." In the post-Cold War era, the affirmative transfer of technology to former adversaries has become an extremely important policy instrument.

[14] The Ukrainian export control system operates on the basis of Presidential and Cabinet of Ministers decress. Unlike the debate over nuclear divestiture, export control policy is not – pending ratification of the comprehensive Export Control Law – subject to the full range of the Ukrainian political system. Since independence, the Kuchma administration manages all export control matters. One Ukrainian official noted that had export control policy been subject to parliamentary involvement, progress on export controls would have suffered from the "institutionalized" political animosity between President and Rada. He explained, "No one [in the government] really knows about export controls. However, they (Rada) would have argued against Kuchma's attempt to develop the system simply because it was Kuchma, not because they were export controls." Author's interview, Ministry of Foreign Affairs, Kyiv, August 1999.

[15] Wendt also concedes that, "The 'problem' with all this is that we lack a self-evident way to conceptualize these entities and their relationship." A. Wendt, "The Agent-Structure Problem in International Relations Theory," *International Organization* 41, no. 3, Summer 1987, p. 388.

[16] A. Wendt, "Constructing International Politics," *International Security* 20, no. 1 (Summer 1995), p. 73.

[17] David Dessler, "What's at Stake in the Agent-Structure Debate," *International Organization* 43, no. 3, Summer 1989, p. 456.

[18] Wendt, "The Agent-Structure Problem in International Relations Theory," p. 362.

[19] Keohane, *After Hegemony*, p. 80.

[20] *Ibid.*, p. 51.

[21] As Max Weber notes: "The generally observable need of any power, or even advantage of life, is to justify itself." M. Weber, *Economy and Society: An Outline of Interpretive Sociology*, Guenther Roth, ed. (Berkeley: University of California Press, 1978), p. 953.

[22] Brian Fry, *Mastering Public Administration: From Max Weber to Dwight Waldo* (Chatham: Chatham House, 1986), Chapter 5.

[23] Terry Moe, "Interests, Institutions, and Positive Theory: The Politics of the NLRB," in *Studies of American Political Development*, vol. 2, Karen Orren and Stephen Skowrenek (New Haven: Yale University Press, 1987), p. 283.

[24] Andrew Moravcsik, "Preferences and Power in the European Community: A Liberal Intergovernmentalist Approach," *Journal of Common Market Studies* 31, October 1993, p. 478. See also, A. Moravcsik, "Taking Preferences Seriously: A Liberal Theory of International Politics," *International Organization* 51, no. 4 (Autumn 1997).

[25] Jeffrey Legro, "Preferences and International Cooperation," paper prepared for annual meeting of the American Political Science Association, 2-5 September 1993, p. 3, archived on www.ciao.org.

[26] For a definition of a "payoff environment," see Arthur Stein, *Why Nations Cooperate*, p. 10.

[27] See, Claus Hofhansel, "German Perspectives on Export Control Policy," in Bertsch, et al., *International Cooperation on Nonproliferation Export Controls* and Harald Müller, *Nach den Skandalen: Deutsche Nichtverbreitungspolitik*, HSFK-Report 5/1989 (Frankfurt: Hessische Siftung Freidens und Konfliktforschung, 1989), pp. 31-32. Müller explains that, despite the lucrative nature of resuming the contract, Bonn forbade Siemens from completing the reactors because of direct US pressure.

[28] Andrew Koch and Jeanette Wolf, *Iran's Nuclear Facilities: A Profile* (Monterey: Center for Nonproliferation Studies, 1999).

[29] See, *Report of the Quadrennial Defense Review: 1999* (QDR) and *Proliferation: Threat and Response 1998, Report of the Secretary of Defense*, US Department of Defense (Washington, DC: Pentagon). For example, the latter report notes, "Iran is trying to acquire fissile material to support development of nuclear weapons and has set up an elaborate system of military and civilian organizations to support its effort.... Iran does not yet have the necessary infrastructure to support a nuclear weapons program, although is actively negotiating for purchase of technologies and whole facilities to support all development strategies. Iran claims it is trying to establish a complete nuclear fuel cycle to support a civilian energy program, but this same fuel cycle would be applicable to a nuclear weapons development program. Iran is seeking foreign sources for many elements of the nuclear fuel cycle. Chinese, Russian, and Ukrainian supply policies are key to whether Iran will successfully acquire the needed technology, expertise, and infrastructure to manufacture the fissile material for a weapon and the ability to fashion a usable device. Russian or Chinese supply of nuclear power reactors, allowed by the NPT,

could enhance Iran's limited nuclear infrastructure and advance its nuclear weapons program."

[30] Evan S. Medeiros, "Russian-Iranian Reactor Contract Restarts Work at Bushehr Complex," *Arms Control Today*, vol. 26 no. 4, May 1996, pp. 25-26. Iran is one of the few countries that has gone beyond its basic NPT commitments by allowing the International Atomic Energy Agency (IAEA) to conduct "special inspections" to disprove reports of a secret nuclear weapon program. Iran claims the United States is violating the NPT by denying Tehran its "inalienable right" under the treaty to peaceful nuclear technology. Tehran has also argued that US opposition to the reactor deal is a double standard because of Washington's promise to supply a similar type of light-water reactor to North Korea in exchange for Pyongyang's pledge to dismantle its nuclear weapon program. North Korea, which was generally considered to be in violation of its NPT commitments, refused repeated IAEA requests for special inspections.

[31] David Albright, "An Iranian Bomb?" *The Bulletin of Atomic Scientists*, January 1995. Albright compares the ability of Washington to pressure Russia and Ukraine, concluding that the former would not yield for political reasons, whereas the latter would most likely succumb to both economic and political pressure.

[32] For a detailed study of the Russian case, see Michael D. Beck, *To Proliferate or Control: Russia and Exports of Strategic Technology*, Ph.D. Dissertation (Athens: University of Georgia, 1998), especially pp. 81-83.

[33] David Albright, "An Iranian Bomb?" and Michael Eisenstadt, *Iranian Military Power: Capabilities and Intentions* (Washington, DC: The Washington Institute for Near East Policy, 1996), p. 106.

[34] Michael Gordon, "Ukraine Decides Not to Supply Key Parts for Ukrainian Reactor," *The New York Times*, 14 April 1997.

[35] Andrew Koch, "Iran's Nuclear Procurement Program: How Close to the Bomb?" *The Nonproliferation Review* 5 no. 1 (Fall 1997), pp. 126-127.

[36] "International Atomic Energy Chief Inspecting Iranian Research Facilities," *Associated Press*, 20 July 1997.

[37] Andrei Ivanov and Judith Perera, "US Squeezes Other CIS Nations Trading With Iran," *Inter-Press Service*, 25 March 1998.

[38] An excellent study of the nonproliferaiton norm is Keith Krause, "Constructing Non-Proliferation and Arms Control: The Norms of Western Practice," in Keith Krause, ed., *Culture and Security: Multilateralism, Arms Control and Security Building* (New York: Frank Cass & Co., 1999).

[39] "Ukraine Waffles on Iran Nuclear Plant," *The Asian Times*, 21 April 1997.

[40] "Ukraine Pressures US on Iran Deal," *Reuters*, 13 November 1997.

[41] Other countries have followed the US-inspired lead regarding Bushehr. For example, under prompting by the US State Department, the Canadian government announced that it had blocked the proposed sale of an experimental nuclear reactor to Iran fearing that the technology might be used to make weapons. Canadian Foreign Ministry spokesman Sean Rowan said that "the rationale for the decision

was that the experimental nuclear facility could indirectly benefit a nuclear weapons program." See, *RFE/RL Iran Report*, 9 September 1999.

[42] Howard Diamond, "US, Ukraine sign nuclear accord, agree on MTCR accession," *Arms Control Today*, vol. 28, no. 2, March 1998, p. 23. The MTCR is a 29-member informal suppliers arrangement which seeks to limit the transfer of ballistic missiles and missile technology for systems capable of delivering a 500-kilogram payload 300 kilometers or more. Ukraine's entry into the MTCR will ease its participation in the global space market, which is dominated by the United States and other MTCR members who restrict their space cooperation with non-member states.

[43] For more on the fractious history between the US and Ukraine over MTCR criteria and membership, see Gary Bertsch and Victor Zaborsky, "Bringing Ukraine into the MTCR: Can US Policy Succeed?" *Arms Control Today* 27, no. 2 (April 1997); Zaborsky, "Ukraine's Niche in the US Launch Market: Will Kyiv's Hopes Come True?" World Affairs 159, no. 2 (Fall 1996) pp. 55-63; Zaborsky and Scott A. Jones, eds., *Missile Proliferation and MTCR: The Nth Member and Other Challenges* (Athens: University of Georgia, June 1997); Zaborsky, "Ukraine Nuke Policy Struggle Over Fate of ICBMs," *Defense News*, November 18-24, 1996; Zaborsky, "US-Ukraine Face Missile Impasse," *Defense News*, July 15-21, 1996; Zaborsky, "US-Ukrainian Talks on MTCR: Is Compromise Possible?" *The Monitor: Nonproliferation, Demilitarization and Arms Control*, vol. 2, no. 3, Summer 1996.

[44] Author's interview, US Embassy, Kyiv, August 1999.

[45] Victor Zaborsky, "Can Ukraine's Launch Market Survive?" *Space News*, 20 September 1999. See also, David Dyker, "FDI in Ukraine: First Results, Tendencies and Prospects," in David Dyker, *Foreign Direct Investment and Technology Transfer in the Former Soviet Union* (London: Edward Elgar Publishing, 1998); and Malcolm Hill and Caroline Hay, eds., *Trade, Industrial Cooperation and Technology Transfer: Continuity and Change in a New Era of East-West Relations* (Aldershot: Avebury, 1993).

[46] Scott Wilson, "Ukraine Vies for Place in World Launch Market," *Aviation Week and Space Technology* 150, no. 2, 11 January 1999.

[47] "Transcript: Remarks by Udovenko, Albright and Kuchma," United States Information Agency (USIS): Kyiv, 09 March 1999.

[48] US company Westinghouse is to supply a fuel reload to the South Ukraine VVER-1000 NPP; the first Western fuel to be burnt in a Russian designed reactor. Upon Kyiv's final decision, the US and Ukrainian governments signed a nuclear cooperation agreement requiring Westinghouse to provide fuel technology transfer, lead test facilities and a fuel reload. Charles Pryor president and chief executive officer of Westinghouse has said the program will benefit all parties. Pryor noted, "Ukraine will benefit because it will have another qualified supplier from which to purchase fuel reloads for South Ukraine Unit 3 and the ten other VVER 1000 nuclear units now operating there. Perhaps more importantly, though, the transfer of Western technology will help Ukraine improve their proficiency in

performing all of the analyses necessary to specify, design and license fuel for the VVER 1000 power plants and to diversify its fuel sources. Westinghouse will benefit in that the agreement will give us technical experience that will facilitate additional VVER fuel business throughout Central and Eastern Europe." "Westinghouse to Supply Ukraine," *Nuclear Engineering International*, 20 July 1999, p. 2.

[49] Presently, lacking enrichment or reprocessing facilities, Ukraine must import its nuclear fuel. While a raw uranium producer, Ukraine is unable to independently meets its nuclear fuel needs. A closed nuclear fuel cycle would allow Ukraine to diminish its reliance on fuel imports, thereby indirectly reducing Russia's ability to use the energy issue to manipulate Kyivol.

[50] Sea Launch is a consortium that includes companies from the United States, Russia, Ukraine, and Norway. It will provide a unique launch service to boost commercial communications satellites into orbit from equatorial waters in the Pacific from a floating platform. Ukraine will supply portions of the launch vehicles. Tim Dolan, "State Department Reinstates Sea Launch License," The Boeing Company, *Press Release*, 30 September.

[51] For example, Taras Kuzio notes, "The secretiveness of the military-industrial complexes in Dnepropetrovsk produced skilled leaders able to maneuver at the highest levels of power, among them Leonid Brezhnev, who encouraged the development of clannish ties and nepotism in non-Russian republics and his protégé, Vladimir Shcherbitskii, the iron-fisted Communist Party chief in Ukraine from 1972 to 1989. In order to reverse the effects of regional deals during his predecessor's tenure, Kuchma needed loyal advisers and a united government to implement a more stringent economic plan requiring a powerful political center. By bringing in a team of "like thinkers and professionals," Kuchma has staffed the administration with regional allies. With the passage of the Constitution in July 1996, the administration acquired the legal means to consolidate this group's hold on power. Kuchma's need for support from his home-town cronies to the exclusion of other interests for the sake of economic and political reform paradoxically permits the continuation of Soviet era policies of favoritism. By dominating Kyiv, the Dnepropetrovsk group has succeeded in securing major deals for their own constituencies." Taras Kuzio, *Ukraine: Back from the Brink*, European Security Study No. 23 (London: The Institute for European Defence and Strategic Studies, 1995), 9 and Kuzio, *Ukraine Under Kuchma*, pp. 63-65. See also, Gwynne Oosterbaan, "Clan Based Politics in Ukraine and the Implications for Democratization," conference proceedings, East Europe Institute, March 1997 (www.ciao.org).

[52] See, William J. Broad "State Dept. Halts a Pioneering Boeing-Russian Space Venture," *The New York Times*, 11 August, 1998.

[53] US Department of State, Summary and Highlights FY 1999 International Affairs (Function 150) Budget Request Resources, Plans & Policy, Office of the Secretary of State, 2 February 1998.

[54] "William Taylor, Acting Coordinator of Assistance to the New Independent States, Visits Kharkiv and Kyiv," United States Information Agency: Kyiv, *Press Release*, 25 November 1998.

[55] US assistance is linked with Ukrainian export control development and cooperation. Each fiscal year, Ukraine, amongst other states, must be certified by the Secretary of State to Congress as complying with US requests in order to release proposed foreign aid. For example, "Secretary Albright reported to Congress on February 18 that Ukraine had made sufficient progress on economic and political reforms to warrant release of all $195 million in Freedom Support Act assistance to Ukraine for fiscal year 1999. Congress had conditioned roughly $72 million of this assistance on the Secretary reporting such progress by February 18. In her report, the Secretary cited a number of significant reform steps, particularly in the recent decision to forgo a nuclear reactor contract with Iran." US Department of State, Office of the Spokesman, "Statement by James Foley, Deputy Spokeman, On Certification," 19 February 1999.

[56] Author's interview with US Department of Energy representative, Kyiv, August 1999.

[57] At a recent meeting of the Gore-Kuchma Commission, MTCR membership figured prominently in the discussions. For example, the Vice President and President [Kuchma] expressed particular satisfaction with the degree of bilateral cooperation in the area of nonproliferation. Ukraine's decision to become a member of the Missile Technology Control Regime signifies its commendable, responsible approach to non-proliferation. The sides noted their common position on the need to curb the spread of weapons of mass destruction. United States Information Service (USIS) Press Release, "US Ukraine Binational (Gore-Kuchma) Commission Joint Statement," 22 July 1999.

[58] Author's interview with SSEC official, Kyiv, August 1999.

[59] "Transcript: Remarks by Udovenko, Albright and Kuchma," United States Information Agency: Kyiv, 9 March 1999.

[60] William Scott, "Ukraine OKs Sale of Tu-160s As Space Launch Platforms," *Aviation Week and Space Technology*, 11 January 1999, p. 444. Increased trade with other partners has also resulted. For example, now a full member of the MTCR, Ukraine and Brazil recently signed an agreement on enhancing bilateral cooperation on the peaceful use of aerospace. Currently, the two countries are building a launching system for Ukraine's "Whirlwind-4" rockets at a Brazilian rocket launching site. After the project is completed, Ukraine and Italy will use the Whirlwind-4 rockets to launch satellites at an estimated rate of 12 times per year starting from the year 2001. "Ukraine, Brazil to Enhance Cooperation on Use of Aerospace," *Itar-Tass*, 18 November 1999.

[61] Sergey Kirzhayev, "Surrender of Bushehr," *FBIS-SOV-98-069*, *Moskovskiye Novosti*, 10 March 1998. With respect to the actual equipment loss, Moscow said that it will produce the turbine itself from a plant near St. Petersburg. Moscow's assessment was shared by Ukrainian President Leonid Kuchma, who said at the

signing ceremony for the nuclear accord, that Russia would have no difficulty in building the turbines for Bushehr themselves.

[62] See, for example, "Ukraine and Iran Sign Energy Deal," RFE/RL Iran Report, 13 September 1999, vol. 2, no. 36; and Nickolay Novichkov, "Ukraine and Iran Cooperate on Aircraft Design and Production," *Aviation Week & Space Technology*, 23 June 1998, pp. 27-29.

[63] See, William Long, *Economic Incentives and Bilateral Cooperation*, p. 75.

[64] Wendt, "Collective Identity Formation," p. 389. For an economic theory equivalent, see Amartya Sen, "Goals, Commitment, and Identity," *Journal of Law, Economics, and Organization* 1 (Fall 1985), pp. 341-355.

Chapter 7

Conclusion: The Evolution of Ukrainian Export Control System: State Building and International Cooperation

> The criterion for judging international relations scholarship is not therefore the extent to which it replaces interpretation with "objectivity." Rather, it is the extent to which it provides *better* historical accounts and raises new questions.[1]

The preceding chapters of this dissertation helped us better understand both the status of efforts to construct a nonproliferation export control system in Ukraine, and assess how useful four international relations approaches are for explaining the export control development observed. It is my contention that this case study offers important policy, methodological and theoretical insights. First, those in the policy community should gain a greater appreciation of the proliferation threats and nonproliferation opportunities emanating from Ukraine. Second, this study employs a method for more objectively measuring export control development in Ukraine, and across states. Third, practitioners gain an understanding of the forces motivating decision-makers in the Ukraine, and can use this to promote more effective export control development both in the former Soviet Union and globally. Finally, the study determines the relative utility of various approaches to international relations for understanding export control development.

    While the Soviet period limited study in the region, the post-breakup period afforded analysts exceptional research opportunities. This is especially the case for the author, who took part in many of the US efforts to promote export control development in Ukraine. In particular, the political changes in the former Soviet Union allowed in-depth examinations of export control development as a part of ongoing state-building efforts. Moreover, because nonproliferation initiatives in the West have focused on enhancing the ability of the FSU to control strategic technology, the study affords the possibility of assessing the impact of these efforts. By examining the driving forces behind the development of nonproliferation export control policies, practices, and procedures in Ukraine, we come to better appreciate what is prompting Kyiv to address the potential leakage of weapons and weapons-related items from its territory. In particular, we can ascertain the importance of varying factors, such as security threats, democracy, identity, material inducements, and domestic politics, for explaining the development of nonproliferation policies.

This concluding chapter briefly summarizes the findings reached in chapters five and six, and puts into context the implications for policy-makers and analysts. First, I discuss and compare the driving forces behind export control development in light of the theoretical approaches employed. And, in closing, I offer the key theoretical and policy implications of the study's findings and some final observations regarding the future of export control development in the FSU.

7.1 Alternative Explanations

> Science may be described as the art of systematic over-simplification – the art of discerning what we may with advantage omit.[2]

The analysis presented throughout this study allows us to draw a number of conclusions regarding the relative strengths and weaknesses of the various theoretical explanations for export control development. First, the expectations drawn from the Realist/Neorealist approach, which emphasizes the role of military security, largely failed to explain export control development in Ukraine. Ukraine did not develop its controls to balance the power or prevent the military gains of other states. As second tier concerns, export controls are not seen as redressing security imbalances or minimizing security threats. Furthermore, Ukraine has sought Western security guarantees and the strengthening of its own military – and not export controls – as the primary vehicles by which to address its security concerns.[3] The findings regarding realist expectations suggest that military security concerns play little role in state export control decision-making in Ukraine.[4] The overall utility of the Realist/Neorealist approach for explaining export control development is, therefore, weak.

The Rational Institutionalist approach provides the strongest explanation for export control development in Ukraine. There was substantial evidence suggesting that explicit calculations of costs and benefits were made. Transaction costs, uncertainty reduction, future interaction and reciprocity were also important factors for Ukraine. Nonproliferation regime rules and norms, moreover, played a marginal, but important role, in affecting export control development. As is evidenced in the Bushehr case, international nonproliferation rules and norms – buttressed by US incentives – were important factors driving decisions related to export control.

The receipt of material incentives in the form of direct and/or side payments (e.g., US assistance through the Nunn-Lugar program) proved to have an overwhelmingly positive effect on the development of export controls in Ukraine.[5] Although direct payments explicitly linked to export control policies, practices and procedures are important determinants affecting state behavior, the evidence suggests that side payments made with implicit connections to responsible security policies were also important factors influencing some state decisions. For Ukraine, these side payments took the form of access to Western markets and technology. The United States, and to a lesser extent other Western countries – made it clear that if Ukraine wanted to market strategic technology and services in the West, and if it wanted Western technology, Kyiv would first need to develop an effective export control system.

Domestic political approaches failed to explain adequately export control motivations and behavior in Ukraine. For example, interest groups, at least as understood in the West, are largely non-existent in Ukraine and were not, therefore, significant factors influencing export control development or the lack thereof. Likewise, the institutional constructs within Ukraine, in terms of degree of centralization, did not positively affect their export control ambitions. Expectations derived from the domestic political approaches do, however, provide some assistance in explaining variance in the level of export control development. Elite perceptions of the national interest and the relative power of export control agencies were relevant factors for Ukraine. The elevation of the State Service on Export Control (SSEC) – an agency dedicated exclusively to overseeing nonproliferation export controls – to Ministerial status, for example, has prevented other domestic commercial interests and other agencies from promoting a very loose system of control. Moreover, government elites in Ukraine argued that export control development was in the "national interest" and called for the creation of agencies with responsibilities for regulating strategic trade. Being a more industrialized part of the former Soviet Union, the Kuchma administration had the most to gain from developing export control systems because such systems would allow them access to Western technology for enhancing their domestic infrastructures. Furthermore, much of the Kuchma administration was former industrial managers, as was Kuchma himself. We see, therefore, that the elite perceptions of export control being in the "national interest" are largely tied to external considerations; namely, the fact that full and normalized trade relations and uninhibited technology transfer with the West required the development of export control systems. Although the evidence suggests that these factors did influence export control behavior in Ukraine, the overall strength of the domestic politics approach in explaining export control development is less robust than the rational institutionalist approach.

Finally, the liberal identity approach offers some general understanding of export control behavior in Ukraine. The empirical record and interview data suggest Ukraine's expressed sense of community with Western, liberal states concerning export control matters. This "sense of community" and identification with the West is further explicated when one considers the use of incentives as a means of ensuring that development and cooperation remain an attractive option. Ukrainian officials have suggested that interaction with the "liberal community," especially the United States, played a role in their efforts to develop national systems of export control. There appears to be a correlation between the amount of interaction (export control conferences, training seminars, etc.) with Western states and the level of export control development when compared with other former Soviet states.[6] It seems, moreover, that the material and personal benefits (e.g., travel to the West) that such interaction provided were of great importance.[7]

The findings reveal, however, that expectations regarding states promoting export controls that were targeted toward illiberal states, as a consequence of a sense of community, were mixed. Clearly, in the case of Iran, Ukraine targeted an "illiberal" state. However, in terms of military trade with China and Pakistan, this expectation is distinctly limited.

7.2 Implications

This case study was guided by theories of international relations. Specifically, I employed four theoretical approaches to determine their relative strengths and weaknesses and to illuminate forces motivating nonproliferation efforts in Ukraine. Based on the analysis, the findings may be generalized to other regions of the world dealing with similar nonproliferation export control issues.

Concerning this study's specific findings, the Rational Institutionalist approach in tandem with Liberal Identity best explained export control development in Ukraine. Three of the four behavioral expectations derived from the approach (cost/benefit calculations; transaction costs/uncertainty/future reciprocity; and material payments) were found to have been important factors affecting export control development in Ukraine. Access to Western markets and Western technology also proved to be a key incentive motivating Ukraine to develop export controls. Future research areas could examine this otherwise overlooked aspect of IR theory.[8] Specifically, such studies could examine how economic and technology incentives can alter the payoff structure of targeted states resulting in non-coercive desired policy adjustments.

To a lesser degree, expectations derived from Domestic Politics enhance understanding of export control development in Ukraine. Domestically, elite perceptions of the national interest and bureaucratic power asymmetries seemed to have an impact on export control behavior. Elitist approaches to state behavior are, therefore, enhanced. Moreover, the existence of liberal democratizing elite seemingly affected export control behavior. Theoretical approaches highlighting the importance of elite activism and its impact on state behavior are, therefore, supported and strengthened.

Existing theories of international politics need to be complemented by approaches that emphasize the interaction of international and domestic influences on state behavior and take seriously the role of ideas: knowledge, values, and strategic concepts. "Ideas," moreover, intervene between material, power-related factors, on the one hand, and state interests and preferences, on the other.[9] For instance, in terms of a classic balance of power framework, the development of an export control system – and nonproliferation cooperation in general – was a Hobson's choice (*vis-à-vis* the US) for Ukraine. While an accurate explanation of state behavior, a complementary, nuanced account would highlight the intervening role of norms *and* material incentives. The role of ideas in the case of Ukrainian policy making is salient and complementary with more traditional approaches.

In other words, "Ideas do not float freely."[10] Decision makers are always exposed to several, often contradictory policy concepts. Research on transnational relations, for example, and, most recently, on epistemic communities of knowledge-based transnational networks, has failed so far to specify the conditions under which *specific* ideas are selected while others fall by the wayside.[11] Transnational promoters of foreign policy change must align with domestic coalitions supporting their cause to make an impact. I argue that the domestic structure of the target state – that is, the nature of its political institutions, state-society relations, and the values and norms embedded in its political culture – determines both access to the political system and the ability to build winning coalitions.

Until recently, the definition of international relations as the study of egoistic competition in an unregulated environment set the terms of debate in the literature. Thus, the "Neorealist-Neoliberal debate" has been primarily concerned with the barriers to cooperation, the relative importance of wealth verses security, and the degree to which institutions can ameliorate the harsher aspects of anarchy.[12] As Robert Jervis points out, for Neorealism the actors' values, preferences, beliefs, and definition of self are all exogenous to the model and must be provided *before* analysis can begin.[13] The preceding pages suggest that in doing so we miss some crucial elements of international politics.

It appears that how "self" and "other" are designated can influence and sometimes change the social environment through which states interact. Power is an important factor in understanding the range of options a given political actor can consider, yet it does not provide *grounds* for purposive or meaningful action, only the *means* to take action.[14] Under some circumstances states may use power to forcibly attain specific ends at the expense of other states. In other situations states may use their power to facilitate more cohesive relations with selected states. As a result, power is also indeterminate.

The Ukrainian case may point to a broader understanding of power. For example, Joseph Nye defines "soft," or "co-optive," power – as opposed to "command" power – as an "indirect way to exercise power. A country may achieve outcomes it prefers in world politics because other countries want to follow it or have agreed to a system *that produces such effects. Co-optive power can rest on the attraction of one's ideas or on the ability to set the political agenda in a way that shapes the preferences the others express.*"[15] In other words, power relations influence both recipient and exerciser in fundamental ways. Similarly, Alexander Wendt contends:

> Repeated acts of cooperation will tend to have two effects on identities and interests. First, the symbolic interactionist concept of "reflected appraisals" suggests that actors form identities by learning, through interaction, to see themselves as others do. The more significant these others are, as measured by material and/or intersubjective dependency of the self upon them, the faster and deeper this process works. By showing others through cooperative acts that one expects them to be cooperators too, one change the intersubjective knowledge in which identities are defined. Second, by teaching others and themselves to cooperate, actors are simultaneously learning to identify with each other – to see themselves as a "we" bound by certain norms.[16]

Conclusion

The link between power, (self-) identity, norms and interest is a rich field for future research.

This study supports the hypothesis that there is a direct positive correlation between what actors do and what they are. Until recently, most of these claims were based on theoretical argumentation. It is only in the past few years that attempts have been made to apply these insights to empirical cases.[17] This study did not attempt to refute material and rationalist-based explanations as much as they seek to expand them. The empirical chapters support the logic of this approach. While identity was clearly a factor in this case, the study also confirms the role of power and interests in influencing the pattern of relationships and political choices that Ukrainian (and to an indirect extent US officials) officials make. Both the theoretical and empirical chapters demonstrate how reflection and interaction among political actors can lead to a change in traditional and emerging roles. According to Wendt:

> Yes, international politics is in part about acting on material incentives in given anarchic worlds. However, it is also about the reproduction and transformation – by intersubjective dynamics at both the domestic and systemic levels – of the identities and interests through which those incentives and worlds are created.[18]

In a practical sense, this study highlights the various factors that contribute to general export control development in Ukraine. The material costs and benefits associated with, and the inducements or side payments received for, export control development were important considerations motivating Kyiv. Moreover, a growing "sense of community," positive, non-material, or value-oriented interaction with Western liberal states, and efforts to implement democratic reforms greatly affected Ukrainian interest in, and support for, export control development.

Because these factors tended to influence constructively export control behavior, Western decision-makers interested in facilitating, achieving and maintaining nonproliferation export control behavior in Ukraine and in the former Soviet sphere should further incorporate such factors into ongoing policy initiatives. Current export control aid programs, such as the US Cooperative Threat Reduction and Nonproliferation Disarmament Fund programs, should be continued in states receiving such funds, and expanded to those that are not while emphasizing *implementation* of export controls so that they are capable of serving the cause of nonproliferation. Implicit export control goals should also be attached to additional nonproliferation assistance and other aid flowing to the region. In addition, Western leaders should further engage their former Soviet counterparts in consistent interaction. Such efforts will undoubtedly foster the budding "sense of community" between Ukrainian and Western officials and enhance nonproliferation activities. Moreover, the Western community should further encourage the development of liberal democratic governments in Ukraine and throughout the former Soviet region.

7.3 The Future of Export Control Development in Ukraine

While this study has emphasized the advances made in the development of nonproliferation export controls in Ukraine, it is quite clear that a great deal of work remains to be done. For example, the need to inform exporters of their responsibilities, in formalizing export control structures and procedures through law, and in minimizing corruption in the system remain undeniable obstacles to further development.

Another reason for possible reluctance stems from the view among many Ukrainian policy-makers that the United States and other Western countries are imposing export controls on them. Export controls were once a major tool of the West to slow economic and technological development in the FSU during the days of the Cold War. Institutions such as COCOM, for example, governed Western attempts to control trade with and to the Soviet Union throughout that era.[19] The issue of export control development, therefore, is often met with reflexive skepticism in Kyiv. Some Ukrainian officials feel that they are now being asked to participate in technology denial efforts that once had severe domestic implications for their societies. Despite such feelings, most leaders have committed to export control development.

An additional point of reluctance involves the difference in threat perceptions between the West and Kyiv. For example, US conceptions of "rogue" states are not necessarily acceptable to many in Kyiv.[20] Despite greater relative participation in NATO – than in the CIS Collective Security grouping – some officials in Kyiv express dismay over the tendentious US worldview. Ukraine, for instance, has established close political and economic relations with countries such as Iran, Pakistan and China – countries which some in the West, particularly the United States, consider to be violators of international nonproliferation norms. These differing perceptions may lead to serious discord with Western states, and especially the United States, concerning targets of export controls, because Ukraine often views such targets as legitimate trading partners and believes that they can simply no longer afford to turn their backs on much needed trade.[21]

Finally, this study has demonstrated that many Ukrainian policymakers do not see export control as a means to reduce security threats. The future of nonproliferation export control efforts may very well hinge on whether or not some agreement can be made concerning the "real" threats to national and international security, and whether the control of sensitive exports addresses these threats. This study has shown that liberal identification between the West and Ukraine effected export control development. As such, a growing consensus on the nature of national and international security threats may now be profitably addressed. A shared liberal, democratic identity may enhance nonproliferation export control efforts insofar as they may contribute to the common perceptions of threats.

Although there may be reasons for Ukraine to discontinue its export control development efforts, there are many reasons why it may not abandon them. Past, present and future export control activities are likely to become more and more institutionalized as standard policy practices. Once institutionalized, export control efforts will be less likely to disappear. Moreover, along with the development of the export control system has come a budding nonproliferation culture that is being embedded in their political operations. Such a culture may ensure the longevity of export control development, if it is adequately nurtured. Ultimately, Ukraine has come a long way toward developing nonproliferation export controls given the numerous political, social and economic impediments to such an effort. For the sake of international nonproliferation efforts, the states of the West and Ukraine can and should work together to minimize the obstacles and maximize the incentives Ukraine is likely to face on its way to truly effective export control development.

Notes

[1] P. Kowert and J. Legro, "Norms, Identity, and Their Limits: A Theoretical Reprise," in Peter J. Katzenstein, ed., *The Culture of National Security: Norms and Identity in World Politics* (New York: Columbia University Press, 1996), p. 495. What counts as a "better" historical argument is too philosophical a question to examine here in any detail. Simply put, however, "good" arguments are a matter of interpretation within the culture of social scientists. This certainly does not mean that all claims to historical "truth" are equally valid; social science offers many criteria for evaluating the performance of theories. These criteria are the social norms that make the professional study of international relations possible.

[2] Karl Popper, *The Logic of Scientific Discovery* (London: Hutchinson, 1980), p. 44.

[3] Contingent upon enacting the Lisbon Protocol, the 1994 Trilateral Agreement, and the NPT, Ukraine predicated nuclear disarmament on Western Security guarantees as the primary means by which to address its security concerns. See, Taras Kuzio, *Ukrainian Security Policy* (Westport: Præger, 1995). The resultant guarantees were formally declared at a 1995 Budapest Organization for Security and Cooperation in Europe (OSCE) conference. For a succinct study on the Ukrainian effort to augment its military structure, see James Joung-Jun Na, "Non-Nuclear Military Security of Ukraine," in Leonid Kistersky, ed., *Security in Eastern Europe: The Case of Ukraine* (Providence: Brown University, 1995), pp. 75-99. And, for an analysis of how Ukrainian security concerns apply to state-building, see Andrea Chandler, "Statebuilding and Political Priorities in Post-Soviet Ukraine: The Role of the Military," *Armed Forces and Society*, vol. 22, no. 4, Summer 1996, pp. 573-597.

[4] For Ukraine, the primary security threat comes from Russia. Export control does not offer an effective tool, however, for addressing this threat. On the other hand, Russia could use export control or an embargo as a form of economic or political coercion designed to bring about policy changes in Ukraine as well as in other states of the FSU.

[5] In a larger study comparing export control developments in the FSU, material inducements were found to be robustly correlated with the level of export control development. Although there is a clear link between material aid from the West and the level of export control development, it is important to note that there was considerable variance in the amounts and types of aid flowing to these countries individually. The countries with the most developed export control systems, for example, received the most aid both specifically for export control activities as well as for general nonproliferation and other purposes. See, Bertsch and Grillot, eds., *Arms on the Market*, especially pp. 213-228.

[6] For example, the Baltic states, Belarus, Ukraine, Russia, and Kazakhstan, which have been the focus of Western export control training efforts also have more developed export control systems. Conversely, the states of Central Asia and the Caucasus have had limited interaction with the West in export control activities and have the least developed export control systems. *Ibid.*, pp. 217-220.

[7] For specific information on US efforts to promote export control in the FSU and perceptions of this assistance see, National Research Council, Office of International Affairs, *Proliferation Concerns: Assessing US efforts to help contain nuclear and other dangerous materials and technologies in the former Soviet Union* (Washington, DC: National Academy Press, 1997), especially pp. 99-108.

[8] For example, William Long observes: "Despite their considerable attention to the role of economic incentives in international politics, scholars have provided little insight into how economic incentives work and operate as a policy instrument ... The popular enthusiasm for, and scholarly neglect of, programmatic economic incentives means this important and increasingly prevalent policy instrument is

poorly or incompletely understood." *Economic Incentives and Bilateral Cooperation*, p. i.

[9] There is a growing body of literature on the role of ideas in foreign policy in contemporary IR literature. With regard to the former Soviet Union, see in particular George W. Breslauer and Philip E. Tetlock, eds., *Learning in US and Soviet Foreign Policy* (Boulder: Westview, 1991); Jeffrey Checkel, "Ideas, Institutions, and the Gorbachev Foreign Policy Revolution," *World Politics* 45 (January 1993), pp. 271-300; Matthew Evangelista, "Sources of Moderation in Soviet Security Policy," in Philip Tetlock, Robert Jervis, Paul C. Stern, and Charles Tilly eds., *Behavior, Society, and Nuclear War* (Oxford: Oxford University Press, 1991), vol. 2; Matthew Evangelista, *Unarmed Forces: The Transnational Movement to End the Cold War* (Ithaca: Cornell University Press, 1999); Sarah E. Mendelson, "Internal Battles and External Wars: Politics, Learning, and the Soviet Withdrawal from Afghanistan," *World Politics* 45 (April 1993), pp. 327-60; Rey Koslowski and Friedrich Kratochwil, "Understanding Change in International Politics: The Soviet Empire's Demise and the International System," in Thomas Risse-Kappen and Richard Lebow, eds., *International Relations Theory and the End of the Cold War* (New York: Columbia University Press, 1996); and Janice Gross Stein, "Political Learning by Doing: Gorbachev as Uncommitted Thinker and Motivated Learner," in Risse-Kappen and Lebow, eds., *International Relations Theory and the End of the Cold War*. On ideas and foreign policy in general, see Emanuel Adler, *The Power of Ideology: The Quest for Technological Autonomy in Argentina and Brazil* (Berkeley: University of California Press, 1987); Judith Goldstein, "Ideas, Institutions, and American Trade Policy," *International Organization* 42 (Winter 1988): 179-217; Judith Goldstein and Robert O. Keohane, eds., *Ideas and Foreign Policy* (Ithaca: Cornell University Press, 1993); Ernst Haas, *When Knowledge Is Power* (Berkeley: University of California Press, 1990); Peter Haas, ed., *Knowledge, Power, and International Policy Coordination, International Organization* (special issue) 46 (Winter 1992); John Odell, *US International Monetary Policy: Markets, Power, and Ideas as Sources of Change* (Princeton: Princeton University Press, 1982); and Kathryn Sikkink, *Ideas and Institutions: Developmentalism in Brazil and Argentina* (Ithaca: Cornell University Press, 1991).

[10] Thomas Risse-Kappen, "Ideas Do Not Float Freely: Transnational Coalitions, Domestic Structures, and the End of the Cold War," in Thomas Risse-Kappen and Richard Lebow, eds., *International Relations Theory and the End of the Cold War* (New York: Columbia University Press, 1996).

[11] On epistemic communities, see P. Haas, *Knowledge, Power, and International Policy Coordination;* and E. Haas, *When Knowledge Is Power*. On transnational relations, see Robert O. Keohane and Joseph Nye, Jr., eds., *Transnational Relations and World Politics* (Cambridge: Harvard University Press, 1971).

[12] See David Baldwin, "Neoliberalism, Neoliberalism, and World Politics," in David Baldwin, ed., *Neorealism and Neoliberalism: The Contemporary Debate*

(New York: Columbia University Press, 1993); and Sean Lynn-Jones and Steven Miller, eds., *The Cold War and After: Prospects for Peace*, expanded ed. (Cambridge: MIT Press, 1993).

[13] Robert Jervis, "Realism, Game Theory, and Cooperation," *World Politics*, vol. 40 (April 1988), p. 319.

[14] An example of linking the material with the intentional in contemporary understanding of power in the international system is Andrew Moravcsik, "Taking Preferences Seriously: A Liberal Theory of International Politics," *International Organization* 51, no. 4 (Autumn 1997).

[15] Joseph Nye, "The Changing Nature of World Power," *Political Science Quarterly*, vol. 105, no. 2 (1990), p. 181; and *Bound to Lead: the Changing Nature of American Power* (New York: Basic Books, 1990).

[16] Wendt, "Collective Identity Formation and the International State," *American Political Science Review* 88 (2), p. 390. This concept is also captured in Ruggie's "embedded liberalism." See Ruggie, "International Regimes, Transactions, and Change: Embedded Liberalism in Post-War Economic Order," in Stephen Krasner, ed., *International Regimes* (Ithaca: Cornell University Press, 1983).

[17] A representative example of empirical treatments using a constructivist approach can be found in Martha Finnemore, *National Interests in International Society* (Ithaca: Cornell University Press, 1996).

[18] A. Wendt, "Collective Identity Formation," p. 394.

[19] For more on the role of COCOM, see Richard T. Cupitt and Suzette R. Grillot, "COCOM is Dead, Long Live COCOM: Persistence and Change in Multilateral Security Institutions," *British Journal of Political Science* 27 (July 1997), pp. 361-389.

[20] For more on the different conceptions of rogueness, see Richard T. Cupitt, "Target Rogue *Behavior*, Not Rogue States," *The Nonproliferation Review* 3, 2 (Winter 1996), pp. 46-54.

[21] It is important to note that the 1990s has seen many disputes between the United States and other members of supply-side nonproliferation arrangements surrounding the targets of export control and sanctions. In other words, Russia and the FSU states are not alone in questioning US policy on the choice of targets (e.g., Iran). See, Michael Klare, *Rogue States and Nuclear Outlaws: America's Search for a New Foreign Policy* (New York: Hill & Wang Publishing, 1997); Michael Klare "The New Rogue States," *The Nation*, vol. 260, no. 18, 8 May 1995, pp. 625-628, and Scott A. Jones, "Is Allah a Rogue: Nonproliferation and the Islamic Bomb," Center for International Trade and Security, *Working Paper*, February 1999 (Athens: University of Georgia).

Bibliography

Emanuel Adler, "Seizing the Middle Ground: Constructivism in World Politics," *European Journal of International Relations* 3 (3), 1997, pp. 319-363.

Gunnar Adler-Karlsson. *Western Economic Warfare* (Stockholm: Alquist and Wiksell, 1968); Michael Mastanduno. *Economic Containment: CoCom and the Politics of East-West Trade* (Ithaca: Cornell University Press, 1992).

Graham Allison, *et al.*, *Avoiding Nuclear Anarchy: Containing the Threat of Loose Russian Nuclear Weapons and Fissile Material* (Cambridge: The MIT Press, 1996).

D. Arel, "Ukraine - The Temptation of the Nationalising State," in Vladimir Tismaneanu and Bruce Parrot, eds., *Political Culture and Civil Society in Russia and the New States of Eurasia. The International Politics of Eurasia*, vol. 7 (New York: M.E. Sharpe, 1995), pp. 157-188.

Anders Aslund, "Ukraine's Resurrection," *American Foreign Policy Interests*, 17/3 (June 1995), pp. 12-17.

Anders Aslund, "Eurasia Letter: Ukraine's Turnaround," *Foreign Policy*, 100 (Fall 1995), pp. 125-143.

Kathleen Bailey, "Nonproliferation Export Controls: Problems and Alternatives," in Kathleen Bailey and Robert Rudney, eds. *Proliferation and Export Controls* (New York: University Press of America, 1993), pp. 49-55.

John Baker, *Nonproliferation Incentives for Russia and Ukraine*, Adelphi Paper 309 (Oxford: International Institute for Strategic Studies, 1997).

Andrew Bennett and Alexander L. George, "Process Tracing in Case Study Research," Paper presented at the MacArthur Foundation Workshop on

Case Study Methods, Belfer Center for Science and International Affairs (BCSIA), Harvard University, October 17-19, 1997.

Peter L. Berger and Thomas Luckmann, *The Social Construction of Reality: A Treatise in the Sociology of Knowledge* (New York: Anchor Books, 1966).

Gary K. Bertsch, Richard T. Cupitt, and Steven Elliott-Gower, eds., *op. cit.*; Gary K. Bertsch and Steven Elliott-Gower, eds., *Export Controls in Transition: Perspectives, Problems, and Prospects* (Durham: Duke University Press, 1992).

Gary K. Bertsch, Richard T. Cupitt, and Steven Elliott-Gower, eds., *International Cooperation on Nonproliferation Export Controls: Prospects for the 1990s and Beyond* (Ann Arbor: University of Michigan Press, 1994).

Gary K. Bertsch and Suzette R. Grillot, eds., *Arms on the Market: Reducing the Risk of Proliferation in the Former Soviet Union* (New York: Routledge, 1998).

Gary Bertsch and Igor Khripunov, "Restraining the Spread of the Soviet Arsenal: Export Controls as a Long-Term Nonproliferation Tool," *Status Report*, Center for International Trade and Security, University of Georgia, March 1996.

Gary K. Bertsch and William C. Potter, eds., *Dangerous Weapons, Desperate States: Russia, Belarus, Kazakstan, and Ukraine* (New York: Routledge, 1999).

Gary K. Bertsch and Victor Zaborsky, "Bringing Ukraine Into the MTCR: Can US Policy Succeed?" *Arms Control Today* 27, 2 (April 1997), pp. 9-14.

Russell Bova, "Political Dynamics of the Post-Communist Transition: A Comparative Perspective," F.J. Fleron and E.P. Hoffman, eds., *Post-Communist Studies and Political Science: Methodology and Empirical Theory in Sovietology* (Boulder: Westview Press, 1993), pp. 239-265.

Glynis M. Breakwell, ed., *Social Psychology of Identity and the Self Concept* (London: Surrey University Press, 1992).

Anne-Marie Burley, "Law Among Liberal States: Liberal Internationalism and the Act of State Doctrine," in *Columbia Law Review*, vol. 92, no. 8 (December 1992).

Barry Buzan, Charles Jones and Richard Little, *The Logic of Anarchy: Neorealism to Structural Realism* (New York: Columbia University Press, 1993).

Glenn Chafetz, "The End of the Cold War and the Future of Nuclear Proliferation: An Alternative to the Neorealist Perspective," in Zachary Davis and Benjamin Frankel, eds., *The Proliferation Puzzle: Why Nuclear Weapons Spread and What Results* (London: Frank Cass, 1993), pp. 127-158.

Andrea Chandler, "Statebuilding and Political Priorities in Post-Soviet Ukraine: The Role of the Military," *Armed Forces and Society*, vol. 22, no. 4, Summer 1996, pp. 573-597.

Jeffrey Checkel, "The Constructivist Turn in International Relations Theory," *World Politics*, 50 (2), 1998, 324-48.

Nikolay Churilov and Tatyana Koshechkina, "Public Attitudes in Ukraine," in Richard Smoke, ed., *Perceptions of Security: Public Opinion and Expert Assessments in Europe's New Democracies* (Manchester: Manchester University Press, 1996), pp. 189-208.

Combat Proliferation of Weapons of Mass Destruction: [Deutsch] Commission Report of the Commission to Assess the Organization of the Federal Government to Combat the Proliferation of Weapons of Mass Destruction (Washington, DC: US Publishing Office, 1999).

C. Craft and S. Grillot, "How and Why We Evaluate Systems of Export Control," *The Monitor: Nonproliferation, Demilitarization and Arms Control* 2, 4 (Fall 1996).

Cassady Craft and Suzette Grillot with Liam Anderson, Michael Beck, Chris Behan, Scott Jones, and Keith Wolfe, "Tools and Methods for Measuring and Comparing Nonproliferation Export Control Development," Occasional Paper of the Center for International Trade and Security (Athens: The University of Georgia, 1996).

Bruce Cronin, *Community Under Anarchy: Transnational Identity and the Evolution of Cooperation* (New York: Columbia University Press, 1999).

Richard Cupitt and Suzette Grillot, "COCOM is Dead, Long Live COCOM: Persistence and Change in Multilateral Security Institutions," *British Journal of Political Science*, 27 (July 1997), pp. 361-389.

Richard T. Cupitt, "Target Rogue *Behavior*, Not Rogue States," *The Nonproliferation Review* 3, 2 (Winter 1996), pp. 46-54.

Jozef Darski, "Quo Vadis Ukraine?" *Uncaptive Minds*, 5/1 (Spring 1992), pp. 59-74.

Zachary Davis and Jason Ellis, "Nuclear Proliferation: Problems in the States of the Former Soviet Union," *CRS Report for Congress* IB91129 (June 28, 1995).

Jane Dawson, *Eco-Nationalism. Anti-Nuclear Activism and National Identity in Russia, Lithuania and Ukraine* (Durham, Duke University Press, 1996).

Nadia Diuk and Adrian Karatnycky, "Ukraine: The Pivotal Nation," in *The Hidden Nations: The People Challenge the Soviet Union* (New York: Morrow, 1990), pp. 72-104.

Paula Dobriansky, "Ukraine: A Question of Survival," *The National Interest*, 36 (Summer 1994), pp. 65-72.

John Dunn, *Towards Real Politics: The First Year of Ukrainian Politics* (Camberley: Camberley Press, 1992).

David Dyker, "FDI in Ukraine: First Results, Tendencies and Prospects," in David Dyker, ed., *Foreign Direct Investment and Technology Transfer in the Former Soviet Union* (London: Edward Elgar Publishers, 1999).

Harry Eckstein, "Case Study and Theory in Political Science," in Fred Green Greenstein and Nelson Polsby, eds., *Handbook of Political Science, Volume 7: Strategies of Inquiry* (Reading: Addison-Wesley, 1975), pp. 79-137.

Economist Intelligence Unit Report, Ukraine, 1st Quarter 1999.

Matthew Evangelista, "Domestic Structure and International Change," in Michael Doyle and John Ikenberry, eds., *New Thinking in International Relations Theory* (New York: Columbia University Press, 1997), pp. 202-28.

Joe R. Feagin, Anthony M. Orum, and Gideon Sjoberg, eds., *A Case for the Case Study* (Chapel Hill: University of North Carolina Press, 1991).

Martha Finnemore, National Interests in International Society (Ithaca: Cornell University Press, 1996).

Steven Flank, "Exploding the Black Box: The Historical Sociology of Nuclear Proliferation," *Security Studies* 3: 1994, pp. 259-294.

Foreign Direct Investment in Ukraine, OECD Working Papers, vol. 5, no. 83 (Paris: OECD, 1997).

Charles Furtado, "Nationalism and Foreign Policy in Ukraine," *Political Science Quarterly*, 109/1 (Spring 1994), pp. 81-104.

Sherman W. Garnett, *Keystone in the Arch: Ukraine in the Emerging Security Environment of Central and Eastern Europe* (Washington, DC: Carnegie Endowment for International Peace, 1997).

Alexander George and Timothy McKeown, "Case Studies and Theories of Organizational Decision Making," in R. Coulam and R. Smith, eds., *Advances in Information Processing in Organizations* (Greenwich: JAI Press, 1985), pp. 21-58.

Anthony Giddens, *Central Problems in Social Theory* (London: Macmillan, 1979).

Anthony Giddens, *The Constitution of Society: An Outline of the Theory of Structuration* (Cambridge: Polity Press, 1984).

Evhen Golovakha, *The Current Political Situation and the Future of the Political and Economic Development of Ukraine* (Washington, DC, 1994).

Joseph Grieco, "Realist International Theory and the Study of World Politics," in Michael W. Doyle/G. John Ikenberry (eds.), *New Thinking in International Relations Theory* (Boulder CO: Westview, 1997), pp. 163-201.

Paul Hare, "Ukraine: the Legacies of Central Planning and the Transition to a Market Economy," in Taras Kuzio, *Contemporary Ukraine: Dynamics of Post-Soviet Transformation* (New York: M.E. Sharpe, 1998), pp. 181-199.

Andreas Hasenclever, Peter Mayer, and Volker Rittberger, *Theories of International Regimes* (Cambridge: Cambridge University Press, 1997).

Ole Holsti, "Foreign Policy Makers Viewed Psychologically: Cognitive Process Approaches," in James Rosenau, ed., *In Search of Global Patterns* (New York: Free Press, 1976), pp. 120-144.

Ted Hopf, "The Promise of Constructivism in International Relations Theory," *International Security*, 23/1, Summer 1998, pp. 171-200.

Christopher Hummel, "Ukrainian Arms Makers Are Left on Their Own," *Radio Free Europe/Radio Liberty (RFE/RL) Research Report*, 14 August 1992, pp. 33-37.

Mohammed Ishaq, "Foreign Direct Investment in Ukraine Since Transition," *Communist & Post-Communist Studies* 32, no. 1 (March 1999), pp. 91-109.

John Jaworsky, *Ukraine: Stability and Instability*, McNair Paper 42 (Washington, DC, August 1995).

Scott A. Jones, "The Evolution of the Ukrainian Export Control System: State Building and International Cooperation," in Gary K. Bertsch and Suzette R. Grillot, eds., *Arms on the Market: Reducing the Risk of Proliferation in the Former Soviet Union* (New York: Routledge, 1998).

Scott A. Jones "Post-Warsaw Pact Arsenal Unbound: Managing Weapons Flows to Conflict Zones," Center for International Trade and Security Occasional Paper, August 1999 (Athens: The University of Georgia).

Scott A. Jones, "Ukraine," Global Evaluation of Nonproliferation Export Controls: 1999, Center for International Trade & Security, University of Georgia, 1999.

Scott Jones and Victor Zaborsky, "Ukraine," in *Restraining the Spread of the Soviet Arsenal: A Status Report*, Center for International Trade and Security (University of Georgia, October 1995).

A. Karatnycky, "The Ukraine Factor," *Foreign Affairs*, 71/3 (Summer 1992), pp. 90-107.

A. Karatnycky, "Ukraine at the Crossroads," *Journal of Democracy*, 6/1 (January 1995), pp. 117-30.

Peter Katzenstein, ed., *The Culture of National Security* (New York: Columbia University Press, 1996).

Robert Keatley, "Ukraine Arms Makers Seek Civilian Pursuits," The Wall Street Journal, 20 April 1992.

Robert Keohane, "Theory of World Politics: Structural Realism and Beyond," in Keohane, *Neorealism and Its Critics: The Political Economy of International Change* (New York: Columbia University Press, 1986), pp. 158-203.

Robert Keohane, "Neoliberal Institutionalism: A Perspective on World Politics," in Keohane, ed., *International Institutions and State Power* (Boulder CO: Westview, 1989), pp. 1-20.

Robert O. Keohane and Joseph Nye, Jr., eds., *Transnational Relations and World Politics* (Cambridge: Harvard University Press, 1971).

Gary King, Robert Keohane, and Sidney Verba, *Designing Social Inquiry: Scientific Inference in Qualitative Research* (Princeton: Princeton University Press, 1994).

Gary King, Robert Keohane, and Sidney Verba, "The Importance of Research Design in Political Science," *American Political Science Review*, 89, June 1995, p. 479.

Leonid Kistersky "General Theory of Ukrainian Security," in Leonid Kistersky, ed., *Security in Eastern Europe: The Case of Ukraine* (Providence: Brown University Press, 1994), pp. 7-17.

Leonid Kistersky and Serhii Pirozhkov, "Ukraine: Policy Analysis and Options," in Richard Smoke, ed., *Perceptions of Security: Public Opinion and Expert Assessments in Europe's New Democracies* (Manchester: Manchester University Press, 1996), pp. 209-227.

Jack Knight, *Institutions and Social Conflict* (Cambridge: Cambridge University Press, 1992).

Vitaly Korotich, "The Ukraine Rising," *Foreign Policy*, 85 (Winter 1991-1992), pp. 73-82.

Stephen Krasner, ed., *International Regimes* (Ithaca: Cornell University Press, 1983).

Stephen D. Krasner, *Defending the National Interest: Raw Materials Investments and US Foreign Policy* (Princeton: Princeton University Press, 1978).

R. S. Kravchuk, *Ukrainian Politics, Economics and Governance, 1991-96* (New York, 1999).

Bohdan Krawchenko, "Ukraine: The Politics of Independence" in Ian Bremmer and Ray Taras, eds., *Nations and Politics in the Soviet Successor States* (Cambridge, 1993), pp. 75-98.

N. S. Krawciw, "Ukrainian Security and Military Doctrine," in Bruce Parrott, ed., *State Building and Military Power in Russia and the New States of Eurasia* (New York: M.E. Sharp, 1995), p. 138.

Taras Kuzio, "The Birth of an Independent Ukraine," *European Security Analyst*, February and April 1992.

Taras Kuzio, *Ukraine: The Unfinished Revolution. European Security Studies 16* (London: Routledge, 1992).

Taras Kuzio, "New Crisis in Ukraine," *Foreign Report (The Economist)*, 4 November 1993.

Taras Kuzio, "Ukraine - Past, Present and Future," *The World in Conflict – Jane's Intelligence Review Yearbook*, 1994/95, pp. 49-53.

Taras Kuzio, *Ukraine: Back From the Brink, European Security Studies* 23 (London, 1995).

Taras Kuzio, "Borders, Symbolism and Nation-State Building: Ukraine and Russia," *Geopolitics and International Boundaries*, 2/2 (Autumn 1997), pp. 36-56.

Taras Kuzio, *Ukraine under Kuchma: Political Reform, Economic Transformation and Security Policy in Independent Ukraine* (New York: Routledge, 1997).

Taras Kuzio, "Ukraine: A Four-Pronged Transition," in Taras Kuzio, ed., *Contemporary Ukraine: Dynamics of Post-Soviet Transformation* (Armonk, NY, 1998), pp. 165-180.

Taras Kuzio, *Ukraine: State and Nation Building* (New York: Routledge, 1998).

Taras Kuzio, ed., *Contemporary Ukraine: Dynamics of Post-Soviet Transformation* (Armonk, NY, 1998).

Taras Kuzio, Paul D'Anieri, and R.S. Kravchuk, *Politics and Society in Ukraine* (Boulder: Westview Press, 1999).

Taras Kuzio and A. Wilson, *Ukraine: Perestroika to Independence* (London: Routledge, 1994).

Roman Laba, "The Russian-Ukrainian Conflict: State Nation and Identity," *European Security*, 4/3 (Autumn 1995), pp. 457-487.

Mark Laffey and Jutta Weldes, "Beyond Belief: Ideas and Symbolic Technologies in the Study of International Relations," *European Journal of International Relations*, 3/2, 1997, pp. 193-237.

Chrystyna Lapychak, "Ukraine's Troubled Rebirth," *Current History*, 92/576 (October 1993), pp. 337-341.

Chrystyna Lapychak and Ustina Markus, "Ukraine's Continuing Evolution," *Transition*, 3/2 (7 February 1997).

Stephen Larrabee, "Ukraine: Europe's Next Crisis?" *Arms Control Today*, July/August 1994, pp. 14-19.

Stacy Larsen, "An Overview of Defense Conversion in the Ukraine," Bonn International Center for Conversion, *BICC paper 9*, June 1997, and Center for Peace, Conversion and Foreign Policy of Ukraine, "Conversion in Ukraine: Problems and Prospects," Analytical Paper Series, October 1998, Kyiv.

Michael Lipson, "The Reincarnation of COCOM: Explaining Post-Cold War Export Controls," *The Nonproliferation Review* 6, no. 2 (Winter 1999), pp. 33-51.

Daniel Little, *Microfoundations, Method, and Causation* (New Brunswick: Transaction, 1998).

William J. Long, *US Export Control Policy: Executive Autonomy vs. Congressional Reform* (New York: Columbia University Press, 1989).

David Marples, "After the Putsch: Prospects for Independent Ukraine," *Nationalities Papers*, 21/2 (Fall 1993), pp. 35-46.

Marget B. McClean and Deborah Palmieri, "Marketization through Defense Conversion: A Policy Prescriptive on the Ukrainian Case," in Deborah Palmieri, ed., *Russia and the NIS in the World Economy: East-West Investment, Financing, and Trade* (Westport, CT: Præger, 1996) pp. 149-60.

Timothy McKeown, "Case Studies and the Statistical Worldview," *International Organization* 53, no. 1, Winter 1999, pp. 161-190.

Helen Milner, *Interests, Institutions, and Information: Domestic Politics and International Relations* (Princeton: Princeton University Press, 1997).

Andrew Moravcsik, "Taking Preferences Seriously: A Liberal Theory of International Politics," *International Organization*, 51/4, Autumn 1997, pp. 513-553.

John Morrison, *Ukraine's First Year of Independence: Russia and CIS Programme Briefing Paper* (London: The Royal Institute for International Affairs, November 1992).

John Morrison, "Pereiaslav and After: the Russian-Ukrainian Relationship," *International Affairs*, vol. 64, no. 9, October 1993, pp. 677-704.

Alexander Motyl, *Dilemmas of Independence. Ukraine After Totalitarianism* (New York, 1993).

Alexander Motyl, "Structural Constraints and Starting Points: The Logic of Systematic Change in Ukraine and Russia," *Comparative Politics*, 29/4 (July 1997), pp. 433-447.

Alexander Motyl and Bodhan Krawchenko, "Ukraine: from empire to statehood," in Ian Bremmer and Ray Taras, eds., *New States, New Politics: Building the Post-Soviet Nations* (Cambridge: Cambridge University Press, 1997), pp. 235-275.

Homer E. Moyer and Linda A. Mabry, *Export Controls as Instruments of Foreign Policy: The History, Legal Issues, and Policy Lessons of Three Recent Cases* (Lanham, MD: International Law Institute, 1988).

Edwin Mroz and Oleksandr Pavliuk, "Ukraine: Europe's Linchpin," *Foreign Affairs*, 75/3 (May-June 1996), pp. 52-62.

National Research Council, Office of International Affairs, *Proliferation Concerns: Assessing US efforts to help contain nuclear and other dangerous materials and technologies in the former Soviet Union* (Washington, DC: National Academy Press, 1997).

Joseph Nye, *Bound to Lead: the Changing Nature of American Power* (New York: Basic Books, 1990).

Joseph Nye, "The Changing Nature of World Power," *Political Science Quarterly*, vol. 105, no. 2 (1990), p. 181.

Nicholas Onuf, *World of Our Making: Rules and Rule in Social Theory and International Relations* (Columbia: University of South Carolina Press, 1989).

Elizabeth Pond, "Poland is Not Yugoslavia. Neither is Ukraine," *The Harriman Review*, 8/2 (July 1995), pp. 1-4.

William Potter, "Before the Deluge: Assessing the Threat of Nuclear Leakage from the Post-Soviet States," *Arms Control Today* 25, 8 (October 1996), pp. 9-16.

Robert Powell, "Anarchy in International Relations Theory: The Neorealist-Neoliberal Debate," *International Organization* 48 (Spring 1994).

Proliferation and Export Controls: An Analysis of Sensitive Technologies and Countries of Concern, Deltac & Saferworld Report (Surrey, 1995).

Proliferation Concerns: Assessing US Efforts to Help Contain Nuclear and Other Dangerous Materials and Technologies in the Former Soviet Union, Office of International Affairs, National Research Council (Washington, DC: National Academy Press, 1997).

George Quester, ed., *The Nuclear Challenge in Russia and the New States of Eurasia* (London: M.E. Sharpe, 1996).

Mitchell Reiss and Robert Litwak, *Nuclear Proliferation after the Cold War* (Washington, Johns Hopkins University Press, 1994).

James Rosenau, "Probing Puzzles Persistently: A Desirable But Improbable Future for IR Theory, in S. Smith, K. Booth, M. Zalewski, *International Theory: Positivism and Beyond* (Cambridge: Cambridge University Press, 1996), pp. 309-320.

John Ruggie, "International Regimes, Transactions, and Change: Embedded Liberalism in Post-War Economic Order," in Stephen Krasner, ed., *International Regimes* (Ithaca: Cornell University Press, 1983).

Bruce Russett, "International Behavior Research: Case Studies and Cumulation," in Michael Haas and Henry Kariel, eds., *Approaches to the Study of Political Science* (Scranton: Chandler Publishing, 1970), pp. 428-429.

Richard Sakwa, "Democratic Change in Russia and Ukraine," *Demokratizatsiya*, 1/1 (Spring 1994), pp. 41-72.

Thomas Schelling, *The Strategy of Conflict* (London: Oxford University Press: 1960).

D.J. Shaw, "Problems of Ukrainian Independence," *Post-Soviet Geography*, 33/1 (January 1992), pp. 10-16.

Stephen Shulman, "Cultures in Competition: Ukrainian Foreign Policy and the "Cultural Threat" from Abroad," *Europe-Asia Studies*, 50/2 (March 1998), pp. 287-303.

Gerhard Simon, "The Ukraine and the End of the Soviet Union," *Aussenpolitik*, 43/1 (1992), pp. 62-71.

Gerhard Simon, "Problems Facing the Formation of the Ukrainian State," *Aussenpolitik*, 45/1 (1994), pp. 61-67.

Roman Solchanyk, "Ukraine: Kravchuk's Role," *RFE/RL Research Report*, 3/36 (6 September 1991).

Etel Solingen, "The Political Economy of Nuclear Restraint," *International Security* 19, 2 (Fall 1994), pp. 126-169.

Angela Stent, "Ukraine's Fate," *World Policy Journal*, 11/3 (Fall 1994), pp. 83-87.

Nicholas Stern, The Future of the Economic Transition," *EBRD Working Paper*, No. 30, July 1998.

Peter Sullivan, *Export Controls: Conventional Arms and Dual-Use Technologies* (Washington, DC: National Defense University, Institute for National Strategic Studies, 1996).

Roman Szporluk, "Nation-Building in Ukraine: Problems and Prospects," in J.W. Blaney, ed., *The Successor States to the USSR* (Washington, DC, 1995), pp. 173-183.

Roman Szporluk, "Ukraine: From an Imperial Periphery to a Sovereign State," *Daedalus*, 126/3 (Summer 1997), pp. 85-120.

B.A. Turner, "Some Practical Aspects of Qualitative Data Analysis: One of Organizing the Cognitive Process Associated with the Generation of Grounded Theory," *Quality and Quantity* 15 (1981), pp. 225-247.

United Nations Development Report: Ukraine 1998, United Nations, Kyiv, 1999.

United States General Accounting Office, "Weapons of Mass Destruction: Reducing the Threat From the Former Soviet Union: An Update," GAO/NSIAD-95-165 (June 1995).

United States General Accounting Office, "Nuclear Nonproliferation: US Assistance to Improve Nuclear Material Controls in the Former Soviet Union," GAO/NSIAD/RCED-96-89 (March 1996).

US Congress, Office of Technology Assessment, *Proliferation and the Former Soviet Union*, OTA-ISS-605 (Washington, DC: US Government Printing Office, September 1994).

Stephen Van Evera, *Guide to Methodology for Political Science* (Cambridge, MA: MIT Press, 1991).

Yaccov Vertzberg, *The World in Their Minds: Information Processing, Cognition, and Perception in Foreign Policy Decision Making* (Stanford: Stanford University Press, 1990).

Oliver Vorndran, *The Constitutional Process in Ukraine: Context and Structure*, Research Papers in Russian and East European Studies, REES97/3, Birmingham, December 1997.

R. B. J. Walker, *Inside/Outside: International Relations as Political Theory* (Cambridge: Cambridge University Press, 1993).

Immanuel Wallerstein, *Unthinking Social Science: The Limits of Nineteenth Century Paradigms* (Cambridge: Basil Blackwell, Ltd., 1991).

Kenneth Waltz, *Man, the State, and War: A Theoretical Analysis* (New York: Columbia University Press, 1959).

Kenneth Waltz, *Theory of International Politics* (Reading, MA: Addison-Wesley, 1979).

Kenneth Waltz, "Anarchic Orders and Balances of Power," in Robert Keohane (ed.), *Neorealism and Its Critics* (New York: Columbia University Press, 1986), pp. 98-130.

Alexander Wendt, "Anarchy is What States Make of It," *International Organization*, vol. 46, no. 2, 1992, pp. 391-425.

Alexander Wendt, "Constructing International Politics," *Journal of International Security*, 20/1 Summer 1995.

Alexander Wendt, Ronald Jepperson, and Peter Katzenstein, "Norms, Identity, and Culture in National Security," in Peter Katzenstein, ed., *The Culture of National Security* (New York: Columbia University Press, 1996).

Andrew Wilson, "Ukraine," *Russia & the Successor States Briefing Service*, 1/1 (February 1993), pp. 2-36.

Andrew Wilson, "The Donbas between Ukraine and Russia: The Use of History in Political Disputes," *Journal of Contemporary History*, 30/2 (April 1995), pp. 265-289.

Andrew Wilson, "Ukraine Under Kuchma," *Russia & the Successor States Briefing Service*, 3/6 (December 1995), pp. 2-17.

Andrew Wilson, "Myths of National History in Belarus and Ukraine," in Geoffrey Hosking and George Schopflin, eds., *Myths & Nationhood* (London: Hurst, 1997), pp. 182-197.

Robert Yin, *Case Study Research: Design and Methods* (Newbury Park, CA: Sage Publications, Inc., 1989).

Victor Zaborsky, "Ukraine's Missile Industry and National Space Program: MTCR Compliance or Proliferation Threat?" *The Monitor: Nonproliferation, Demilitarization and Arms Control*, vol. 1, no. 3, Summer 1995.

Victor Zaborsky, "Ukraine's Niche in the US Launch Market: Will Kiev's Hopes Come True?" *World Affairs*, Fall 1996, vol. 159, no. 2.

Victor Zaborsky, "Ukraine Nuke Policy Struggle Over Fate of ICBMs," *Defense News*, November 18-24, 1996.

Victor Zaborsky, "US-Ukraine Face Missile Impasse," *Defense News*, July 15-21, 1996.

Victor Zaborsky, "US-Ukrainian Talks on MTCR: Is Compromise Possible?" *The Monitor: Nonproliferation, Demilitarization and Arms Control*, vol. 2, no. 3, Summer 1996.

Victor Zaborsky, "Ukraine and Nonproliferation Regimes," in *Arms Trade and New Independent States* (in Ukrainian by the National Institute for Strategic Studies, Kyiv, 1997).

Victor Zaborsky, "US Missile Nonproliferation Strategy Toward the NIS and China: How Effective?" *The Nonproliferation Review*, Fall 1997, vol. 5, no. 1, pp. 88-94.

Victor Zaborsky, "Export Control Developments in Ukraine," in Gary K. Bertsch and William C. Potter, eds., *Dangerous Weapons, Desperate States: Russia, Belarus, Kazakstan, and Ukraine* (New York: Routledge, 1999).

Victor Zaborsky, "Ukraine Restructures Arms Export Controls," Jane's Intelligence Review, November 1999, pp. 19-22.

Victor Zaborsky and Scott Jones, eds., "Missile Proliferation and MTCR: The Nth Member and Other Challenges" (Athens: Center for International Trade and Security, June 1997).

Index

Afghanistan, 201
Allison, Graham, 11, 37, 46, 56
Armenia, 12, 66-68
Australia Group, 42, 62, 74, 94, 124
Azerbaijan, 66-68, 103, 145

Belarus, 1, 12, 66, 73, 79, 88, 95, 100, 104, 106, 121, 129, 142, 145, 146, 152, 155, 158, 165, 200
Bertsch, Gary, 12, 13, 14, 15, 16, 17, 56, 89, 90, 91, 95, 142, 150, 155, 185, 200
Buzan, Barry, 35, 38, 40, 140

Case study research, 7-9, 17, 44-59, 191, 194
Catch-All, 9, 64, 82, 96
Chemical Weapons Convention, 43, 62
CIS, 5, 72, 101, 102-103, 104, 107, 113, 126, 144, 149, 151, 158
COCOM, 3, 16, 39, 62-64, 73, 4, 89, 90, 91, 198, 202
Cold War, 1, 3, 11-12, 13, 16, 60, 61, 62, 70, 90, 152, 156, 160, 183, 184, 198, 200, 202
Common standards, 9, 52, 62-69
Constructivism, 8, 27, 29, 41, 153
Cooperative Threat Reduction. *See* CTR
Co-optive power, 17, 43, 169, 184, 196
Coordinating Committee on Multilateral Export Control. *See* COCOM
CTR, 43, 68, 88, 102, 128-133, 141, 153, 157, 160-164, 172-173, 176, 180
Czechoslavakia, 15, 19, 107, 141

Deutsch, Karl, 26, 39
Domestic Political Processes, 7, 18, 52

Elements of an export control system, 9, 64-68, 92
Equifinality, 51

Finland, 77, 90, 95, 164
Finnemore, Martha, 16, 154, 183, 202

Georgia, 66-68, 103, 151
Germany, 72, 77, 90, 133, 160, 164
Gore-Kuchma Commission, 118, 128, 129, 139, 154, 155, 174, 189
Governmental Commission on Export Controls. *See* GCEC
GUUAM, 99, 103, 104

Habermas, Jürgen, 39, 45, 55
Hungary, 4, 15, 90, 95, 100, 107
Huntington, Samuel, 13, 151, 158

IMF, 15, 103, 115, 127, 142, 145, 151, 169
International relations. *See* IR
IR, 10, 28, 30, 28-34, 195, 201
Iran, 90, 96, 99, 119, 123, 125, 133-134, 138, 141, 158, 162-163, 166-181, 194, 199
    Bushehr, 96, 133, 134, 136, 138, 141, 162, 166-181, 193

Japan, 63, 77, 86, 88, 90, 160, 161

Kazakstan, 1, 12, 66, 88, 95
Keohane, Robert, 19, 29, 31, 35, 36, 37, 40, 41, 42, 50, 55, 57, 160, 170, 171, 182, 183, 185, 201, 202

Kranser, Steven, 37, 41, 42, 188, 202
Kyrgyzstan, 66-68

Liberal Identity, 7, 8, 11, 18, 26, 30, 39, 52, 88, 115, 122, 138, 155, 158, 166, 194, 195
Libya, 73, 90, 99, 119, 123, 125, 126, 135, 172, 174

Missiles, 4, 5, 74, 81, 99-100, 107, 125-126, 138, 147, 163, 175, 187
Moldova, 12, 68, 100, 103, 107, 142, 143, 146
Morgenthau, Hans, 21, 35, 36, 40
MTCR, 4, 5, 14, 43, 74, 75, 78, 94, 109, 124, 126, 134-136, 146-147, 160, 163, 175-177, 178, 181, 187, 189, 190

NATO, 89, 99, 101, 102, 104, 105, 108, 112, 114, 118, 120, 121, 128, 129, 133-135, 144, 147, 155, 156, 157, 159, 162, 166, 173, 179, 189, 199
PfP, 99, 101, 102, 144,
Neorealist, 16, 19-22, 27, 36, 40, 192, 196
Newly independent states. *See* NIS
NIS, 1, 2, 6, 7, 23, 25, 30, 66-68, 70, 73, 88, 91, 127
Nonproliferation regime, 1, 16, 32, 33, 43, 62, 69, 70, 71, 74, 75, 86, 89, 92, 119, 122-125, 135, 155, 193
North Korea, 3, 28, 90, 100, 119, 123, 168, 186
Norway, 77, 90, 134, 160, 188
Nuclear Nonproliferation Treaty (NPT), 43, 75, 119, 148, 154, 157, 173-175, 186, 200
Nuclear Suppliers Group. *See* NSG
Nuclear Weapons, 3, 11, 16, 23, 28, 47, 74, 86, 96, 99, 100, 104, 106, 118, 119, 128, 133, 140, 145, 154, 157, 158, 163, 68, 171, 173, 186, 187
Nunn, Sam, 11, 129, 162
NSG, 43, 74, 75, 78
Nye, Joseph, 17, 39, 42, 43, 95, 169, 183, 184, 196, 202

Poland, 15, 90, 100, 107, 142, 148

Rational choice theory, 29-31, 41, 59
Rational Institutionalism, 7, 18, 30, 33, 52, 88, 124, 136, 138, 166
Realism/Neorealism, 7, 18-19, 22, 35, 52
Rogue States, 99, 133, 162, 176, 188, 202
Romania, 99, 100, 107, 141, 143
Russia, 1, 63-66, 98-121, 133, 141, 168, 173-176, 180
 Chernomyrdin, Viktor 105, 128, 146
 Duma, 106, 142, 149
 Gazprom, 103
 MINATOM, 133, 173
 Yeltsin, Boris, 105, 173

Sea Launch, 134-135, 175-176, 188
START, 179
State Service on Export Controls. *See* SSEC

Tajikistan, 12, 66-68
Turkmenistan, 66-68

Ukraine
 Black Sea Fleet, 99, 104-105, 143, 146
 Cabinet of Ministers, 76, 78, 82, 83, 85-87, 95-96, 112, 135, 150, 156, 162, 184
 Chernobyl, 106, 126, 165, 176
 Constitutional Court, 111, 150
 Council on National Security and Defense, 78-79

Index

Crimea, 99-100, 104, 105, 108, 116, 146, 159
Dnipropetrovsk, 14, 81, 84, 86, 113, 135, 136
Export control system, 98-142
GCEC, 76, 83, 85, 114
Golubchenko, Anatoly, 8, 119, 156
Horbulin, Volodymyr, 101, 104, 126, 144-145, 153-155
Kravchuk, Leonid, 102, 108, 110, 111, 119, 144, 149, 161, 163
Kuchma, Leonid, 4, 5, 14, 77-78, 80, 82, 95, 101-123, 128-129, 135, 137, 139-140, 142, 174-176, 179-180, 184-187, 188, 189
Kuzmuk, Olexander, 114
Ministry of Defense, 76, 112, 114, 152
Ministry of Foreign Affairs, 76, 95, 112, 148, 155-156, 160-161, 163, 185
Ministry of Foreign Economic Relations, 73, 76, 95, 114
Ministry of Machine Building, 5, 87, 95, 112
SSEC, 75-85, 112, 114, 132-133, 152-153, 155, 161, 189, 193
State Customs Service, 78-79
Turboatom, 133, 162, 173-175, 180
Ukrspetsexport, 83, 114
Verkhovna Rada, 82, 99, 112, 150, 184-185
Yuzhnoye, 4, 113, 135, 148, 176

United States *See* US
University of Georgia, 64, 121
US, 8, 52, 70, 75, 77, 86, 98, 108, 113-136, 140-142, 167-181, 195-199
  Albright, Madeline, 161, 172, 175-177, 186, 188-189
  Clinton, Bill, 92, 128, 141, 173, 175, 176
  Department of Commerce, 77, 82, 87, 96, 121, 128, 131-133
  Department of Defense, 121, 127, 131-133, 177
  Department of Energy, 77, 121, 131-133
  Department of State, 33, 131-133
  FREEDOM Support Act, 33, 127
  Lab-to-Lab, 77, 121
  US Customs, 77, 121, 131-133
US-Ukrainian Binational Commission. *See* Gore-Kuchma Commission
USSR, 117, 129, 153, 155, 158
Uzbekistan, 66-68

Waltz, Kenneth, 21, 35, 37
Wassenaar Arrangement, 3, 43, 63, 74, 78, 90, 114, 118, 123
Weapons of Mass Destruction. *See* WMD
Weber, Max, 49, 57, 185
Wendt, Alexander, 39, 40, 41, 122, 139, 141, 154, 155, 158, 165, 170, 181, 184, 190, 196, 197, 202
WMD, 1-3, 6, 10, 108, 128-129